The University as a Settlem

The 1960s and the 1970s marked a generational shift in architectural discourse at a time when the revolts inside universities condemned the academic institution as a major force behind the perpetuation of a controlling society. Focusing on the crisis and reform of higher education in Italy, *The University as a Settlement Principle* investigates how university design became a lens for architects to interpret a complex historical moment that was marked by the construction of an unprecedented number of new campuses worldwide.

Implicitly drawing parallels with the contemporary condition of the university under a regime of knowledge commodification, it reviews the vision proposed by architects such as Vittorio Gregotti, Giuseppe Samonà, Archizoom, Giancarlo De Carlo, and Guido Canella, among others, to challenge the university as a bureaucratic and self-contained entity, and defend, instead, the role of higher education as an agent for restructuring vast territories. Through their projects, the book discusses a most fertile and heroic moment of Italian architectural discourse and argues for a reconsideration of architecture's obligation to question the status quo.

This work will be of interest to postgraduate researchers and academics in architectural theory and history, campus design, planning theory, and history.

Francesco Zuddas is Senior Lecturer in Architecture at Anglia Ruskin University, UK. He studied at the University of Cagliari and the Architectural Association, where he also taught. His research sits on the edge of the discourses of architecture and urbanism, with a specific interest in understanding the pedagogy of the city, and his writings have appeared in *AA Files*, *Domus*, *Oase*, *San Rocco*, *Territorio* and *Trans*.

Routledge Research in Architecture

The *Routledge Research in Architecture* series provides the reader with the latest scholarship in the field of architecture. The series publishes research from across the globe and covers areas as diverse as architectural history and theory, technology, digital architecture, structures, materials, details, design, monographs of architects, interior design and much more. By making these studies available to the worldwide academic community, the series aims to promote quality architectural research.

Narratives of Architectural Education
From Student to Architecture
James Thompson

Migrant Housing
Architecture, Dwelling, Migration
Mirjana Lozanovksa

Architecture, Space and Memory of Resurrection in Northern Ireland
Shareness in a Divided Nation
Mohamed Gamal Abdelmonem and Gehan Selim

Open Architecture for the People
Housing Development in Post-War Japan
Shuichi Matsumura

Ruined Skylines
Aesthetics, Politics and London's Towering Cityscape
Günter Gassner

Architecture and Silence
Christos Kakalis

The University as a Settlement Principle
Territorialising Knowledge in Late 1960s Italy
Francesco Zuddas

For a full list of titles, please visit: https://www.routledge.com/Routledge-Research-in-Architecture/book-series/RRARCH

The University as a Settlement Principle

Territorialising Knowledge in Late 1960s Italy

Francesco Zuddas

Routledge
Taylor & Francis Group

LONDON AND NEW YORK

First published 2020
by Routledge
2 Park Square, Milton Park, Abingdon, Oxon OX14 4RN

and by Routledge
605 Third Avenue, New York, NY 10017

First issued in paperback 2021

Routledge is an imprint of the Taylor & Francis Group, an informa business

Publisher's Note
The publisher has gone to great lengths to ensure the quality of this reprint but points out that some imperfections in the original copies may be apparent.

Every attempt has been made to contact copyright holders and we would be pleased to rectify any errors should copyright holders come forward after publication.

British Library Cataloguing in Publication Data
A catalogue record for this book is available from the British Library

Library of Congress Cataloging-in-Publication Data
Names: Zuddas, Francesco, author. | Routledge (Firm)
Title: The university as a settlement principle : territorialising knowledge in late 1960s Italy / Francesco Zuddas.
Other titles: Routledge research in architecture.
Description: First Edition. | New York : Routledge, 2020. |
Series: Routledge research in Architecture |
Includes bibliographical references and index.
Identifiers: LCCN 2019029879 (print) | ISBN 9781138054615 (Hardback) |
ISBN 9781315166537 (eBook)
Subjects: LCSH: Campus planning--Italy. |
College buildings--Italy--Planning. |
College campuses. | Space (Architecture)--Italy. |
Community and college--Italy.
Classification: LCC LB3223.5.I8 Z84 2020 (print) |
LCC LB3223.5.I8 (ebook) | DDC 378.45--dc23
LC record available at https://lccn.loc.gov/2019029879
LC ebook record available at https://lccn.loc.gov/2019029880

ISBN 13: 978-1-03-208952-2 (pbk)
ISBN 13: 978-1-138-05461-5 (hbk)

Typeset in Sabon
by Taylor & Francis Books

To Sabrina and Lorenzo

Contents

List of figures   ix
Acknowledgements   xii
Timeline   iv

Introduction: University by (urban) design   1

PART I
Beyond campus: Chronicle   15

Prologue I: Another campus   17

1 The campus phenomenon   21

2 Imagining an urban Italy   39

3 Reform or revolution   56

4 Architecture or system: A parable in four episodes   75

Epilogue to Part I: End of an illusion   107

PART II
Academic territories: Four takes   111

Prologue II: The principle of concentration   113

5 Exemplars of order: Vittorio Gregotti, Giuseppe Samonà, and
   academic gigantism   116

6 Information *à la carte*: Archizoom and territorial de-
   institutionalisation   141

7 Reversing the pyramid: Giancarlo De Carlo and the dilution of
   the university   160

8 The anti-city: Guido Canella and the nomadic university   183

Epilogue II: Academic instability   205

Conclusion: Towards academic commons   208

Appendix 1: Conference on university design, ISES (Istituto per lo
*   Sviluppo dell'Edilizia Sociale), Rome, 1–2 October 1970*   212
Appendix 2: Designing the Italian university: Four competitions   213
Appendix 3: Higher education: An international architectural
*   discourse, 1960–1977*   218
Bibliography   224
Index   236

Figures

0.1 Timeline. The project of the university settlement, 1790s–1970s.   xiv

0.2 The university as a settlement principle. Vittorio Gregotti *et al.*,
     project for the University of Calabria (1972–74). General scheme.   xvi

1.1 Campus between finiteness and indeterminateness: Thomas
     Jefferson's University of Virginia.   25

1.2 The ultimate campus.   28

1.3 The staircase principle: Student housing at the University of East
     Anglia (architects: Denys Lasdun and Partners).   30

1.4 The industry of learning: Perspective of transfer area, Potteries
     Thinkbelt, North Staffordshire, England (architect: Cedric Price).   33

2.1 Designing a new urban dimension. Competition for the new
     neighbourhood Barene di San Giuliano, Mestre, 1959. Entry by
     Ludovico Quaroni *et al.*   43

2.2 The form of a tertiary society. Competition entries for a *Centro
     Direzionale* in Turin, 1963. Entries by: Ludovico Quaroni *et al.*;
     Giuseppe Samonà *et al.*; Carlo Aymonino *et al.*; Luca Meda,
     Gianugo Polesello and Aldo Rossi.   48

2.3 The new dimensions of a city-territory.   51

3.1 The battle of Valle Giulia, Rome (1 March 1968).   63

3.2 Planning the modern Italian university. Città Universitaria, Rome
     (master planner: Marcello Piacentini, 1932–35).   65

4.1 The Italy-UK diatribe on the international design competition for
     the University of Florence (1970–71).   79

4.2 Competition panels for the University of Florence, 1970–71.
     Project: *Aquarius*. Architects: Pier Luigi Cervellati and Italo
     Insolera (second prize).   81

4.3 Competition entry for the University of Florence, 1970–71. Project:
     Sistemi Congiunti Tre. Architects: Ludovico Quaroni *et al.* (third prize).   83

4.4 Competition entry for the University of Cagliari, 1971–73.
     Architects: Luisa Anversa Ferretti *et al.* (first prize). Territorial
     plan and project of the university node.   85

4.5 Competition entry for the University of Calabria, 1972–74.
     Architects: Carlo Aymonino, Costantino Dardi *et al.* General plan.   91

4.6 Competition entry for the University of Calabria, 1972–74.
Architects: Guido Canella *et al.* Bird's-eye view with the student
residencies (foreground), research and teaching centre (middle
ground, right), office for regional consultancy (middle ground,
centre), cultural and social centre (middle ground, left), and
laboratories and sports complex (background).   93
4.7 Competition entry for the University of Salerno, 1973–75.
Architects: Mario Ingrami *et al.* (first prize). Explanation of a
typical technological module.   97
4.8 Competition entry for the University of Salerno, 1973–75.
Architects: Mario Ingrami *et al.* (first prize). Taxonomy of the
spatial modules.   98
4.9 Competition entry for the University of Salerno, 1973–75.
Architects: Uberto Siola *et al.* (second prize ex-aequo). Bird's-eye
view of the complex and project of the large courtyard unit.   101
5.1 Vittorio Gregotti *et al.*, project for the University of Calabria
(1972–74). Model.   117
5.2 Giuseppe Samonà *et al.*, project for the University of Cagliari
(1971–73). Competition model.   118
5.3 Vittorio Gregotti *et al.*, project for the University of Calabria
(1972–74). Longitudinal section.   125
5.4 Vittorio Gregotti *et al.*, project for the University of Calabria
(1972–74). Cutaway axonometric of a typical section of the
complex showing the departmental buildings attached to the
central three-tier bridge.   126
5.5 Vittorio Gregotti *et al.*, project for the University of Florence
(1970–71). General plan of the territory between Florence and Sesto
Fiorentino.   130
5.6 Vittorio Gregotti *et al.*, project for the University of Florence
(1970–71). The university complex with the departmental slabs and
the service and leisure podium.   132
5.7 Vittorio Gregotti *et al.*, project for the University of Florence
(1970–71). Bird's-eye view of the university complex with one of
the departmental slabs in the foreground.   133
5.8 Vittorio Gregotti *et al.*, project for the University of Florence
(1970–71). Perspective view of the freeway crossing the university
complex.   134
5.9 Giuseppe Samonà *et al.*, project for the University of Cagliari
(1971–73). Competition model of a typical portion of the university
settlement.   136
6.1 Archizoom Associati, project for the University of Florence (1970–71).
Competition panel 4.   142
6.2 Archizoom Associati, project for the University of Florence (1970–71).
Competition panels 1 and 2: Comparison of urban plans and sections. 150

6.3 Archizoom Associati, project for the University of Florence (1970–71).
Competition panel 6: Surface for the distribution of information.   154

7.1 Student protest in Milan, 4 October 1968.   161

7.2 Giancarlo De Carlo, project for Collegio del Colle, Urbino
(1962–66). General plan showing the structural elements.   164

7.3 Giancarlo De Carlo, competition entry for University College
Dublin (1962–64). General plan, scale 1:500.   167

7.4 Giancarlo De Carlo, urban plan for the University of Pavia (1971–
76). General plan, scale 1:10000.   173

8.1 Photo taken outside of the Politecnico di Milano during the student
occupation in May 1971. In front of the military, from left: Fredi
Drugman, Guido Canella, Paolo Portoghesi (with megaphone),
Federico Oliva, Pierluigi Nicolin.   184

8.2 Guido Canella, Project for a theatrical system in Milan, produced
in the architectural design studio led by Canella at the Politecnico
di Milano (1965).   192

8.3 Guido Canella, Lucio Stellaro D'Angiolini *et al.*, territorial plan for
a new university in Calabria, produced in the architectural design
studio led by Canella and D'Angiolini at the Politecnico di Milano
(1967–69).   196

8.4 Graffiti against the technical committee appointed by the
government to restore order at the school of architecture of the
Politecnico di Milano (197?).   199

Acknowledgements

This book has been a long time in the making. So much so that thinking back at its origins reminds me (or warns me?) how fast the last ten years have passed. My interest in studying higher education as a spatial problem started during the Master's programme in Housing and Urbanism at the Architectural Association in London, a cradle to which I have returned various times during this decade and where I also have had the fortune of contributing as a teacher. My first thanks go to the teachers and, subsequently, colleagues in H&U, especially Elena Pascolo, who, I guess, really should be credited as the original person responsible for this work through her exhortation to question universities as players in the urbanistic gamble. The supervisor of my Master's thesis, the late and sorely missed Hugo Hinsley, contributed with his knowledge to my initial understanding of the ambitions and contradictions of British higher education reform in the 1960s. This in turn spurred a more decisive jump back in history to investigate, through the Italian vicissitudes in that same period, how the path was diverted from the dream of an open university projected onto a vast territorial scale to a reality in which higher education is vigorously enclosed and treated like any other commodity.

The most immediate precursor to the text published here is my doctoral thesis, of which this book is a thorough rewriting, with some additions but especially substantial revision and synthesis, plus the careful editing by Stephen Pigney, who polished my English and improved the readability of my narrative – my most sincere thanks for that. I developed the PhD at the University of Cagliari under the supervision of Martino Tattara and I owe a lot to him and his honest criticism, rigour, and exemplar passion for teaching. Most importantly, I am thankful to have living proof that academic relations can turn into real friendship.

During my doctoral studies I had the opportunity to spend a year as a Visiting Research Scholar at the Graduate School of Architecture, Planning and Preservation of Columbia University. There, I could not hope for a better academic sponsor than the one I found in Grahame Shane. For the many chats, focused recollections, and the infinite digressions into unpredictable paths – thank you, Grahame.

The research behind this book has led me to explore various archives and institutions, and listen to the recollections of individuals who took an active part in the story I recount here. Aware of some inevitable – certainly not deliberate – omission of names, I express my deepest gratitude to: Archivio Bottoni, Milan; Archivio Gregotti, Milan (especially Elisabetta Pernich); Centro Studi Archivio Comunicazione, Parma; IUAV Archivio Progetti, Venice; Università degli Studi di Cagliari, Ufficio Tecnico; Università degli Studi della Calabria, Ufficio Tecnico; Università degli Studi di Firenze, Ufficio Tecnico; Università degli Studi di Salerno, Archivio and Ufficio Tecnico; Luisa Anversa Ferretti, Francesco Barbagli, Cristoforo Bono, Giovanni Maria Campus, Riccardo Canella, Pierluigi Cervellati, Gilberto Corretti, Enrico Corti, Giorgio Fiorese, Vittorio Gregotti, and Joseph Rykwert.

Many things can change in ten years but some need to remain constant. This book is dedicated to the one constant in my life that is also (co)responsible for the biggest (so far) change: thank you, Sabrina, and welcome, Lorenzo.

Timeline

USA [1] 1792 Yale University — John Trumbull

USA [2] 1812 Harvard University — Charles Bulfinch

USA [3] 1813 Union College — Joseph-Jacques Ramée

USA [4] 1817 University of Virginia — Thomas Jefferson

USA [5] 1856 Davidson College — Alexander Jackson Davis

USA [6] 1866 College of California (Berkeley) — Frederick Law Olmsted

USA [7] 1887 Stanford University — Frederick Law Olmsted

USA [8] 1893 University of Chicago — Henry Ives Cobb

USA [9] 1894 Columbia University — McKim, Mead & White

USA [10] 1899 University of California, Berkeley — Emile Bénard (1st prize)

USA [11] 1904 Johns Hopkins University — Parker, Thomas & Rice (1st prize)

USA [12] 1910 William M. Rice Institute — Cram, Goodhue & Ferguson

USA [13] 1913 Massachusetts Institute of Technology — William Welles Bosworth

France [14] 1920 Cité Universitaire, Paris

Spain [15] 1929 Ciudad Universitaria, Madrid — Lopez Otero

1800s   1850s   1900s   1910s   1920s   1930s

Germany [31] 1962 Ruhr Universitat Bochum — Candilis, Josic & Woods (competition)

Germany [32] 1962 Ruhr Universitat Bochum — Bakema & Van der Broek (competition)

Germany [33] 1962 Ruhr Universitat Bochum — The Architects Collaborative (compet.)

Germany [34] 1962 Ruhr Universitat Bochum — Arne Jacobsen (competition)

USA [35] 1962 State University of New York at Albany — Edward Durrel Stone

USA [36] 1962 State University College at Potsdam — Edward Larrabee Barnes

USA [37] 1962 State University College at Fredonia — I.M. Pei & Partners

UK [38] 1963 University of Warwick — Arthur Ling and Alan Goodman

UK [39] 1963 University of Essex — Architects' Co-Partnership

UK [40] 1963 University of Lancaster — Bridgewater, Shephard and Epstein

UK [41] 1963 University of East Anglia — Denys Lasdun and Partners

Germany [42] 1963 Freie Universitat Berlin — Candilis, Josic & Woods (1st prize)

Germany [43] 1963 Freie Universitat Berlin — Henning Larsen (2nd prize)

Ireland [44] 1963 University College Dublin — Giancarlo De Carlo (competition)

Ireland [45] 1963 University College Dublin — Shadrach Woods (competition)

1963

UK [61] 1966 Potteries Thinkbelt — Cedric Price

UK [62] 1966 University of Surrey — Building Design

UK [63] 1967 University of Stirling — Matther, Johnson-Marshall & Partners

Italy [64] 1967 Libera Università Gabriele D'Annunzio — BBPR (1st prize)

Italy [65] 1967 Libera Università Gabriele D'Annunzio — Romano Chirivi (competition)

Germany [66] 1968 Universitat Bielefeld — Herzog, Kopke, Kulka and Siepmann

Belgium [67] 1968 Université Catholique de Louvain — Groupe Urbanisme et Architecture

Belgium [68] 1969 Université libre de Bruxelles — Maresquier, Ducharme, Faunsilber (1 prize)

Italy [69] 1970 Università degli Studi di Firenze — Vittorio Gregotti (1st prize)

Italy [70] 1970 Università degli Studi di Firenze — P.L. Cervellati, I. Insolera (2nd prize)

Italy [71] 1970 Università degli Studi di Firenze — C. Aymonino, C. Dardi (competition)

Italy [72] 1970 Università degli Studi di Firenze — Archizoom Associati (competition)

Italy [73] 1971 Università degli Studi di Cagliari — Luisa Anversa Ferretti (1st prize)

Italy [74] 1971 Università degli Studi di Cagliari — Giuseppe Samonà (2nd prize)

Italy [75] 1971 Università degli Studi di Cagliari — C. Aymonino, C. Dardi (competition)

1967   1968   1969   1970   1971

Figure 0.1 Timeline. The project of the university settlement, 1790s–1970s.

Country	No.	Year	Institution	Architect
Italy	16	1932	Città Universitaria, Rome	Marcello Piacentini
USA	17	1938	Florida Southern College	Frank Lloyd Wright
USA	18	1939	Illinois Institute of Technology	Ludwig Mies van der Rohe
Venezuela	19	1944	Ciudad Universitaria de Caracas	Carlos Raul Villanueva
Finland	20	1949	Helsinki University of Technology	Alvar Aalto
Mexico	21	1951	Ciudad Universitaria, Mexico City	Mario Pani, Enrique de Moral
Iraq	22	1957	University of Baghdad	The Architects Collaborative
UK	23	1959	University of Sussex	Basil Spence
Punjab	24	1959	University of Punjab	Doxiadis Associates
UK	25	1960	University of Leeds	Chamberlin, Powell and Bon
Sweden	26	1961	University of Stockholm	Henning Larsen (1st prize)
USA	27	1961	University of Illinois at Chicago Circle	Walter Netsch - SOM
UK	28	1962	University of York	Matthew, Johnson-Marshall & Partners
UK	29	1962	Brunel University	Sheppard, Robson & Partners
Brasil	30	1962	Universidade de Brasilia	Oscar Niemeyer

1940s   1950s   1960   1961   1962

Country	No.	Year	Institution	Architect
Canada	46	1963	Simon Fraser University	A. Erikson, G. Massey (1st prize)
USA	47	1963	University of California Irvine	William L. Pereira & Associates
USA	48	1963	University of California Santa Cruz	John Carl Warnecke & Associates
USA	49	1963	Southern Massachusetts University	Paul Rudolph
Canada	50	1964	Scarborough College	John Andrews and Partners
UK	51	1964	University of Kent	William Holford
UK	52	1964	University of Edinburgh	Percy Johnson-Marshall
Germany	53	1964	Phillips Universitat Marburg	K. Scheide
France	54	1964	Université de Paris - Jussieu	Edouard Albert
UK	55	1965	University of Bath	Matthew, Johnson-Marshall & Partners
Zambia	56	1965	University of Zambia	J. Elliot, A. Chitty
USA	57	1966	State University College at Purchase	Edward Larrabee Barnes
UK	58	1966	Loughborough University of Technology	Arup Associates
Denmark	59	1966	Odense Universitet	Bureau Khron, Rasmussen (competition)
USA	60	1966	Tougaloo College	Gunnar Birkerts & Associates

1964   1965   1966

Country	No.	Year	Institution	Architect
Italy	76	1971	Università degli Studi di Cagliari	C. Manzo, U. Siola (competition)
Italy	77	1971	Università degli Studi di Pavia	Giancarlo De Carlo
Italy	78	1972	Università degli Studi della Calabria	Vittorio Gregotti (1st prize)
Italy	79	1972	Università degli Studi della Calabria	C.Aymonino, C.I.Dardi (competition)
Italy	80	1972	Università degli Studi della Calabria	Guido Canella (competition)
Italy	81	1972	Università degli Studi della Calabria	Giuseppe Samonà (competition)
Italy	82	1972	Università degli Studi della Calabria	Ludovico Quaroni (competition)
Italy	83	1973	University of Somalia	Ludovico Quaroni
Italy	84	1973	Università degli Studi di Salerno	Mario Ingrami (1st prize)
Italy	85	1973	Università degli Studi di Salerno	Uberto Siola (2nd prize)
Italy	86	1973	Università degli Studi di Salerno	Riccardo Dalisi (competition)
Italy	87	1975	Università degli Studi di Lecce	Ludovico Quaroni
Italy	88	1975	Università degli Studi di Messina	BBPR (1st prize)

1972   1973   1975

Figure 0.1 (Cont.)

Figure 0.2 The university as a settlement principle. Vittorio Gregotti *et al.*, project for
the University of Calabria (1972–74). General scheme.
Source: C.A.S.V.A., Comune di Milano. Archivio Gregotti.

Introduction
University by (urban) design

'The University is becoming a transnational bureaucratic corporation, either tied to transnational instances of government such as the European Union or functioning independently, by analogy with a transnational corporation.'[1] Bill Readings wrote these words in the mid-1990s as part of a more general declaration: the university, he claimed, was in ruins. Through a journey across the history of the modern university – that creature emerging under the auspices of German idealism in the early 1800s – Readings spoke of an academic institution that by the late twentieth century had lost its main referent, namely, the State. Since Wilhelm von Humboldt's reforms at the University of Berlin, the modern university has operated to shape national culture, and its existence has been inextricably related to a geopolitical order constituted of centralised nation states. With the decline of the latter and the creation of a new world order of supra-national economic and political powers, the university no longer had as its main role the creation of subjects that share principles and beliefs associated with clear territorial demarcations.

Readings's argument complements other analyses of the condition of late twentieth-century societies, such as Jean-François Lyotard's 1979 diagnosis of the 'end of grand narratives' as the central phenomenon in the shift from a modern to a postmodern condition,[2] and Zygmunt Bauman's reflections on the idea of a postmodern university. Is there, Bauman asked in 1997, 'any "common feature" left to the variegated collection of entities called universities, and to the equally variegated interior of any one of them ... that upholds the claim of their unity?'[3] His response was charged with optimism, as he believed it to be

> the good luck of the universities that there are so many of them, that there are no two exactly alike, and that inside every university there is a mind-boggling variety of departments, schools, styles of thoughts, styles of conversation, and even styles of stylistic concerns. It is the good luck of the universities that ... they are not comparable, not measurable by the same yardstick ...[4]

Bauman's postmodern optimism was more than an attempt to find sense in the proliferation of higher education institutions that have claimed the status of university during the last four decades of the millennium, for it was also an uncanny anticipatory warning for what lay in wait for European universities: the Bologna Process, the inter-ministerial agreement initiated in 1999 to create a single European higher education area capable of countering American domination.[5] To take on the competitor, the national ministries of education agreed, it was necessary to assume the competitor's identity. Hence, curricula were homogenised (resulting in a common structure for bachelor's and master's degrees), and there was a growing aspiration both to the corporatisation of attitudes, protocols and language and to the commercialisation of the campus in the form of paraphernalia, gadgets and memorabilia. And by no means the least important aim was cross-border academic mobility, which has pushed established exchange programmes like Erasmus, leading to recent students' experience of higher education being very different from that of their parents.

Despite the indubitable enrichment deriving from the encounter with different cultures, the mobility promoted during recent decades has been part of a wider strategy that, instead of enabling individuals, still imposes directives from the top. This is, in other words, an idea of mobile higher education that differs little from authoritarianism – the same enemy fought by the mothers and fathers of the Erasmus generation in 1968. Evidence of this is the general homogeneity that is kept together by the mobile system, as students encounter very limited variety in their pilgrimages. Their wanderings from place to place are not accompanied by experiences of really different ideas of the university; rather, they are confronted with a bureaucratic system on a transnational scale, one that administers an extensive process of converting exams and credits to adapt to the curricula of different institutions. Mobility has come to act more like a training ground for a forced life on the move – the age of the precariat[6] – than as the postmodern constitution of self through the piecing together of true differences. Underpinning this is a reality in opposite to Bauman's *fin-de-siècle* optimism: universities are, in essence, almost the same everywhere.

Bureaucracy and commodity combine in the transnational university – where 'transnational' sits alongside 'corporate', 'global', 'entrepreneurial', and so on, as one of the rubrics intended to make sense of the current state of higher education.[7] Statements made less than two decades ago about the postmodern university being 'a knowledge and research emporium – a multi-centred, if not in fact centreless, learning "centre" that is radically de-centralized',[8] as argued by Carl Raschke in 2002, might appear to hold true today, when the numbers of students are at a historical peak and higher education is offered by multiple institutions. Yet this de-centralisation is superficial, for the university today is mostly the result of a mix of multiplied sameness and colonisation, with more institutions aspiring to the status of 'the' university while the strongest ones franchise themselves around the world. The narrow case of architecture as an academic discipline is perhaps illustrative: the proliferation of visiting schools in the last decade has surely offered precious occasions for debate and confrontation, but it is ultimately worthless in a world that only values official transcripts, certificates, and titles granted by 'real' universities. Thus, the postmodern realisation of the university has been restricted only to the idea of the 'emporium' (in Raschke's quotation above). In the emporium, everything – tutorials, research, discussions – is exchanged for money.

Many critical diagnoses of the contemporary state of the university, especially in advanced neoliberal economies, highlight the disappearing academic mission of unimpeded critical enquiry under the blows of commercialised knowledge.[9] What is teaching, other than a service bought by the students? What is research, if not the direct satisfaction of predetermined goals for the creation of utilitarian knowledge?

Profound modifications in the very language of universities are linked to these questions, as we assist 'the elaboration of an ad hoc vocabulary that is located between the jargon of entrepreneurship and the nomenclature of a scientific laboratory'.[10] Anyone familiar with the visual slides and oratory adorning lunchtime continuing professional development seminars might recognise their experience in this recent statement by Giorgio Agamben. A widespread rhetoric throughout higher education not only appropriates words from the business sphere but also distorts academic terminology. So, a most beloved entry in the academic vocabulary is 'excellence', about which Readings had issued a warning in the mid-1990s:

> The point is not that no one knows what excellence is but that everyone has his or her own idea of what it is. And once excellence has been generally accepted as an organising principle, there is no need to argue about differing definitions. Everyone is excellent, in their own way ...[11]

Next to 'excellence' sits 'research', the main terminological contribution of von Humboldt. As Agamben has observed, 'research' has come to almost entirely subsume and substitute the older term 'studying'. Whereas research is a circular activity around an object that is still to be found, he explains, study has already found its object and, as such, is motivated only by the desire to know, which for the philosopher is enough reason to consider it 'a higher knowledge paradigm than researching'.[12] Applying similar reasoning to the realm of architectural pedagogy, Joan Ockman has recently reflected on the critical status of history and theory studies inside schools of architecture:

> Instead of history/theory today, what we now have is research. Research is the holy grail of contemporary architecture education, and the 'laboratories' in which it is carried out – by white-coated architectural technicians, figuratively speaking – are its shrines. As for criticism: arguably, we now have something like 'curation'. History/theory has turned into research/curation.[13]

In this current higher education predicament, writing a book on the topic on the fiftieth anniversary of 1968 has an inescapably symbolic aspect, particularly if the book tells the story of the events that shaped that period of intense dissent and revolution, and of the time when the loss of the referent diagnosed by

Readings – and with it the various other drifts mentioned above – first became apparent. Although my opening remarks locate the general topic and its problems within a wide sphere that encompasses sociology, economics, pedagogy and philosophy, the book, by necessity, operates within a more confined domain: architecture, a discipline that has long struggled to define itself 'scientifically', and which has displayed an uncertain mix of love and hate for extra-disciplinary excursions. The history of twentieth-century architectural theory, and especially that of the second half of the century, offers a perfect reflection of this uncertainty, one that stretches between the opposites of disciplinary autonomy and interdisciplinary engagement.

This book contributes to the history of precisely that period. It focuses on the specific geographical context of Italy and a time frame of about fifteen years from 1963 to 1977. Without expanding on the reasons for these particular dates – which will be explained later – it suffices here to introduce the chapters that follow by recalling that, in architecture, discourse is built through artefacts that span the spectrum from the physical to the immaterial, the visual to the textual, the built to the imagined. On special occasions, a topic can channel interest and attention to such an extent that all artefacts cluster around it, indissolubly linking a certain moment with that topic. Between 1963 and 1977, this topic was higher education and its reform. Innumerable drawings of new universities, written statutes for and magazine articles on new universities, and buildings for new universities were produced during a turbulent period that pivoted on the events of 1968. The centrality of the topic in the architectural preoccupations of that period was best encapsulated by Joseph Rykwert, who claimed that universities had become the paradigm (or archetype) of all that was being built.[14]

To be sure, interest in universities has not dissipated over the half-century that separates us from Rykwert's claim. A crisis of higher education continuously makes the headlines, triggered by anxiety about the rampant commodification of learning, and the construction of universities has all but stopped since 1977, the end point of this book's story. Academic buildings still occupy a favourite role in the portfolio of major international architects, and universities themselves, especially the bigger ones, take pride in reclaiming a role in large-scale urban development.[15] Before jumping into the past in the remainder of the book, it is worth reflecting further on the current situation.

The present status of higher education in relation to the architectural and urban design of universities and to the type of scholarship on the topic that has been produced over the last few decades can be sketched as follows. A central role for universities is reclaimed by many urban studies scholars in relation to a wider reconceptualisation of the value of cities that has taken place over the last couple of decades. This reconceptualisation can be summarised under the larger umbrella of the knowledge economy. Nevertheless, in the mid-1990s, the urbanism of a new economy and society based on a commercial use of knowledge (because that is what knowledge economy actually indicates, rather than a misleading statement about our times being more knowledge-based than in the past) could be studied in terms of 'technopoles'. Since the 1960s, these had been built as the territorial outposts of a new type of industry encompassing science and technology parks, business parks, and the like, which followed in the footsteps of universities as part of a migration from inner-city areas to outlying sites. The exile shaped an image of the new economy that Manuel Castells and Peter Hall defined as 'a series of low, discreet buildings, usually displaying a certain air of quiet good taste, and set amidst impeccable landscaping in that standard real-estate cliché, a campus-like atmosphere'.[16]

Over the last twenty years, a turn to the knowledge economy associated with a parallel reconsideration of the inner city has attempted to modify the idyllic image described by Castells and Hall, transforming it into the image of a dense urban neighbourhood. This, however, does not necessarily coincide with a complete return to the city of the knowledge-based components that have been incubated for years outside of it. The variously labelled 'mega-research parks' or 'innovation hubs' of the early 2000s do not replace the older peripheral clusters.[17] Rather, they act as their allegedly urbanised complement, where urbanised equals an attempt to provide them both with the density of activities and with the built mass proper to an inner-city area. When the return to the city actually happens, as in the case of the 'innovation district' 22@Barcelona, a blurring of the logics of an urban residential area and of a specialised campus occurs.[18] These new urbanised campuses add to the geography of workplaces aimed at the contemporary workforce of 'talents' – the knowledge workers, increasingly divided between waged labourers for large corporations and self-entrepreneurs nurtured inside start-up incubators that, in turn, are connected to universities.

According to Ali Madanipour: 'Now that knowledge is announced as the driving force of economic development, universities find an even more central role, both economically and spatially.'[19] Similar statements reposition the centrality of the university by ultimately allowing it to take on a role as a proper urban developer – to make it, as it were, 'a university of, not simply in, the city'.[20] There is an emerging new relationship between the city and the university that, as Sharon Haar put it in her study of Chicago as a testing ground for various ideas of higher education during the twentieth century, is 'based on the common mission to acknowledge and accommodate diverse people, ideas, and technologies and to advance knowledge directed toward global interactions'.[21] In an attempt to answer the question 'how did the city, once claimed to be anathema to American higher education and pedagogy, come to find itself so intertwined in the future of both?', Haar argues that, in Chicago

> the urban campus is imbricated in the city by virtue of the need to produce urban citizens and, equally important, to research social and urban forms that will lead to new ideas about urban migration, calls for urban reform, and ultimately, new models of urban planning and design.[22]

Like other attempts to reconsider the urban nature of the university,[23] Haar develops an argument against the common understanding of the American university as a rejection of the city. Today, the overlapping missions of university and city, she suggests, provide a clear example of the partiality of the pastoral conception of higher education that has been traditionally promoted in America and was exported internationally as a canon in the 1960s. Haar's work shows that city and university are today inextricably related by what could be described as bi-directional opportunism. On the one side, the city takes advantage of hosting a university to brand itself as a 'knowledge hub', and thus looks to position itself in the global competition among cities. On the other hand, the university exploits the city as a source for its research purposes. If the latter is a phenomenon that shaped from the outset the modern urban university (with its prototype, the University of Chicago, whose famous school of urban sociology took as its object of scientific study the city of Chicago itself), the increasingly user-centred production processes of today make this opportunistic relationship even more relevant today — one might think of the feedback mechanism that turns users into active participants in the production chain for new ICT applications (the idea of Living Labs).[24]

The Janus-faced nature of the situation hardly passes unnoticed. In fact, opposition is as strong as endorsement of the allegedly new urban role for the academic institution. Madanipour has suggested that 'what appears to be spaces of knowledge might actually be spaces of speculation and market-making'.[25] Such doubt legitimately applies to many of the recent large-scale urban operations of some of the most prestigious world universities, including Columbia University's Manhattanville campus in West Harlem,[26] the Allston Master Plan of Harvard University,[27] the expansion plan Penn Connects of the University of Pennsylvania in Philadelphia,[28] the creation of so-called Loop U as a network of universities in Chicago's centre,[29] and the expansion projects of the Université de Paris on the Rive Gauche.[30] All these development proposals cause conflicts with the local communities, and fierce criticism, following a Marxist line, has dubbed them as 'factories of knowledge':

> The university is becoming an actor in the intertwined strategies of the real estate market and infrastructure policy: the upgrading of city districts, gentrification, and the transformation of formerly industrial or working-class neighbourhoods into zones occupied by the creative economy have become functions of university management.[31]

This climate of accusation ties in with the declaration of a university in ruins, with which I opened this Introduction and which, in turn, finds today even more dramatic statements declaring 'the slow death of universities'.[32] And while scholars of urban studies fluctuate between acceptance and accusation of the present higher education/urban design nexus, a voice that was central fifty years ago recedes unnoticed into the background: the voice of architects. This is not to say that architectural projects for academic spaces are disappearing: a glance at any web portal of recent projects immediately proves the opposite. It is perhaps more correct to state that, over the last few decades, a combined process of scaling down and a concentration on academic buildings rather than academic settlements is noticeable. Despite some large-scale master plans for new and whole campuses – especially in countries undergoing rapid economic development[33] – since the 1990s, the story of university design is mostly a tale of single buildings. Examples are numerous and encompass canonical case studies of contemporary architecture by the likes of OMA (from Educatorium, 1997, to Millstein Hall, 2001, and ongoing), Bernard Tschumi (Lerner Hall, 1999), Morphosis (41 Cooper Square, 2006), SOM (The New School University Centre, 2014), Stanton Williams (Central Saint Martin, 2011), Grafton Architects (Bocconi University, 2008), Diller & Scofidio +Renfro (Roy and Diana Vagelos Education Centre, 2017), among many others. A common characteristic of these projects is that, by often declaring their interior spatial complexity to be aimed at compensating for a perceived loss of a capacity by the city to nurture social bonds, they end up providing just a single answer: a sealed interior. In fact, these spaces that are often emphatically labelled with an urban vocabulary – streets, forums, boulevards, and the like – are trapped in the logics of today's society of control, often resulting in buildings inaccessible to the person on the street and hardly open even to the free appropriation by the individuals for whom they are ostensibly designed, controlled as the spaces are by top-down complex bureaucratic mechanisms of space booking.

It is relevant to recall that many of the projects listed above are the products of designers who received their architectural education around 1968. To mention but the more obvious, Rem Koolhaas and Bernard Tschumi's theories of the unprogrammed and 'event spaces' stemmed from the 1968 ideology against top-down authority and paternalism. The 'universities of the street' proposed by their own architectural teachers and colleagues at the time remained also for them no more than paper projects for a long time. The first realised event spaces arrived around the mid-1990s, at a time when the bottom-up dreams of 1968 had been largely neutralised and all that could be produced – as their projects did – was form with corrupted utopia.

Let's go back, therefore, to before this neutralisation, and take a closer look at that time of contradiction and polemic when architects occupied a central role in the advancement of ideas to reform higher education. As already noted, the 1960s were a period of unprecedented reflection on higher education all over the Western world, and it produced a similarly unprecedented expansion of the physical substance of academic environments. The historical accounts that have been produced from a review of this university building boom have suggested a phenomenon led by the UK, in Europe, and by the US, on the other side of the Atlantic, with other countries following suit (most notably France and Germany).[34] The story I tell in this book considers a case that has been undetected by the radar of historiography: Italy. Yet I aim to argue for a level of general validity as to the relevance of this circumscribed episode, adding that such validity can be verified as much within the times in which the actions took place as it can with hindsight. However, besides these introductory remarks that refer to a present condition, I will refrain from making clear allusions to the 'lessons' that could or should be learned today by looking at that moment in the past. I prefer leaving to the reader the choice of whether or not that might be a relevant approach. I will thus limit my efforts to interpreting how a series of projects operated as mediums between various domains spanning the architectural, the political and the pedagogic – aspects that, I believe, are universally valid independently of historical time.

Synthetically summarised, the story that will be discussed in this book unfolds as follows. By the early 1960s, Italy, after twenty years of a democratic turn following the also two-decade-long fascist dictatorship up to 1945, had to address the issue of modernising its educational system to maintain and further sustain a period of unprecedented affluence (the so-called postwar Italian economic miracle, whose highpoint historians locate between 1958 and 1963).[35] Disagreement on educational reform, particularly as far as higher education was concerned, led to delays in decision-making, while growing numbers of prospective applicants accumulated at the doors of the country's overpopulated universities. The inability to reach agreement inside the official halls of politics had architects and urbanists suddenly called into action to provide an ad hoc expansion of the existing built stock. Besides missing policy guidance, an additional problem was those architects' lack of previous experience in the field of university planning and design. Yet, their response was enthusiastic, which they demonstrated by flocking to enter the architectural competitions launched by some Italian universities in the early 1970s, of which I will discuss four: those for the universities of Florence, Cagliari, Calabria and Salerno. More than an attempt to fill their design specialisation gap, however, the enthusiasm expressed by some of the leading mid-twentieth-century Italian architects stemmed from their instrumental interest in the new brief to continue a conversation on large urban territories – a conversation that had begun in the 1950s. For the likes of Ludovico Quaroni, Giuseppe Samonà, Vittorio Gregotti, Giancarlo De Carlo, Carlo Aymonino, Archizoom and Guido Canella – to mention the most notable names – the creation of new university settlements outside cities appeared to be the right opportunity to drive urban order at a large scale. Despite adopting very different, even opposite, viewpoints, all agreed that the outlying character of the settlements would not be a replica of the dominant planning solution that was being applied across the Western world: Italian universities, they claimed, would not be campuses.

Without 'spoiling' more of the plot, what emerges from this synopsis is an anticipatory response to the argument proposed by Bill Readings thirty years later about the loss of the referent for the (post)modern university. This response finds in the city the possible remaining referent for a late twentieth-century academic institution. Or, more appropriately, the referent can be the vast, regional urban territories that many postwar Italian architects aimed to demonstrate could be designed. In summary, this is a joint story of university, architectural and urban design – that is to say, three objects connected by the shared property of designability. The political dilemma associated with the story is whether – and, if so, to what extent – the new idea(s) of higher education proposed by the architects mentioned above really managed (or even aimed) to break away from traditional authoritarianism and discipline to accede to the requests made by students around 1968 for freer pathways to higher learning. A fundamental historical parameter in the story is that the projects that I will discuss were produced after 1968, as opposed to many other international cases of new universities that were conceived, designed and built ahead of revolution, as was the case of the British 'plateglass' universities, which will constitute the main contrasting case in the coming pages. Thus, whereas the latter landed more swiftly on earth, the Italian projects were from the outset mired in controversy coming from all sides: from the general social turmoil of the time; from the political incapacity to agree on higher education reform; and from the inner conflicts of the Italian architectural debate.

The episode narrated here is anything but a coherent, choral experience. Instead, it is made of singular voices that at times came together in discussion and debate, but, more often, operated in the solitude within which they had been left by politics. Yet the lack of guidance from central government was ultimately received as liberation, for the architects could operate autonomously. Hence, university design became a brief on which to project wider preoccupations and, often, the ego of each individual architect.

I will tell this story twice, according to two different narrative structures. As such, this Introduction serves also as a disclaimer about the inevitable repetitions that will be encountered by the reader who decides to read through the whole book. Of course, the double narrative is not a mere stylistic experiment, as the two parts into which the book is divided are ultimately complementary and work to the advantage of a general argument: reflecting on the university, as a central institution of humankind, reveals insights into architectural and urban theory.

The first story is told as a chronicle, reconstructing the facts as they unfolded over time. Architectural journals and magazines of the period provide the main sources of information for the chronicle, making the first part of the book an operation of historiographical systematisation for a mostly neglected episode in the university building boom of the 1960s, but also in the narratives of the Italian postwar debate. One reason for the latter might be found in the architects' disillusionment with the State's real intentions and its capacities to implement their far-reaching visions that reached a peak by the time the projects for the Italian universities were commissioned in the early 1970s.

The second narrative breaks with chronology and opts for a fragmentary structure that is developed 'through the eyes' of a selection of architects. Among the leading voices of the Italian architectural scene of the time, I have chosen to focus on Gregotti, Samonà, Archizoom, De Carlo and Canella, although names that would have similarly offered insights into the topic could have been Carlo Aymonino, Costantino Dardi and Ludovico Quaroni (who are discussed more synthetically in Part I). The choice has pragmatic reasons related to the availability of primary and secondary materials and the need to limit the overall length of the text. Nevertheless, the four positions they represent (considering Gregotti and Samonà as a unity) provide a wide enough spectrum to understand how university design was used as a lens to magnify insights into architectural theory, with particular relation to the 1960s–1970s urgency of defining architecture's response to growing urban societies.

Before finishing these introductory notes, a comment on the choice of title for the book, and, in particular, on the term 'settlement principle', is needed. I use the term 'principle' (*principio*) in a threefold sense: (1) a kick-starting element of something new; (2) a rule (or a set of rules); and (3) a paradigm, that is, an exemplary instance providing criticism of its context. In turn, 'settlement' adds a spatial characterisation that avoids the usage of other terms, such as city or town; in fact, I will not look at the university as a town or city in miniature, as it is often referred to more or less rhetorically. Instead, the university will be here considered as something that is in constant dialectical relation with towns and cities – or, more generally, with territories. Saying that the university acts as a settlement principle, therefore, means recognising its crucial role in shaping a critical consciousness that encompasses both immaterial and material dimensions – from the intellectual contents of academic thought all the way to the very form of the built environment.

To be true, mine is not any terminological invention, for I have borrowed the term from a project of one of the architects discussed in the following pages: Vittorio Gregotti's University of Calabria (Figure 0.2). About the project, Gregotti and his associates wrote:

> Our project seeks above all to direct the construction of the new University of Calabria towards a principle of settlement. The choice of such a principle is preliminary to any subsequent operation as its main role is to establish a relation among the various parts composing an architectural organism and the site; in our case, this is a relation among the various parts of a residential university organism: teaching and research spaces, residences, and the collective services that are open to an outside public. A correct relation among these parts and the site turns the University from being the representation and functional model of an institution to a model of a new settlement.[36]

While related to the specific theoretical investigations of their main proposer – as I will discuss later – these words have a general applicability that extends to the whole episode narrated in this book, for the architects who approached the design brief of new universities in Italy shared a belief that this brief implied the more general elaboration of statements about the city and about what the very term 'city' meant in a period of rapid urbanisation.

As anticipated, telling a story of events happening around 1968 on the fiftieth anniversary of the events of that year charges the book with a symbolic meaning that can easily take a celebratory route, albeit one that is unlooked for.

While a slippery route for anyone, it could be even more so for one of the sons of the 1968 generation who views it from a distance of time over which society has changed deeply. Hence, when I claimed in passing that universities are not so different now from how they were before 1968, my statement was intended as an answer to a general question: has the university really changed during these fifty years? Is the institution we know today fundamentally different from the one our parents went to? The answer would probably be more negative than positive if some of the more radical proposals made fifty years ago to profoundly alter the university by creating alternatives to dominant models are considered. As well as proposals by some influential radical thinkers and pedagogues, many of those proposals were elaborated by architects who were taking advantage of a singularly heroic moment in the history of their discipline: a moment when modernism, with its ethical agenda, was not too far in the past, while the formal extravaganza of a more recent age was still an unpredictable scenario.

Notes

1 Bill Readings, *The University in Ruins* (Cambridge, MA: Harvard University Press, 1996), 3.
2 Jean-François Lyotard, *The Postmodern Condition: A Report on Knowledge* (Minneapolis, MN: University of Minnesota Press, 1979).
3 Zygmunt Bauman, 'Universities: Old, New and Different', in *The Postmodern University? Contested Visions of Higher Education in Society*, ed. Anthony Smith and Frank Webster (Buckingham: Society for Research into Higher Education & Open University Press, 1997), 20.
4 Ibid., 24.
5 The Bologna Process is so called because of a declaration signed in the Italian city in June 1999 by 29 European ministers of education that set the European Higher Education Area. Its official definition and objectives are stated as follows:
   The Bologna Process is an intergovernmental cooperation of 48 European countries in the field of higher education. It guides the collective effort of public authorities, universities, teachers, and students, together with stakeholder associations, employers, quality assurance agencies, international organisations, and institutions, including the European Commission, on how to improve the internationalisation of higher education. The main focus is: the introduction of the three-cycle system (bachelor/master/doctorate); strengthened quality assurance; and easier recognition of qualifications and periods of study.
   Available at: https://ec.europa.eu/education/policies/higher-education/bologna-pro cess-and-european-higher-education-area_en (accessed 28 December 2018).
6 See Guy Standing, *The Precariat: The New Dangerous Class* (London: Bloomsbury Academic, 2011); and Isabell Lorey, 'Becoming Common: Precarization as Political Constituting', *eFlux Journal* 17 (2010), retrieved from: www.e-flux.com/journal/17/ 67385/becoming-common-precarization-as-political-constituting/ (accessed 28 December 2018).
7 See Roland Barnett, 'The Idea of the University in the Twenty-First Century: Where's the Imagination?', *Yüksekögretim Dergisi* 1, no. 2 (2011): 88–94.
8 Carl A. Raschke, *The Digital Revolution and the Coming of the Postmodern University* (New York: RoutledgeFalmer, 2003), 11.
9 For a critique of contemporary higher education and its commodification, see Michael Bailey and Des Freedman, *The Assault on Universities: A Manifesto for*

Resistance (New York: Pluto Press, 2011); Derek Curtis Bok, *Universities in the Marketplace: The Commercialization of Higher Education* (Princeton, NJ: Princeton University Press, 2003); Edu-factory, *L'università globale: Il nuovo mercato del sapere* (Rome: Manifestolibri, 2008); Terry Eagleton, 'The Slow Death of the University', *The Chronicle of Higher Education*, 6 April 2015. For a more general inquiry into the idea of the university today, see Stefan Collini, *What Are Universities For?* (London: Penguin, 2012).

10 Giorgio Agamben, 'Studenti', 15 May 2017, retrieved from: www.quodlibet.it/gior gio-agamben-studenti (accessed 28 December 2018). My translation.

11 Readings, *The University in Ruins*, 32.

12 Agamben, 'Studenti'.

13 Joan Ockman, 'Slashed', *eFlux Journal*, 27 October 2017, retrieved from: www. e-flux.com/architecture/history-theory/159236/slashed/ (accessed 28 December 2018).

14 Joseph Rykwert, 'Universities as Institutional Archetypes of Our Age', *Zodiac* 18 (1968): 61–63.

15 See David C. Perry and Wim Wiewel, *The University as Urban Developer: Case Studies and Analysis* (Cambridge, MA: M.E. Sharpe, 2005). See also the case studies that formed part of the research project 'University-Led Urban Regeneration', at UCL Urban Laboratory (project initiated by Clare Melhuish), retrieved from: www. ucl.ac.uk/urbanlab/research/university-regeneration (accessed 28 December 2018).

16 Manuel Castells and Peter Hall, *Technopoles of the World: The Making of Twenty-First-Century Industrial Complexes* (New York: Routledge, 1994), 1.

17 See 'The Global Economy's Latest Weapon: The Mega Research Park' (Special Report), *Business Week*, June 2009; and *Creative Urban Regeneration: The Case of 'Innovation Hubs'*. INTELI, Intelligent Cities Programme, 2007, retrieved from: www.inteli.pt/uploads/documentos/documento_1220959067_7946.pdf (accessed 28 December 2018). For a discussion of architecture and urbanism in the knowledge economy, see Sabrina Puddu, 'The Urbanisation of Innovation Environments: Architecture and Urbanism in the Post-Fordist Economy', unpublished PhD thesis, Dottorato di Ricerca in Architettura, Università degli Studi di Cagliari (2011).

18 See Sabrina Puddu and Francesco Zuddas, 'Cities and Science Parks: The Urban Experience of 22@Barcelona', *Territorio* 64 (2013): 145–152.

19 Ali Madanipour, *Knowledge Economy and the City: Spaces of Knowledge* (New York: Routledge, 2011), 154.

20 Thomas Bender, 'Scholarship, Local Life, and the Necessity of Worldliness', in *The Urban University and Its Identity*, ed. Herman van der Wusten (Dordrecht: Springer Netherlands, 1998), 18. In the 1980s, Thomas Bender resurrected an interest in the urban university as opposed to the pastoral paradigm that ruled the American academic ideal. In 1985, he organised a conference at New York University on 'The university and the city' to review and discuss the European origins of the university as an institution inextricably embedded in the urban environment. See Thomas Bender, ed., *The University and the City: From Medieval Origins to the Present* (New York: Oxford University Press, 1988).

21 Sharon Haar, *The City as Campus: Urbanism and Higher Education in Chicago* (Minneapolis, MN: University of Minnesota Press, 2011), xiii.

22 Ibid., xiv.

23 For more recent contributions on the relation between universities and cities (besides the work of Thomas Bender cited in note 20), see Kerstin Hoeger and Kees Christiaanse, eds., *Campus and the City: Urban Design for the Knowledge Society* (Zurich: GTA Verlag, 2007); Paul Benneworth, David Charles and Ali Madanipour, 'Building Localized Interactions between Universities and Cities through University Spatial Development', *European Planning Studies* 18, no. 10 (2010): 1611–1629; Roberta Capello, Agnieszka Olechnicka and Grzegorz Gorzelak, eds., *Universities, Cities and Regions: Loci for Knowledge and Innovation Creation* (London:

Routledge, 2013); and John Goddard and Paul Vallance, *The University and the City* (New York: Routledge, 2013).

24 The European Network of Living Labs offers the following definition: 'Living Labs (LLs) are defined as user-centred, open innovation ecosystems based on systematic user co-creation approach, integrating research and innovation processes in real life communities and settings.' See https://enoll.org (accessed 28 December 2018).

25 Madanipour, *Knowledge Economy and the City*, 212.

26 See Caitlin Blanchfield, ed., *Columbia in Manhattanville* (New York: Columbia Books on Architecture and the City, 2016).

27 See www.bostonplans.org/planning/institutional-planning/higher-ed/harvard-universi ty-allston-campus (accessed 28 December 2018).

28 See www.pennconnects.upenn.edu (accessed 28 December 2018).

29 See Haar, *The City as Campus*.

30 See Florence Accorsi, *Universités dans la ville = Università in città = Universities in the City* (Brussels, Paris and Milan: AAM Editions; SEMAPA; Ante Prima; Silva-naEditoriale, 2009).

31 Gerald Raunig, *Factories of Knowledge, Industries of Creativity* (Los Angeles, CA: Semiotext(e), 2013), 38.

32 Eagleton, 'The Slow Death of the University'.

33 See Zhu Wenyi, 'Two Campuses Harmonious in Difference: Guangzhou University City Group 3', in *Campus and the City: Urban Design for the Knowledge Society* (Zurich: GTA Verlag, 2007), 99–109.

34 See Stefan Muthesius, *The Postwar University: Utopianist Campus and College* (New Haven, CT: Yale University Press, 2000).

35 See Paul Ginsborg, *Storia d'Italia dal dopoguerra a oggi* (Turin: Einaudi, 1989), 160–199.

36 Vittorio Gregotti *et al.,* 'Università degli Studi della Calabria: Progetto per la cost-ruzione del Dipartimento di Chimica. Relazione Generale', July 1975. Archivio Gregotti, Milan.

Part I

Beyond campus

Chronicle

Prologue I

Another campus

In common speech, 'town-and-gown' and 'ivory tower' are interchangeable labels that attach a sense of exclusivity to the institution of the university. Together, they encapsulate an idea of friction with and necessary detachment from the university's surroundings that convey the sense of the university as an enclave hosted within foreign territory. 'Campus' is the most commonly used word to refer to this enclave occupied by a university, and it is a term almost synonymous with the word 'university' itself. It is also a term that has departed from its original attachment to academic environments to signify an increasingly wide array of corporate settlements that wave the flag of 'knowledge': knowledge clusters, knowledge hubs, knowledge districts, knowledge parks, and so on. The myth of autonomy is central to the promotion of such places, either because of their location on peripheral sites or, more generally, for their potential to shape corporate identity within clearly identified boundaries. Yet the idea of knowledge as a pure and uncontaminated domain – which is an ideal aspired to on one view of the enclave of the campus – is an impossibility, and this is as true in today's condition of alleged total connectivity as it is historically. Institutions of knowledge have always been embedded within a socio-political context, and they have very rarely managed to function in real isolation and independence. This reality should be sufficient to demystify any idea of higher education institutions as pure and safe havens set in retreat from the distractions and imperfections of the wider world.

Nevertheless, the idea of a safe haven has ruled over the architectural history of higher education, particularly since modernity has led to such history becoming self-conscious. The pre-modern university has inhabited various spaces, from the cloistered monasteries of the Middle Ages to the palaces of the Renaissance and the Enlightenment – a parasitical use of existing space rather than the construction of a specific, dedicated and new space. Even when structures were designed to purposely fulfil higher education needs – as, for instance, in the case of the Archiginnasio in Bologna – the modest size of the institution did not require thinking beyond the single building. The expansion and new codification of knowledge resulting from the development of modern science since the seventeenth century led to the complication of universities, resulting in larger institutions made of an increasing array of components that corresponded to a widening set of branches of knowledge and methods of inquiry. The birth of the modern university in Berlin in the early nineteenth century paved the way for such complication to unroll over the following centuries – a way that came to be walked with particular confidence on the other side of the Atlantic. Despite its origins in early colonial times – that is, before the new German codification of a university devoted to the indissoluble dyad of research and teaching – the American campus is commonly discussed as the only properly conceived academic space that has managed to interpret the growing complexity of higher education in the conditions of modernity.

One argument of this book (developed in Chapter 1) is that what we call a campus today is the result of a historical trajectory that transformed the original status of the campus as an open-ended spatial diagram into a closed and self-contained spatial object oriented to shaping a community of peers. This historical trajectory resulted in the campus losing its capacity to confront and critique the territorial logics of its time; instead, it gradually took part in the processes of urbanisation, eventually ending up being digested by them. On this reading of the campus trajectory, I build my narrative of this book's central case study: the debates over and design of universities in Italy at the beginning of the 1970s. My contention is that the type of thinking that grounded these debates and design proposals were closer to an original understanding of the campus than to our conception of it today. Crucially, the present-day conception of the campus was codified and spread internationally precisely in the period that I shall be discussing.

As the baby boomer generation of the 1940s approached college age, and as industrialised societies irreversibly moved towards service-based economies requiring a more educated workforce, the reform and expansion of higher education systems became a paramount priority for Western governments. A quantum leap in the history of universities took place, as never had higher education been so widely debated across a vast spectrum of actors, among whom were state governors, city administrators, vice chancellors, educationalists, sociologists and economists. The debates went hand in hand with a historically unprecedented expansion of higher education. This expansion manifested itself most evidently in the substantial number of new university buildings and entirely new academic settlements that popped up all over the industrialised world. Urban planners and architects were also part of both the debates and the expansion, and their key role in pushing higher education reform in the 1960s has been studied as a central architectural phenomenon of that period. The profound effect of this development on the culture of higher education was wittily captured in a student journal published at the State University of New York, one of more than sixty institutions to receive entirely new or expanded campuses under the auspices of Nelson Rockefeller's government in the mid-1960s:

> Because of the great New Paltz population boom, we found, in our community, another phenomenon of expansion called the LINE. There were breakfast LINES, lunch LINES, dinner LINES, bookstore LINES, registration LINES, snack bar LINES, library LINES, ticket LINES, fee LINES,

laundry LINES, and LINES to get on to LINES that head no-one-knows-where. And, beginning in September, there will undoubtedly be another LINE added for paying tuition. AND, the more students, the longer the LINES. [1]

To this day, this story's narrative has been centred mostly within an Anglo-American context, and it is Anglo-American ideas of higher education that have become a model for most other countries. Inextricably linked to these ideas was the promotion of the university as a specific moment in the life of an individual that required a similarly specific, possibly self-contained and safe environment for it to be nurtured – and even, perhaps, incubated – within. Stemming from these ideas and this way of thinking was the 1960s' codification of an international campus phenomenon. It is this phenomenon, which I discuss in Chapter 2, that defines, mostly by way of contrast, the fundamental context for understanding the Italian case. I show how its main assumptions and beliefs – namely, that a university campus could be an urban environment on its own, even if located outside a city for pragmatic reasons of cheaper land and easier possibilities of clustering and planned future growth – were actually trapped in a general incapacity to cope with a drastically changing condition that, as I will discuss, has been described as an 'urban revolution'.

A central ambiguity of the university expansion of the 1960s is located at the intersection between a desire for urbanity and its rejection by a retreat into the countryside. Italy did not escape this ambiguity, as evidenced by the briefs of four architectural competitions launched in the early 1970s that, invariably, indicated expansion and consolidation of higher education in out-of-town sites. Yet an assessment of the Italian case should not be abandoned simply because of this apparent conformity with the international campus phenomenon of that age – an abandonment that, instead, happened at the time of the events, in turn, causing the subsequent almost wholesale disappearance of this chapter from the official histories of postwar university design and, more generally, from architectural historiography. A more comprehensive reading of the Italian architectural and urbanistic response to higher education reform around 1968 requires consideration of the multiple discourses that intersected in ways unique to Italy. In Chapter 2 and Chapter 3, I discuss those Italian discourses, which can be categorised into three main strands: (1) the Italian postwar architectural debate on a changing urban condition; (2) the political debate on higher education reform during a period of centre-left government and reformism; and (3) the counter-debate of the students protesting inside and outside Italian universities and factories. It is only by considering the overlaps, idiosyncrasies and ambiguities of these debates that a better understanding can be achieved of the Italian projects for new universities, and in particular their attempt to prove that higher education could not be limited to a campus – no matter how big or beautifully conceived – but required more expansive thinking and ideas.

The products of the four architectural competitions that I discuss in Chapter 4 – for the universities of Florence, Cagliari, Calabria, and Salerno, in chronological order – clearly stand out from many of their contemporary international counterparts for their megalomania. However, I will argue that they cannot be fully assessed on the same terms as most of the projects that manifested infatuation with the possibilities of building big and that have been historicised under the label of 'megastructure'. In keeping with a widely accepted reading of Italian architectural culture of that period, the projects for universities can be seen as part of the ideologically imbued approach of a mostly left-oriented architectural community aiming to define a future for Italian urbanisation along the lines of rationally conceived regional dispersion rather than metropolitan concentration. My reading of the four competitions depends on this premise and proposes interpreting the competitions as a parable that recounts the euphoria about an idea of architecturally and formally defined city-territory in the first two competitions suddenly changing into a preoccupation that architecture had succumbed to the force of a growing technological systems-approach.

My narrative argues for the intrinsic value of a type of discussion – chaotic as it proved to be – that I believe has gradually got lost since the 1970s and certainly not only in Italy. This value resides in the attempt to consider higher education as a large-scale issue that cannot be reduced either to the perfection of a building or an array of buildings or to being a mere agent of the opportunistic and authoritarian urban development that creates 'knowledge districts'.

Note

1 N.A. *Paltzonian: Yearbook of the State of New York College of Arts and Sciences New Paltz* (New York: New Paltz, 1963), 7.

1 The campus phenomenon

Urban revolution

In the years following the Second World War, an unprecedented identity crisis impacted Western societies, which was eventually poured into the design of new higher education environments that proliferated as the main architectural brief of the 1960s. After three decades of global conflict and totalitarianism, the dawning of a democratic turn was not only immediately immersed in the insecurity of a new bipolar world order and the associated spectre of a nuclear war, but it was also accompanied by the sudden awakening of a radically different relationship between humans and the built environment. In 1970, Henri Lefebvre called this situation a complete urbanisation.[1] Central to his analysis of urbanised societies was the distinction between the industrial and the urban. Whereas the former tended 'toward homogeneity, toward a rational and planned unity of constraints', the latter tended towards difference: 'each place and each moment exist[s] only within a whole, through the contrasts and oppositions that connect it to, and distinguish it from, other places and moments'.[2] Thus, the hierarchy of the industrial condition, which had its key reference point in the large factory,[3] was swept away in a new situation that dissipated any fixed references, leaving only a reality of 'concrete contradiction'[4] shaped by the opposing forces of centralisation and decentralisation, territorialisation and deterritorialisation.

'How to impose order in this chaotic confusion?'[5] For Lefebvre, the response to this question required a substantial break with the status quo of reasoning and planning that wrongly equated the urban and the industrial and, just as wrongly, aimed to address the urban with the mindset of the industrial. Inherent to such a break was a critique of authority and bureaucracy, both of which Lefebvre accused of connivance with the commodification of values that was shaping modern consumer societies. Modernity and its associated act of industrialisation, he claimed, had turned the relation between humans and the built environment from being an act of free inhabitation to become a ritual enacted within limits imposed from the top.[6] Baptised as 'habitats', these controlled environments included all those products provided by postwar welfare states behind a promise of social equality: housing estates, transport systems, educational and service complexes.[7]

The history of architecture in the second half of the twentieth century has in large part been a history of the production of such social infrastructure. It has told a story in which the advocates of reformist, controlling apparatuses are opposed to the dreamers of a future world of liberated individuals. As Colin Rowe and Fred Koetter put it in the mid-1970s, the architectural debate of the postwar years has clustered around the opposing poles of the proposers of a 'brave new world' and the defenders of a lost past consisting of tight communities.[8] Reality, as it does with most intellectual dichotomies, produced an amalgam of the two opposites in the form of three-dimensional products that usually contained elements of both. From behind a cloak of new architectural splendour enabled by the achievements of advanced technological and scientific societies, the British new towns, the French *grands ensembles*, and the Italian neo-realist *quartieri* of the 1940s–1960s could not avoid retaining some level of anachronistic attachment to a lost past of alleged social cohesion. According to Lefebvre, these new environments were responses to the modern urban condition that came from an industrial mentality controlled from the top and promoted as a way of overseeing society by breaking it down into manageable space-products.[9]

During the 1960s, university campuses were added in large numbers to the palette of controlling apparatuses that made up Lefebvre's 'habitat'. Conceived as necessary responses to an urgently required expansion of higher education for advanced industrial and tertiary societies, they confirmed the urbanistic crisis of their age through their carefully crafted utopianism.[10] Built during the 1960s and 1970s in unprecedented numbers across Europe, the US, and the developing world, the new universities were the favourite testing grounds of architectural experimentation for over a decade, and they manifested precisely the coexistence of forward-oriented vision and backward-looking anachronism.

Certainly, not all the vast architectural production of academic environments can be put into the same category. Responses varied quite substantially between the small, compact university settlements built in the UK, the quasi-industrial complexes designed in Germany, the large new campuses with detached build-ings on landscaped grounds that populated both coasts of North America, the megastructural gestures superimposed on the Canadian landscape, and the uni-versity-cities that revived colonialism in developing countries. Yet all these responses had as a baseline a common ambition towards completeness, enclo-sure and self-sufficiency that was promoted as the means to restore a lost sense of community to urban civilisation. As such, the university campuses produced by the welfare state hardly contributed to shaping a new condition. Instead, they expanded the old condition based on the industrial logics of spatial con-centration, so that the campuses came to represent the new factories of the late twentieth century. What became 'universal' in the new universities was the simplistic practice of fencing themselves off within a discreet – although some-times very large – compound.

At the same time, the new campuses also signalled the drama of a society that had been deprived of a capacity to inhabit the world and was left with only two options: either to accept life structured according to imposed rules, or, as would happen during the 1960s, to totally oppose authority. The latter choice charged the academic environments that staged the 1968 protests, as they reclaimed criticism both as the basic role of higher education institutions and as a counter to the growing utilitarianism with which knowledge was administered from the top down in industrially advanced societies. Placed in a historical perspective, the use of campuses as a place of criticism was a revival of a capacity that had been ingrained in the earliest codifications of these particular apparatuses. To understand the university building boom of the 1960s, it is thus necessary briefly to consider the origins and modifications of the term 'campus'.

The fate of Jefferson: Campus neutralised

University campuses were not an invention of the 1960s.[11] As Paul Venable Turner has shown, the campus is an 'American planning tradition' that started with the colleges established in the seventeenth-century British colonies in North America.[12] Constituting an integral part of the colonisation plans for the new continent, the colleges of Yale, Harvard and Princeton marked a new birth for higher education that moved universities beyond the monastic nature of their British counterparts. This change was achieved through some spatial differences from the British colleges: whereas the latter had a traditionally enclosed nature, the new American universities were projected over their surrounding territories. The term 'campus' was originally used to signal this new approach to space and territory.

According to Turner, the earliest recorded use of the term was in a letter written by a Princeton student in January 1774 recounting an event evidently inspired by the Boston Tea Party: 'Last week to show our patriotism, we gathered all the steward's winter store of tea, and having a fire in the Campus, we there burnt near a dozen pounds, tolled the bell and made many spirited resolves.'[13]

Rather than indicating a three-dimensional product, 'campus' bore the more elementary meaning of mere spatial expanse separating an academic building from the street. In this early use of the term, the spatial specificity of the university was inscribed in a simple act of detachment that, differently from the British colleges built around enclosed quadrangles, did not completely fence off academic space from urban space.[14]

Continuity between the urban and the academic was embedded in the earliest master plans that regulated the future growth of the colonial colleges, which were to act not as self-contained environments but as the nuclei of new towns. City and university weaved through one another, and it was only when, at the turn of the twentieth century and supported by neo-Gothic revivalism, the ideal of the British quadrangle came back into fashion that the colonial colleges began fencing themselves off from their surroundings.[15] Since then, the ideal of the segregation of the university from the urban environment would hardly ever be challenged.

With Thomas Jefferson's design for the University of Virginia, developed between 1817 and 1825, the university decisively entered the realm of the architectural project.[16] Jefferson's project marked a pivotal moment in the history of the campus and, by extension, in the conception of a university. It simultaneously marked the highpoint of the idea of the university as an open-ended spatial diagram, which had been represented by the earlier colonial colleges, and accomplished the ultimate objectification of the university as a spatial and intellectual model that could be replicated. Famously, the University of Virginia provided a novel spatial representation of the idea of academic community. Its horseshoe configuration partially enclosed a stepped lawn between two parallel rows of student rooms that alternated with pavilions containing classrooms on the ground floor and the professors' residences on the first floor. In subsequent additions to the project, Jefferson reinforced the idea of a spatial diagram made of parallel built rows and gardens by adding a second row behind the original horseshoe.

As built, the Virginia campus manifests quite a different idea from that expressed in the first sketches by Jefferson. A clear focal point – the Rotunda library, added on at the suggestion of Benjamin Latrobe[17] – provides a spatial hierarchy to the whole complex, and the presence of a built fourth side of the lawn fronting the library – that is, on the side that was originally left open in Jefferson's design – hints at a self-contained settlement. By contrast, the original drawings unveil how the essence of the project lies elsewhere, in some sort of anticipatory urbanistic thinking that has been overshadowed in the built artefact. An axonometric drawing, probably executed around 1820, before the construction of the Rotunda, depicts the university as a fragment of a wider space. Showing an open ladder made of only the four parallel rows of pavilions, dormitories and gardens, it provides a snapshot of an indefinite piece of architectural order in the open landscape. This drawing unveils an urbanistic intention that must be placed in the context of its age: more than a self-contained community, the University of Virginia was a germ of urbanistic thinking that relied on a confrontational attitude both towards the status quo of the surrounding territory and, most importantly, towards the prospect of its future change. In an anticipatory move to the logic of boundless urban growth, which arose from the urbanistic codes and planning techniques in mid-nineteenth-century Europe, Jefferson devised a spatial diagram ambiguously poised between finiteness and openness and one that expressed a desire both to exorcise the city-countryside dichotomy that shaped European territories and to avoid the oil-spill nature of nascent modern urban planning (Figure 1.1). With his design for the University of Virginia, Jefferson was using higher education as a testing ground for an idea of urbanity – that is, as a settlement principle – and in the process offering a different vision of urban planning to the continuous extension of the city proposed a few decades later across the Atlantic by Ildefons Cerdà in his theory of urbanisation of 1867.

More than a century later, architects in the 1960s again found themselves faced with the goal of testing ideas about the city on the design of new universities. Yet, the degree of success in using higher education as the motivating force for redirecting urbanisation was significantly lowered by the inability to deal with the urban condition from inside its complexity. At most, universities

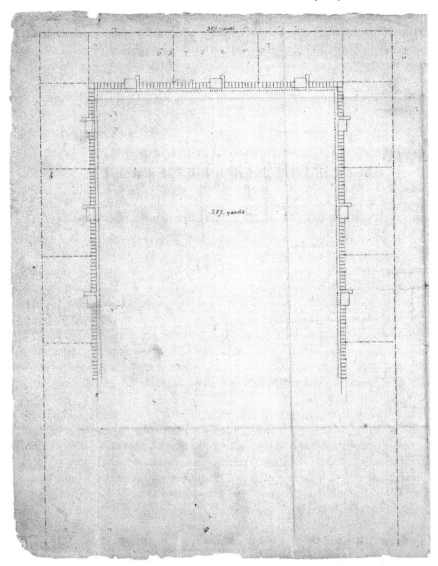

Figure 1.1 Campus between finiteness and indeterminateness: Thomas Jefferson's University of Virginia.
Source: Thomas Jefferson Architectural Drawings for the University of Virginia, circa 1816–1819, Accession #171, Special Collections, University of Virginia Library, Charlottesville, VA.

were treated like places to experiment with architectural solutions, but always within well-defined limits, and wider debates about what a university could mean and do for rethinking vast territories were rarely attempted. An explanation of this situation might be found in the meaning that, by the 1960s, had been widely attached to the term 'campus', and which stands in sharp contrast to the original indication of mere expanse of space denoted by the term. The story of Jefferson's university, with its fourth side being built and its original settlement principle of an open ladder diagram being turned into a closed figure, lent itself to the subsequent vicissitudes in the design of campuses, with the result that the history of campuses ended up being written as a history of enclosures.

1963: Academic community dissolved and reclaimed

And now – the education explosion ...[18]

If the key moment in the massive expansion of higher education during the 1960s were to be identified, then it would be the year 1963. For there were several crucial developments in that year that shaped the idea(s) of a new university for an open society. The first was the publication of *The Uses of the University* by Clark Kerr, the president of the University of California. In this book, Kerr introduced the concept of a 'multiversity' as an unplanned result of the evolution of the university in the US.[19] The multiversity was no longer a tight community, as academic institutions had traditionally been, but multiple communities clashing with one another. It was not an 'organism' because 'parts could be added and subtracted without harming the system',[20] rather, it had become a 'mechanism kept together by administration and activated by money', with academics themselves being more preoccupied with administration than with scholarly concerns.[21]

Kerr was sketching a gigantic and incoherent administrative machine populated by an affluent faculty with interests extending beyond the university because the institution was now 'called to merge its activities with industry in an unprecedented way'.[22] Hence, the traditional goal of a university – the pursuit of knowledge – was relegated by the multiversity to being no more than a memory. In the multiversity, knowledge had to be useful, thus threatening the survival of research and intellectual inquiry free from its instrumentalisation for economic purposes, an outcome that Abraham Flexner had already alarmingly signalled in 1939.[23]

As a space, the multiversity was an institution with the scale of a large industrial complex located 'between a middle class district on the verge of becoming a slum and an ultra-elitist industrial park, so that students can live in the former and faculty in the latter'.[24] Composed of many, different and specialised buildings clustered on vast university grounds, it found representation in Kerr's own University of California, where new campus plans at Irvine, San Diego and Santa Cruz were among the highlights of 1960s' American campus planning.[25] These new campuses were large academic compounds designed on the principles of plot subdivision, zoning, ring roads and landscaped grounds – features that were officially codified in Richard Dober's *Campus Planning*, also published in 1963 and the second significant development of that year.[26]

In the Introduction to his book, Dober stated: 'The size of the problem we face is not common knowledge. Between now and 1975 we will have to duplicate (quantitatively) all the campuses which have been constructed from 1636 to 1963.'[27] Adding the disclaimer 'I am not a historian and educator nor a scholar',[28] the author was presenting the professional practice base of the new planning discipline. By doing so, he was also confirming the leading role played by practising architects for a praxis-based reconceptualisation of vast urban territories in the postwar United States, major examples of which are Victor Gruen, the inventor of the regional shopping mall, and Eero Saarinen, a significant contributor to the architecture of suburban corporate complexes.[29] Dober's contribution was the university campus, which he dissected into its constituting parts, or 'planning modules' as he called them. These 'modules' categorised different needs of academic life into a set of functions that were then translated into space requirements. The result was the accommodation of each function in a single building or specific area of the campus, in a mighty demonstration of zoning practice (Figure 1.2).

Opening the book with a photograph of Jefferson's University of Virginia, Dober claimed to have distilled the components, as well as the rules for recombining the components, from a few centuries of American campus history. His claim testified to the objectification of Jefferson's campus, whose original sense of a more ambiguous and open-ended settlement principle was totally neglected. Central to Dober's science of the campus was an idea of self-containment, to which he gave mathematical precision by indicating an optimum size of 400 acres (160 hectares), possibly on a flat site. All that was needed once such a limit had been defined was to correctly design and arrange the components – the 'Instructional Facilities', 'Libraries and Museums', 'Research', 'Housing', and 'Sports, Recreation and Physical Education'[30] – possibly in the company of a good proportion of open parkland, and then to add a ring road around the campus together with generous parking areas along the edge. The result was *the* university campus, whose variations would depend on the capacities of its designers, but which would always be an iteration made from the same impeccable recipe.

Against this recipe, and in particular against the idea of a large academic campus comprising detached buildings, came a response elaborated in the United Kingdom. The third key development of 1963 formulated this response, coming in the form of a government document that triggered a vast programme of national reform and expansion of higher education: the *Robbins Report on Higher Education*. [31] The report played a fundamental role in pushing the British academic landscape beyond the status quo composed of Oxford, Cambridge, the University of London, and the so-called redbrick or civic universities founded in the late nineteenth and early twentieth centuries, to provide tertiary education in British industrial cities.[32]

As explained by Stefan Muthesius in his reconstruction of the British season of university building in the 1960s, the Robbins Report was not properly the origins of the new institutions that popped up throughout the country, for

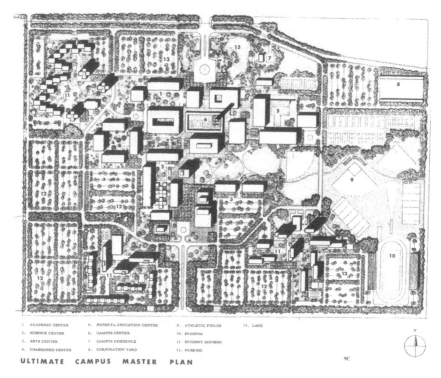

Figure 1.2 The ultimate campus.
Source: Richard Dober, *Campus Planning* (New York: Reinhold, 1963). Courtesy of John Wiley & Sons.

various of them had been agreed prior to 1963 and even as early as 1958.[33] In particular, the first seven were all independently founded by 1961 at Sussex, York, East Anglia, Essex, Kent, Warwick and Lancaster, and are often referred to as the 'British seven' to distinguish them from the wider category of the 'plateglass universities' that also includes the other institutions created in the 1960s.[34] The impact of the report, Muthesius notes, was to move away from the autonomous conception of new institutions and towards a clearer unitary governmental programme of higher education expansion; in other words, the new universities were turned into the object of welfare state planning while they were being built.[35] In fact, by proclaiming the expansion of higher education as a matter of national urgency, the report boosted the construction of the new settlements, and, by 1966, all of the seven had opened their doors to the first students.

Despite being gradually subsumed to the State, the new universities represented a novelty in the British higher education landscape because of their unprecedented level of autonomy. Although funded by taxpayers' money, the new institutions were not directly managed by the State but by the University Grants Committee, an organisation established to mediate between the national and the local levels. This arrangement gave to the new institutions two things they had sought: autonomy and difference from their competitors, the existing and established universities. Indeed, their founders rejected the elitism of Oxbridge, the structure and size of the University of London (at the time, the largest university in the country), and the unplanned nature of the redbricks (which had not been the result of cohesive planning, but consisted rather of an array of large non-residential buildings located inside the urban fabric of their host towns). Moreover, the new British universities differentiated themselves from their American counterparts. Refusing the hectic idea of a multiversity, they argued instead for tightness of community, which was represented in the projected student numbers, with five out of the seven planning for an initial population of 3,000 students.[36] Smallness was not limited to student population or plot size but was more generally a principle that the new universities extended to their pedagogical approaches. Seminars and individual tutorials were emphasised over large-audience lectures, and inter-disciplinary initiatives, such as a common first year for all students and the creation of Schools of Studies to bridge various departments, were implemented to create closer ties across the academic population.[37]

Architecturally, the new institutions proposed to nurture sociality within compact environments that often adopted an urban character, where urban was synonymous with a traditional dense townscape. This was particularly evident at the universities of Essex and Lancaster, which were conceived almost as continuous, horizontally built masses where a central 'spine' or 'street' accessed a series of squares with the proportions proper to a pre-modern urban space. These universities were also those that most explicitly wished to break with Oxbridge collegiate traditions, refusing the ideas of colleges and hall of residences in favour of more informal and urban types of accommodation in tower blocks that resembled the housing solutions proliferating across the UK at the time.[38] The idea of small sub-communities of students sharing common facilities as if residing in a real urban environment also applied to the University of East Anglia, where the Vice Chancellor and his architect Denys Lasdun 'turned back for inspiration, not to the college, but to what some would regard as its secret strength: the staircase'.[39] Here, groups of twelve students shared a dwelling unit that was independently accessible through a staircase inside ziggurat-style residential blocks, which in turn were plugged into a continuous 'teaching wall' housing the university's academic functions (Figure 1.3).

Of the designs for the original seven plateglass universities, Lasdun's project was unquestionably the most innovative for its ability to overcome the mere resemblance to urban environments and instead to interpret in an original way the relationship with the open landscape that constituted the territorial condition of the new universities.[40] Not coincidentally, Lasdun's subsequent project for the Institute of Education, set within an inner-city site in London as part of a master plan by Leslie Martin,[41] also demonstrated how an architect could interpret a project for a special piece of city in ways that went beyond the reiteration of the townscape mentality that flourished in British postwar architectural culture, and to which the universities of Essex and Lancaster were indebted.

Figure 1.3 The staircase principle: student housing at the University of East Anglia
        (architects: Denys Lasdun and Partners).
Source: Tony Birks and Michael Holford, *Building the New Universities* (Newton
Abbot: David and Charles, 1972).

Indeed, the universities of Lancaster and Essex approached the university as
an ideal town, finding in academic space the testing ground for ideas of urban
planning that were at the centre of debate in the 1960s – ideas such as the differentiation of types of movement on multiple levels, the achievement of a
completely pedestrian-friendly environment, and the confinement of cars to the
periphery of the settlement. Vice chancellors and architects alike proclaimed
the urbanity of their development plans, coupling, for example, statements that

'the central street should be an Essex equivalent of a town centre [with] neon lights [and] a certain amount of controlled vulgarity'[42] with declarations of 'attempts to make the University itself a kind of small town with its own modest range of small shops, restaurants and coffee-bars'.[43]

Eventually, the new universities' hopes of urban community utopianism were compromised by their having been conceived in isolation from a wider territorial picture, defined as they were as detached small communities set in calm isolation at an average distance of 2–6 kilometres outside provincial towns. Forced to be themselves small towns as the only way of compensating for the loss of city, their desired differentiation from the American campuses was quickly overshadowed by the reality of

> an Americanisation of university life for the British student, for the campuses, like American colleges, are total environments. When you leave your lecture room, go shopping, visiting or even walking, you are still in the university and you are not necessarily in contact with any other kind of life.[44]

Joseph Rykwert was the first to notice how the urban claims of the new universities were trapped within the sin of mere urban mimicry. As a recently appointed professor at Essex in 1968, Rykwert took that university as an example of the inherent contradiction behind the planning and architectural rationale of the British new institutions. This contradiction was the proclaimed desire to create new model towns while ultimately failing to go beyond the concept of density as a category for understanding urbanity. In an article that became widely quoted in discussions on the architecture of universities, Rykwert claimed that the university was the institutional archetype of its age.[45] What his declaration suggested was that the conception of the new settlements as loci for architectural experimentation needed coupling with a wider acknowledgement of the type of society of which those settlements were a paradigmatic example: 'It is a society organized around differentiation and disagreement; its freedom is the token of the open society.'[46] There could not be more dissonance between Rykwert's words and those of the new universities' architects who claimed: 'We had a strong feeling that a university, if it meant anything at all, should be a "coherent society".'[47]

Cedric Price: The large scale of higher education

The smallness aspired to by the new British universities in their pursuit of the impossible dream of a coherent society proved to be a desperate cry for an anachronistic dream of harmonious communities. Despite claiming difference from the status quo of higher education, the new universities ultimately confirmed higher education as a privileged service for the few to whom they provided, in the words of Cedric Price, 'containers [that] are dressed up to look like a medieval college with power points and are located in gentlemanly seclusion'.[48] Price condemned the results of the Robbins Report and their presumptuous offer of democratic accessibility to higher learning, and he proposed instead a counter-project for a radically different idea of the university. While remaining isolated from the mainstream solution of self-contained campuses, Price's Potteries Thinkbelt project unashamedly wedded the contradictions of its time and looked outside the self-contained academic compound to provide, eventually, a soulmate for the large-scale thinking that characterised the Italian architectural response to higher education reform in the early 1970s.

In 1966, by when several new British universities had opened their doors to the first student cohorts, Price commented on these outcomes of the Robbins Report:

> The prime weakness of the advanced educational system in Britain is a lack of awareness of both the correct scale and intensity at which such education should occur. Institutions today are too small and too exclusive ... The fashionable analogy between existing Universities and ideal towns is dangerous.[49]

Conceived as 'an advanced educational industry', Potteries Thinkbelt envisaged the redevelopment of a vast area of more than one hundred square miles in Staffordshire with the aim to put an end to its economic stagnation resulting from the progressive deindustrialisation of the Midlands.[50] In an early example of post-industrial reasoning, Price suggested reusing the existing infrastructure, in particular the railway system, to implement a territorial system of housing, work and education that differed from a traditional town/countryside arrangement. The project was located within a triangular territory on whose vertexes stood three 'transfer areas' that were conceived as multi-modal transport nodes for national and international air links, the railway and the highway system (Figure 1.4). The transfer areas were also imagined as production plants in which work and living intermingled through the juxtaposition of workshops, test-bed zones, teaching areas, a 'flexible faculty zone', and residential towers. They subverted the common understanding of what makes a university, which was reflected in Price's drawings and collages that depicted environments hardly associable to canonical academic spaces. They also imagined the academic faculty not as a set group of discipline-specific individuals, but as a much more unstable array of activities and people that needed the constant injection of new fields of expertise to accommodate the growth of knowledge-based production processes.

Accepting the inevitable prospect of utilitarian knowledge for advanced technological societies, a radical innovation of Price's idea of the university was the eradication of the distinction between the production of knowledge (university) and the production of material goods (industry). Potteries Thinkbelt blurred conception and production, theory and praxis, and promoted an idea of life fully devoted to production. Price did not conceal the reality of an economised and commodified understanding of knowledge, and, as such, he was

Figure 1.4 The industry of learning: Perspective of transfer area, Potteries Thinkbelt, North Staffordshire, England (architect: Cedric Price).
Source: Cedric Price fonds. Canadian Centre for Architecture.

ideologically closer to the uncomfortable idea of a multiversity than to the presumptuously accommodating self-contained communities of the plateglass universities.

Yet Potteries Thinkbelt also went beyond the point where Clark Kerr's ruminations stopped, namely, at the door of new large campuses. It ultimately broke with the two pillars on which the proliferation of self-contained campuses generally relied: the fixity of space and time. The campus implemented an idea of the university as a special time in life – roughly occurring between the ages of 17 and 23 – whose contents and structure were fixed by curricula and a set of planned distractions and paraphernalia for forced socialisation (student unions, clubs, sport facilities, dining halls, and so on). Although offering knowledge that was preparatory to a future working life, the campus did not dare desecrate the traditional understanding of the university as a special experience that clearly distinguishes being a student from being – in a following stage of life – a worker. Conversely, positing a conception of university as already a working environment, Price argued that education was an integral part of life across a much wider time scale. In his university, there was no difference between a worker and a university student simply because that distinction was naturally being eroded in a world requiring a more skilled and knowledgeable labour force capable of working with increasingly complex machinery and protocols. Potteries Thinkbelt thus anticipated the notion of lifelong learning that would become paramount in subsequent discussions on knowledge societies.[51]

Price's counter-project was, more generally, a radical comment on the meaning of democratic education. Potteries Thinkbelt showed that the equality of opportunity to access higher education – which the Robbins Report and other national reform plans had promised – was trapped in the re-enactment of the elitist idea that education is reserved for a restricted group. The idea of the university behind the new campuses remained an enactment of an authoritarian system that equated learning with instruction controlled from the top, as Price explained in 1968 in the editorial of an issue, tellingly entitled 'What about Learning?', of *Architectural Design*:

> Education is today little more than a method of distorting the individual's mental and behavioural life span to enable him to benefit from existing social and economic patterning. Such an activity, benevolently controlled and directed by an elite can, in relation to the physical structuring that its system requires, do little more than improve on the range and network of structures it already has under its control.[52]

Claiming that to create a truly equitable society there was no need to build more universities and more campuses of the traditional type, Potteries Think-belt suggested alternative paths to welfare state infrastructural planning that would enable individuals to personalise their learning, potentially freeing them from a traditional understanding of industrial, dependent labour and opening up wider possibilities for self-entrepreneurship.

Urbanistically, the project pointed in a direction that interpreted Lefebvre's depiction of a completely urbanised civilisation in which it was necessary for citizens to regain decision-making rather than being subject to a continuing cascade of services provided by top-down authorities. Just as cities in the past had been created from commercial or political activities, Potteries Thinkbelt argued that they could also be created from learning activities. Price believed that the Thinkbelt would kick-start a virtuous cycle leading towards increasing levels of civicness in the area. Yet this was no traditional city, nor was it a repetition of an industrial mentality positing possible fixed points of reference in a territory. The Thinkbelt aimed at a constant reterritorialisation in which material and immaterial production found their synthesis in an incessant pro-duction of space – as marvellously envisaged in Price's photomontages of a landscape unremittingly in the making and having to accept its own mortality. Indeed, integral to the project and in keeping with Price's reasoning about the built environment and architecture, a timeline indicated the predicted lifespan of the structure making up the new university territory.

Ultimately, Price's counter-proposal was as much an argument about the condition of higher education as it was a critique of architectural and urbanistic discourse. This was made explicit in 'Life Conditioning', his 1966 essay in *Architectural Design* that introduced the project.[53] Price kept the text separate from the actual description of the project, since the latter was intended to pro-pose a more general *modus operandi* for architects rather than a specific solu-tion to a contingent problem. Arguing that architects were dramatically lagging behind as contributors to an increasingly consumerist and technological society,[54] Price's main polemic targeted architecture's inability to respond to any problem beyond simplistically translating it into 'three-dimensional pack-aged ammunitions'.[55] Such a response, he claimed, was increasingly lacking meaning as the problems of society were becoming more ephemeral. Education was one such problem, and the new campuses were nothing but old-fashioned packaged solutions that played safe and did not challenge the basic structure of society. Instead, he advocated a radically different conception of education, claiming that 'if it is to become a continuous human-servicing service run by the community, [education] must be provided with the same lack of peculiarity as the supply of drinking water or free teeth'.[56] This sentence summarised the subversive charge of Potteries Thinkbelt, the most radical counter-proposal to the mainstream reform of higher education by means of a proliferation of self-contained campuses until the problem entered the Italian architectural debate.[57]

Italian architecture switched its attention to the problem of higher education at a later date than its British counterpart, approximately around the time that Price began working on his counter-project. As will be discussed later, the rea-sons for this delay can be attributed to the more convoluted political situation in Italy, where reform proposals for the university remained in the air well into the 1970s without reaching agreement. Crucially, the delay meant that the starting point of architectural reasoning followed the climax of the student protests in 1968. Not only did this occurrence charge the Italian spatial responses with more polemical ideology than their British precedent, but they also added fire to a desire to define original approaches to the problems of a changing society. As I will explain in Chapter 2, this desire was widely declared by Italian architects, and rethinking the country's universities became a crucial opportunity to advance evidence of this desired originality – which was inevi-tably measured in opposition to the British achievements and, more generally, against British planning and architectural culture.

Back in 1963, the frame of reference of the British approach to university planning had clearly been set in terms of the inside/outside-the-city dichotomy, as expressed by Lionel Brett:

> Any activity (with the exception no doubt of pure contemplation) that takes itself out of the city or refuses to come into it impoverishes the city and impoverishes itself. For the city it is the loss of youth in its streets and pubs and coffee bars, the loss of a bit of help in shouldering the burden of urban renewal, the loss of a bit of variety and vitality in the townscape. For the university it is the subtle threat of a new kind of public school segre-gation amongst goal posts.[58]

The Italian responses to university design built on a decade of debate among the leading national architects on the topic of a changing urban dimension. From this debate, they derived and elaborated a rejection of a way of reasoning in terms of inside/outside cities that clearly grounded Brett's statement. Instead, they argued for the possibility of vast city territories that could be rationally organised through the design of architectural form at a new, larger scale.

Produced by architects who did not necessarily always share the same architectural, planning or political ideology – at a time when the three continuously merged with one another – their ideas aligned with Cedric Price's attempt at breaking the status quo of campus design. Indeed, the reasoning of the Italian architects shared Potteries Thinkbelt's ambition to rethink higher education on a large scale, and it suggested the possibility of starting a new city out of a reconceptualisation of learning, which they instrumentally seized, much as Price had done, in order to answer the question posed by Lefebvre: 'How to impose order in this chaotic confusion?'

Notes

1 Henri Lefebvre, *The Urban Revolution* (Minneapolis, MN: University of Minnesota Press, 2003; originally published in French as *La révolution urbaine*, 1970).
2 Ibid., 37.
3 Massimo Cacciari, *La Città* (n.p.: Pazzini, 2004).
4 Lefebvre, *Urban Revolution*, 39.
5 Henri Lefebvre, 'The Right to the City', in *Writings on Cities* (Oxford: Blackwell, 1996; originally published in French as *Le droit à la ville*, 1968), 82.
6 Ibid.
7 Mark Swenarton *et al.*, eds., *Architecture and the Welfare State* (New York: Routledge, 2015).
8 Colin Rowe and Fred Koetter, *Collage City* (Cambridge, MA: MIT Press, 1978).
9 Lefebvre, 'The Right to the City'.
10 Stefan Muthesius, *The Postwar University: Utopianist Campus and College* (New Haven, CT: Yale University Press, 2000).
11 On campus planning and design, see, in particular, Richard P. Dober, *Campus Planning* (New York: Reinhold, 1963); Richard P. Dober, *Campus Design* (New York: John Wiley & Sons, 1992); Paul Venable Turner, *Campus: An American Planning Tradition* (Cambridge, MA: MIT Press, 1984); Thomas A. Gaines, *The Campus as a Work of Art* (New York: Praeger, 1991); M. Perry Chapman, *American Places: In Search of the Twenty-First Century Campus* (Westport, CT: Praeger Publishers, 2006).
12 Turner, *Campus*.
13 Ibid.
14 Ibid.
15 Ibid.
16 On Jefferson's project for the University of Virginia, see Richard Guy Wilson, ed., *Thomas Jefferson's Academical Village: The Creation of an Architectural Masterpiece* (Charlottesville, VA: Distributed by University Press of Virginia, 1993); Mary N. Woods, 'Thomas Jefferson and the University of Virginia: Planning the Academic Village', *Journal of the Society of Architectural Historians* 44, no. 3 (1985): 266–283; Turner, *Campus*, 76–87.
17 The earliest sketches for the University of Virginia were drawn by Jefferson in May 1817. Latrobe's suggestion of adding the central Rotunda came in July of the same year. The library building would eventually become the focus of interest for subsequent illustrations, as demonstrated by a view of the university drawn in 1856, which depicted the library evidently scaled up and out of proportion to emphasise its importance in the spatial composition of the complex. See Woods, 'Thomas Jefferson and the University of Virginia'.
18 'Editorial', *Architectural Forum* 116, no. 2 (1962): 51.

19 Clark Kerr, *The Uses of the University* (Cambridge, MA: Harvard University Press, 1963).

20 Ibid., 30–31.

21 Ibid., 32.

22 Ibid., 106.

23 Abraham Flexner, *The Usefulness of Useless Knowledge* (Princeton, NJ: Princeton University Press, 2017; first published in *Harper's Magazine* in 1939).

24 Kerr, *Uses of the University*, 109.

25 For the University of California campus projects, see Donald Canty, 'New Frontier of Higher Education', *Architectural Forum* 118, no. 3 (1963): 96–103; Clark Kerr, 'California's New Campuses', *Architectural Record* 136, no. 5 (1964): 175–199.

26 Dober, *Campus Planning*.

27 Ibid., 'Foreword' (by Dober).

28 Ibid.

29 For the work on shopping malls by Victor Gruen, see Victor Gruen, *Shopping Towns USA: The Planning of Shopping Centers* (New York: Reinhold, 1960); Alex Wall, *Victor Gruen: From Urban Shop to New City* (Barcelona: Actar, 2005). For a discussion of Saarinen's corporate campus projects, see Reinhold Martin, *The Organizational Complex: Architecture, Media, and Corporate Space* (Cambridge, MA: MIT Press, 2003).

30 See Dober, *Campus Planning*, table of contents.

31 *Report of the Committee Appointed by the Prime Minister under the Chairmanship of Lord Robbins* (London: HMSO, 1963).

32 See William Whyte, *Redbrick: A Social and Architectural History of Britain's Civic Universities* (Oxford: Oxford University Press, 2015). The civic universities were Durham (1832), London (1836), Manchester (1880) and Wales (1893). The redbrick universities were Birmingham (1900), Liverpool (1903), Leeds (1904), Sheffield (1905) and Bristol (1909). These were all located inside urban centres, and they were supplemented by other new universities founded in the mid-1900s such as Nottingham (1948), Southampton (1952), Hull (1954), Exeter (1955), Leicester (1957) and Newcastle-upon-Tyne (1963).

33 Muthesius, *Postwar University*, 95. The UK government officially announced the University of Sussex as the first of the new institutions in 1958. Since 1957, British architectural discourse had started directing its attention to higher education reform and university design. See Nikolaus Pevsner, 'Universities: Yesterday', *The Architectural Review* 122, no. 729 (1957): 234–9; Lionel Brett, 'Universities: Today', *The Architectural Review* 122, no. 729 (1957): 240–51.

34 Muthesius, *Postwar University*, 305. The British new universities were established in two main stages, with the first seven (1958–61) being succeeded by a second wave consisting of the upgrade to university status of the former colleges of advanced technology, which resulted in the universities of Bath (established in 1962, first buildings started in 1964), Brunel (1962, 1965), Surrey (1964, 1966) and Loughborough (1964, 1967). These latter institutions were all opened to their first students by the fall of 1968. See also Michael Brawne, ed., *University Planning and Design: A Symposium* (London: Lund Humphries for the Architectural Association, 1967).

35 Muthesius, *Postwar University*, 107.

36 The only exceptions were the universities of Essex and Warwick, both of which questioned the small number and aimed at 10,000 and 15,000 students respectively. See Brawne, *University Planning and Design*.

37 Ibid., 40.

38 See Miles Glendinning and Stefan Muthesius, *Tower Block: Modern Public Housing in England, Scotland, Wales, and Northern Ireland* (New Haven, CT: Yale University Press, 1993).

39 Frank Thistlethwaite (Vice-Chancellor of the University of East Anglia), in Brawne, *University Planning and Design*, 39.

40 On the University of East Anglia, see, in particular, Peter Dormer and Stefan Muthesius, *Concrete and Open Skies: Architecture at the University of East Anglia, 1962–2000* (London: Unicorn, 2001).

41 Leslie Martin, 'The Grid as Generator', in *Urban Space and Structures*, ed. Leslie Martin and Lionel March (London: Cambridge University Press, 1972), 6–27.

42 Brawne, *University Planning and Design*, 49. Similarly, C.F. Carted, Vice-Chancellor of the University of Lancaster, stated: 'We wanted to have a fairly dense urban type of development which would encourage the mixing of people as much as possible. We wanted also to make sure that the site remains alive until late at night, and was not an area which shut at five o'clock': ibid., 67.

43 A.E. Sloman (Vice-Chancellor of the University of Essex), in Brawne, *University Planning and Design*, 48.

44 Tony Birks and Michael Holford, *Building the New Universities* (Newton Abbot: David and Charles, 1972), 43.

45 Joseph Rykwert, 'Universities as Institutional Archetypes of Our Age', *Zodiac* 18 (1968): 61–63.

46 Ibid., 63.

47 Andrew Derbyshire (partner at Robert Matthew, Johnson-Marshall and Partners, architects for the University of York), in Brawne, *University Planning and Design*, 33.

48 Cedric Price, 'Life Conditioning', *Architectural Design* 5 (1966): 483.

49 Cedric Price, 'PTb. Potteries Thinkbelt: A Plan for an Advanced Educational Industry in North Staffordshire', *Architectural Design* 5 (1966): 484.

50 Before being published in *Architectural Design*, the project appeared in *New Society*: Cedric Price, 'Potteries Thinkbelt', *New Society* 192, no. 2 (1966): 14–17.

51 On lifelong learning, see John Field and Mal Leicester, *Lifelong Learning: Education across the Lifespan* (London: RoutledgeFalmer, 2003).

52 Cedric Price, 'Learning: Editorial', *Architectural Design* 5, (1968): 207.

53 Price, 'Life Conditioning'.

54 'I consider it unlikely that architecture and planning will match the contribution Hush Puppies have made to society today, let alone approach that of the transistor or loop': Price, ibid., 483.

55 Ibid.

56 Ibid.

57 There has been renewed interest in Potteries Thinkbelt, and Price's *œuvre* more generally, recently, as demonstrated by the following publications: Samantha Hardingham and Kester Rattenbury, eds., *Cedric Price: Potteries Thinkbelt* (Abingdon: Routledge, 2007); Pier Vittorio Aureli, 'Labor and Architecture: Revisiting Cedric Price's Potteries Thinkbelt', *Log* 23 (2011): 97–118.

58 Lionel Brett, 'Site, Growth and Plan', *The Architectural Review* 134, no. 800 (1963): 258–259.

2   Imagining an urban Italy

Anxiety

From cinema to literature and popular music, the city features obsessively as a disquieting presence in the artworks of postwar Italian culture. In 1966, at the sixteenth Italian song festival held yearly in Sanremo, the song, 'Il ragazzo della via Gluck', told a modern version of Aesop's fable, 'The Town Mouse and the Country Mouse'. In the song, two boys from a rural area on the periphery of Milan discuss the upcoming relocation of one of them to a new job in the city. The boy who is to relocate expresses negative feelings about the prospect of abandoning greenery to 'breathe concrete', epitomising a more general anxiety regarding the continuing conquest of rural land by the advances of the built urban environments in Italy during the so-called 'economic miracle' – a period of remarkable welfare and growth that elevated Italy from a state of disrepair after the destructive impact of the war to being one of the world's leading economies.[1] Between 1958 and 1963, Italian society was thoroughly modified by its embrace of consumerist culture, which had been enabled by the economic prosperity deriving from unprecedented industrial development. At the same time as social habits were changing, the country grew increasingly divided between a rich and urbanising north and the continuing depression of rural southern regions, a gap that was further exacerbated by the migratory fluxes from south to north that saw over nine million people relocate.[2]

Not all commentary, however, shared the same negative tones as the 1966 song. From his first novel, *Ragazzi di vita* (1955), to cinema classics like *Accattone* (1961), *Mamma Roma* (1962) and *The Hawks and the Sparrows* (1966), Pier Paolo Pasolini found in the peripheries of Rome then under construction the lyrical background for a depiction, as poetic as it was tragic, of the life of Italian society's lower strata on the edges of modern civilisation. The political significance of that background was most unashamedly manifested in his third film, the short movie *La ricotta* of 1963, in which, with an unsurpassed mix of poetry, comedy, tragedy and farce, the new peripheries of Rome were the stage for a revisited Passion of Christ, narrated as the struggle between the Italian underclass and the bourgeoisie – 'the most illiterate people, the most ignorant bourgeoisie in Europe', in the words of the protagonist, played by Orson Welles.

Moreover, it was in the early 1960s that Vittorio De Sica, whose *Shoeshine* and *Bicycle Thieves* had driven neo-realist cinematographic representation to international acclaim two decades earlier, focused the camera on the outlying new neighbourhoods popping up in the 1950s. With unspoiled satirical drive, his 1963 film *Il boom* staged the vices of the affluent middle class that was reshaping Italian society to fit the possibilities offered by new economic ventures, of which the building industry represented a favourite paradise. De Sica exaggerated the absurdity of this social state of affairs, telling the story of an aspiring building speculator who agrees to give up one of his eyes in order to maintain the bourgeois status to which he and his wife aspire.

With more documentary intentions, Francesco Rosi's *Hands over the City* (1963) dug into real facts to denounce the collusion of politics and building speculation in Naples through the story of a land developer who manages to get himself elected as city councillor for town planning in order to pursue his speculative activities. On a similar topic, and again in 1963, Italo Calvino reissued *La speculazione edilizia* (*Building Speculation*), a short novel originally published in 1957, in which he intended to 'depict an epoch of low morals'[3] by telling the story of a Genoese intellectual-turned-wheeler-dealer whose investments in the building industry failed miserably.

The recurring date of these works – 1963 – is not merely a fortunate coincidence with the significance of that year for the definition of new ideas of higher education at an international level (as discussed in Chapter 1). For the year 1963 has a particular significance for Italy. On a political level, it was when the first proper centre-left government came to power to pursue reformist policies that, among other aims, sought to restructure the education system that still worked according to the rules defined under the fascist regime of four decades earlier. On a more general level, it also marked the climax of the economic miracle, as growth rates started to diminish after 1963. With the fruits of a decade of change now at the disposal of commentary, the clustering of so much cultural and intellectual production is not a coincidence. From Genoa to Rome to Naples, from the north to the south of the country, and across the whole social spectrum from Pasolini's underclass to Calvino's intellectual in crisis, writers, poets, musicians and screenwriters painted a nation that was impotently accepting urbanisation. Their eyes focused on the middle stage of a process whose future oscillated between, on the one hand, a complete corruption of values and, on the other, the hopes of finding ways of dwelling in a new urban dimension.

During the same period, the Italian architectural community joined forces to discuss how to turn an out-of-control situation into a governable project. Again not coincidentally, 1963 was also a pivotal year for the architectural debate, temporarily putting on hold a line of thinking about the urbanisation of the country that had been under discussion since the late 1950s and that revolved around some central notions – *nuova dimensione urbana, città regione*, and *città territorio* – and a few paradigmatic applicative test beds – *quartieri, centri direzionali*, and *centri universitari*.[4] The latter succeeded one another between

the early 1950s and the 1970s as the spatial products through which the architectural community could prove a thesis. According to this thesis, the expanding urban condition could find in a set of exemplary large-scale architectural
interventions its surviving critical conscience against the prospect of private-led
urban growth so widely denounced in movies, music, and literature.

A new urban dimension

The urbanistic problems of the city cannot be solved within its walls.[5]

The story of the Italian postwar architectural debate has been told many times.[6]
As will be discussed below, the year 1963 marked an important moment of
reflection on what had been accomplished up to that point, but it was another
year, 1959, that historical accounts agree was pivotal for the formulation of an
Italian architectural approach to urban growth.

In 1959, three events – a congress, a competition, and a book – redirected
the ways in which architects had been dealing with urban expansion during
the preceding decade. Covering the whole spectrum of the architecture profession, from diagnosis and theorisation to proposal, the Seventh Congress
of the Italian Institute of Urbanism (INU), the competition for the Barene di
San Giuliano neighbourhood, and Giuseppe Samonà's book, *L'urbanistica e
l'avvenire della città negli stati europei*, combined to solidify the figure of
the architect as a critical antagonist to the growing cohort of technocratic
planners.[7]

Resisting an urbanistic approach based on numbers, codes, and protocols
became a key concern in the early 1960s for many Italian architects, who
advocated continuity with early modernist architecture's capacity for moving
across scales from the building to the city, which they believed had been lost
after the war. The urgency of reconstruction, coupled with demographic changes and increasing migrations from the countryside to urban areas, made multi-
scalar thinking an imperative to cope with the ultimate exhaustion of the significance of the very word 'city'. This urgency was first highlighted at a
roundtable discussion held during the Seventh INU Congress in Lecce,[8] where
Ludovico Quaroni and Giancarlo De Carlo spoke on a 'changed scale of human
life and of the urban scene'[9] and declared the inappropriateness of dichotomist
thinking about city versus countryside. Unlike other advanced industrial
economies, Italy was still at an early stage in its path towards massive urbanisation. Therefore, while *a posteriori* remedial practices were necessary elsewhere – such as in the megalopolis of the 'northeastern seaboard of the United
States' famously observed by Jean Gottman in 1961,[10] or in the large European
metropolises of London and Paris – Italy could count on the benefit of time to
develop solutions ahead of catastrophe. Quaroni and De Carlo claimed that
architecture was capable of directing a process of urbanisation in which city
and countryside would merge in an orderly way with the guidance of public
authorities.

The congress was also an important occasion for self-criticism, which particularly involved Quaroni as a protagonist of Italian architecture since the 1940s and one of the key figures around which younger architects clustered in the postwar years.[11] During the 1950s, Quaroni had been one of the designers of new housing complexes that populated the urban peripheries depicted in neorealist movies and novels. His own project for the *quartiere* Tiburtino in Rome, designed with Mario Ridolfi in 1949, became the urbanistic equivalent of neorealism, demonstrating a willingness to apply the rationalising power of modernism to a renovation of popular and vernacular architecture and its associated traditional social bond. Among the most publicised products of what came to be baptised the 'politics of the neighbourhood' (*politica del quartiere*), the philosophy that grounded Tiburtino, as well as many other satellite neighbourhoods built throughout Italian cities under the auspices of a national housing programme (INA Casa),[12] came under attack from its own creator in the late 1950s. In 1957, Quaroni criticised the ideology behind the new complexes, which handled the city through finite elements that presumptuously promoted social self-sufficiency.[13] 'On the way to the city, we stopped in the village',[14] he claimed, providing a written description of the desolate images of new housing complexes that inhabited the *œuvre* of Pasolini, De Sica, and Fellini. A major reason triggering the critique was that the isolation of the new complexes was not neutral; rather, acting as magnets of private development, they destructively impacted on the processes of urbanisation. Reassessing the ideology of *quartieri* thus implied a more general reconsideration of the role of public authority planning as a front for rampant speculation.

At the 1959 roundtable, Quaroni reiterated this criticism and sketched the main traits of a different approach to urbanisation. In the new urban dimension, he maintained, architecture was called to develop a cultural project still grounded on humanistic principles but not one intended to fashion anachronistic ideal communities. The reason for this was that the main subject of planning had changed from the village peasant, who had been part of a tight community network, to an urban human being, who was 'left alone'.[15] This change required the creation of environments capable of guaranteeing 'maximum sociability, solitude, freedom, and individual responsibility',[16] which justified setting aside the self-contained *quartiere* and switching instead to novel ideas. Quaroni thus began advocating *piano-processo* (plan-process) and *opera-aperta* (open work) as more vaguely defined formal statements that could interpret the ultimate instability of a new urban dimension.[17]

Not surprisingly, Quaroni himself authored the project that first envisaged the switch from the formal stability of the earlier *quartieri* to an 'aesthetics of indeterminism', as Manfredo Tafuri has described Quaroni's competition entry for the new neighbourhood at Barene di San Giuliano, on the mainland facing Venice (Figure 2.1).[18] Quaroni's project depicted large crescent structures between which a thinner fabric was sketched with an intentional lack of peculiarity and definition. With this project, urban design switched from the demarcation of definitive spatial configurations to the design of relations.

Figure 2.1 Designing a new urban dimension. Competition for the new neighbourhood Barene di San Giuliano, Mestre, 1959. Entry by Ludovico Quaroni *et al.*
Source: *Casabella* 242 (September 1960).

Moreover, the normative role of the architectural drawing changed from one of complete formal definition to one of specifying selected relations between the main components within an overall system that was ultimately left open to successive ad hoc detailing. A perfectly contained first-generation *quartiere*, such as the 'horizontal unit' designed by Adalberto Libera at Tuscolano in Rome (1950–54), thus found its diametrical opposite in Quaroni's competition drawings for San Giuliano. The result was a scaling-up of the ordering apparatus that Libera – and most other designers of *quartieri* in the 1950s – still timidly kept at the level of a tight community.

Inherent to Quaroni's drawings was the intention to smooth the edges between humanism and visionary modernism. Therefore, the door was potentially still open for the vernacular to dwell between the monuments of a new urban dimension that elected as its main cultural reference the famous geographical visions by Le Corbusier for North Africa and South America from the late 1920s and early 1930s. Those large-scale architectural gestures became a constant presence in the Italian debate on the new urban condition. Either in words or drawings, they populated the pages of early 1960s' issues of *Casabella*, as well as the writings of Carlo Aymonino, Manfredo Tafuri, Vittorio Gregotti, and Giuseppe Samonà, among others. Samonà, in particular, used them as the counter-images to the mainstream attitude of coping with urban growth by dreaming of harmonious communities set in peaceful continuity with the countryside.

This mainstream approach constituted the main target of attack in Samonà's book *L'urbanistica e l'avvenire della città negli stati europei*, the third milestone of 1959 and a publication hailed by Quaroni as 'the first Italian book on urbanism'.[19] The director of the Institute of Architecture in Venice (IUAV) since 1945, Samonà might be credited with inventing the term 'new dimension', which he used in the title of one of his articles – also written in 1959[20] – and which became the general topic of his book. Centred on a critique of the idea of the Garden City, *L'urbanistica* owed an important debt to the work of Carlo Doglio, a sociologist of anarchist persuasions whom Samonà had appointed professor at IUAV. In 1953, Doglio published the essay, 'L'equivoco della città giardino'[21] ('The Garden City's Misunderstanding'), where he criticised the Garden City movement as a technocratic act that merely 'worked' but was not motivated by a socialist charge comparable to that which had moved William Morris, Charles Fourier, and Robert Owen, despite the enthusiastic appraisal of the movement by his fellow sociologist, Lewis Mumford. In fact, Doglio's essay played an important role in setting the intellectual distance between an Anglo-American way of coping with the nexus of industrialisation and urbanisation and what eventually emerged as a reclaimed original Italian position on the same phenomenon.

In the Garden City idea, as originally formulated by Ebenezer Howard and subsequently imported to America by Clarence Stein and Henry Wright – authors of the 1929 plan for an appropriately sized community in Redburn, the alleged proof that a social bond was still possible even in the automobile era – Mumford had found the antidote to the uncontrolled megalopolis: he hailed Howard as 'the first modern thinker about cities who has a sound sociological conception of the dynamics of rational urban growth'.[22] Conversely, Doglio claimed that the Garden City merely remained at the level of a financial scheme with no real social ideology.[23] Its success was due to it being a perfect technical formula, but socially it could only reinforce an affluent middle class rather than propose a more equitable society.[24] The 'misunderstanding' that Doglio pointed out in the reception of the Garden City idea had long-lasting consequences, since it not only influenced the work of Stein and Wright or its British precedents by

Parker and Unwin, but it also went on to become the core of mid-twentieth-century planning ideology, finding in the British new towns its main formulation.

Following Doglio, Samonà similarly condemned the Garden City–new towns ideology as technocracy hidden under a cloak of philanthropic socialism. He claimed that this ideology approached the city 'from the outside' rather than from within the urban problematic. As such, it promoted only exile from the city as the logical response to the problems of congestion and the lowering of living standards that afflicted the world metropolises. Samonà condemned Howard's idea as an expression of bourgeois culture that had found a way of adapting itself to the explosive process of urbanisation by defining an ideal form of settlement that deceitfully promised the harmonious balancing of dwelling and workplace.[25] A middle class of professional workers thus started shaping a new city that merely resulted in the delocalisation of residential and industrial areas outside the city.

Samonà considered this process to have accelerated during the postwar years, as 'exceeding population' and 'non-homogeneous activities' had become the basic tropes of urbanistic speech trapped within an overall incapacity to deal with a pervasive urban condition. This incapacity was demonstrated by the continuing conception of decentralisation as a remedial practice for urban congestion, which was based on the anachronistic distinction between the interior of what was traditionally called the city and its exterior, the countryside. By declaring that 'the urbanistic problems of the city cannot be solved within its walls', Samonà warned that a different understanding of decentralisation was needed, and that the urban had to be discussed in terms of 'relationships between large structures'.[26] It was on the basis of this that the alternative ideas of *città regione* and *città territorio* were elaborated in the early 1960s as the intellectual categories for designing Italy's urban future.

Città regione ...

Initially used as synonyms, *città regione* and *città territorio* gradually became two opposing forces that increasingly distanced themselves from one another in a common search for approaches to the new urban dimension. Whereas the former remained the flag of Italian planners, the latter became associated with a response to the new urban dimension sustained by architects who emphasised the potential of physical form over regulations and codes.

Città regione tied into the wider ideas of regional planning that were being internationally debated in the 1950s and which had in Lewis Mumford its main proponent. Arguing against dense urban areas, Mumford claimed that 'what the clotted metropolis did in the past, the region will have to do in the future', and he defined the regional city as 'a congeries of cities, big and small, including hamlets, villages, and townships'.[27] Mumford's ideas were popularised in Italy via Adriano Olivetti's magazine *Comunità*, which, in 1957, published his article, 'La nascita della città regionale'.[28] In particular, they were echoed in the work of a group of planners that constituted the Centro di Studi e Piani

Economici (from here on shortened to Centro Piani), a research centre based in Rome that in the 1960s produced the first and second National Economic Plans. These plans, as ambitious as they were generic, were early instances of strategic planning that sketched a large-scale restructuring of the Italian territory in accordance with ideas of linear cities located within vast expanses of parkland.[29] The theoretical underpinnings of the two plans were discussed in *La città regione in Italia* (1966),[30] which argued that a capitalistic and market society needed to consider economic theory and urban planning as two sides of the same coin. The related postulate was that formal configuration should be downgraded in urban reordering, thus placing architecture on the periphery of planning. Whereas Samonà had condemned the technocracy of Howard, the Centro Piani attacked the empty formal utopias of nineteenth-century socialist architectural proposals – the likes of the phalanstère and the familistère – and their modernist reformulations – such as the large-scale visions of Le Corbusier, so beloved of Italian architects. Instead, their set of references included unplanned realities like the diffused cities of the Netherlands and of the Italian north-eastern regions.

Centro Piani aligned with Samonà's claim that the problems of cities could no longer be resolved from their interior. However, their approach ignored the possibility of formal experimentation, which was an inextricable part of Samonà's argument in defence of a unity between architecture and urbanism. Against it, they categorically stated, 'Le style viendrà par sucroît' – style will come later.[31] With this assumption, a wall was built to divide the technocrats – as the members of Centro Piani came to be considered with scorn – and the architect–urbanists, who argued for the centrality of form in the definition of a new urban dimension. To be sure, some architects cautiously positioned themselves between these two fronts; for example, Giancarlo De Carlo's definition of *città regione* as 'a dynamic relation that replaces the static condition of the traditional city'[32] neither posited nor condemned formal configuration. Conversely, other architects explicitly expressed their formalist faith against the generality of strategic planning.

In the article, 'Nuovi problemi' ('New Problems'), published in *Casabella* in 1962, Aldo Rossi clearly opposed the views of Centro Piani and reclaimed for the architect a role of 'defining spatial order for a changing reality, and creating forms capable of interpreting the new condition'.[33] Diagnosing the city as an entity made of parts – an idea that would be central to his most famous theoretical contribution, *The Architecture of the City* (1966) – Rossi joined Quaroni's criticism of the 1950s' practice of dislocating and dispersing discreet residential compounds, arguing instead for a massive scalar leap:

> Shopping centres, universities, cultural centres, and public buildings will all regain their formal importance: they will be the monuments of a wider metropolitan territory marked by an impressive public transport network capable of augmenting and multiplying movement, contacts, and participation of every man in the spirit of the new city.[34]

Rossi's list of new monuments hinted at the growing importance of service infrastructure for an urban civilisation. His article preceded by a few months the launch of a competition in Turin in 1963, when Italian architects (Rossi included) first confronted one another on the possible architectural format for a service infrastructure catering to an expanded urban territory. Such infrastructure took the name of *centro direzionale*.

... or *città territorio*

The programmatic brief of the Turin competition required mixing, on a 70-hectare site on the periphery of the city, the headquarters of banks and corporations, the administration offices of national institutes, commercial and leisure activities, and hotels and other complexes for collective living. In a special issue of *Edilizia moderna* discussing the various architectural, social, cultural, and political events of 1963, Vittorio Gregotti presented the competition as 'the long sought after opportunity for the Italian architect–urbanists to advocate priority and autonomy in the deployment of the urban restructuring hypotheses that have been proposed by the urbanistic culture over the last years'.[35] This opportunity now took on the official name of *centro direzionale*, which came to be conceived as the hinge between the space of dwelling and reproduction – the traditional city – and the space of production – the countryside – with the final objective of abolishing this dichotomy. In turn, *centro direzionale* was the apparatus that allowed an architectural definition of city-territory rather than that proposed by planners; it was, as Carlo Aymonino summarised it, 'the starting node of *città territorio*'.[36] In other words, the architects' idea of a city-territory posited a physical condition that could be enabled through the initial rational reorganisation and concentration of all service activities necessary to serve both city and countryside, with the intention of creating a vast urbanised territory that would eradicate the city–countryside dichotomy.

In Turin, rival operative solutions to the starting node of a city-territory were put forward by the leading Italian architects. The proposals included: the towers-on-a-plinth presented in Quaroni's winning entry to construct a new 'acropolis' in Turin; Samonà's indeterminate layering of horizontal slabs; Aymonino's silo-like monuments presented as a 'living organism';[37] Guido Canella's earliest formulation of *fuori scala*, which interpreted the project as a continuation of the metropolitan infrastructural system; the proposal by Architetti e Urbanisti Associati (AUA, which included a young Tafuri) that more faithfully adhered to the 1960s' international ideology of megastructure, as evidenced by the use of the A-section typical of many large-scale architectural visions of the time;[38] and the abstract gigantic cube of Aldo Rossi, Gianugo Polesello, and Luca Meda, 'a project of architecture on a metropolitan scale; a radically urbanised architecture'[39] that refused the complex articulations of the other entries and proposed instead an elementary form as a clear counterforce to the disorder of the urban periphery (Figure 2.2).[40]

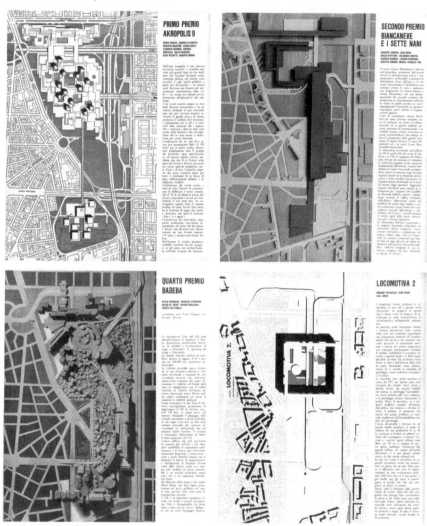

Figure 2.2 The form of a tertiary society. Competition entries for a *Centro Direzionale* in Turin, 1963. Entries by: Ludovico Quaroni *et al.*; Giuseppe Samonà *et al.*; Carlo Aymonino *et al.*; Luca Meda, Gianugo Polesello and Aldo Rossi.
Source: *Casabella* 278 (August 1963).

These formal variations immediately raised suspicions from within architectural circles themselves. In an article polemically entitled 'Affluent Urbanism', Paolo Ceccarelli questioned the cultural basis of the competition's functional-mix ideology, arguing that it was not grounded on 'justifications of an ecological, sociological, or urbanistic nature'[41] and attacking the participants' silent acceptance of the prospects of an affluent society. Ceccarelli pointed out that the creation of an affluent society – the social form proper to postwar advanced industrial economies – consisted of the growth of one large middle class that permeated the rest of society with its values and vices, eventually 'destroying collective solidarity to the advantage of individual competition'.[42] While this process was still in its infancy in Italy when compared to other advanced economies, its repercussions were still to be fully understood. Ceccarelli lamented that

> the urbanistic hypotheses built on excessive confidence about generic interpretations of the current processes of social change are lacking in criticism, and risk remaining reactionary utopias … Unless we unreservedly accept and study the consequences of the only precise reference at our disposal – the development model of an 'affluent society' – all alternatives and oppositions to the system based on functional rationalisation and urbanistic planning are fictitious and mystifying.[43]

In the defence of some of the participants against Ceccarelli's accusations, it should be recalled that many of them had actively contributed their reflections on the new urban dimension and its socio-political implications. Among them was a cohort that taught at the School of Architecture in Rome and included Aymonino, Tafuri, and Giuseppe Samonà's son, Alberto. In 1961–62, they taught together on a design course, led by Saul Greco, that asked students to develop proposals for restructuring the eastern areas of Rome along a new development axis (*asse attrezzato*) supporting the city's *sistema dei centri direzionali*.

In an article published alongside Rossi's 'Nuovi problemi' and later reproduced in *La città territorio* (1964), a book that reflected on the Roman teaching experience,[44] Carlo Aymonino elaborated on the term *centro direzionale*. Focusing on the adjective *direzionale*, he hinted at the existence of a wider objective than that identified by Ceccarelli, who discounted it as merely a functional mix in one location or under one roof. A *centro direzionale*, he argued, was a way of giving new direction to a large-scale arrangement of the city, 'an urban landscape that is different, freer, and more complex than the one produced by the brutal indifference of real estate speculation'.[45] To achieve this goal, it had to be placed within the realm of architectural experimentation, because what was needed were, as Rossi put it with clear modernist tones, 'new forms that fit the new condition'.[46] As such, a *centro direzionale* was a physical entity that could be comprehensively handled only by the architect, and not by the urban strategist, the city administrator, the planner, or any other professional figure who competed for authorship in urban planning.[47]

Another elaboration on the idea of a city-territory was Tafuri's view that there was a 'need to deploy completeness for a society that is increasingly incapable of carving its own space [while at the same time] offering possibilities for freedom within such completeness'.[48] At an early stage in his career, and before monastically switching attention away from practice and towards history, Tafuri operatively contributed to the 1960s' urbanistic debate through projects produced in partnership with Giorgio Piccinato and Vieri Quilici, teaching activity in Rome, and articles written for *Casabella* magazine, where he was a member of the editorial team. One of these articles, 'La città territorio: Verso una nuova dimensione', elaborated on his idea of a possible dialogue between freedom and formal completeness. Illustrated with images of the components of a new urban dimension – highways, airports, housing, and industrial complexes – the article diagnosed the urban territory as the interplay of 'large containers' and communication infrastructures (Figure 2.3).[49] A contradictory entity located between determinacy and indeterminacy, this *città territorio* required the type of thinking that Quaroni had managed to show in his scheme for Barene di San Giuliano. However, whereas Quaroni's project still focused on the theme of housing, *città territorio* required widening the gaze to the multiple dimensions of an affluent society and to the processes of tertiarisation that were the motivating force of some important exemplars of new international architectural production.

Claiming originality: A temporary pause

The definition of a form for a city whose population was increasingly composed of an expanded middle class of tertiary workers was at the core of some large-scale proposals that became popular in Italy in the early 1960s. Two in particular, Kenzo Tange's Tokyo Bay Plan, and Louis Kahn's Plan for the Center of Philadelphia – both projects that received international recognition in 1959 at the final CIAM meeting in Otterlo, thus contributing to the signalling of a crucial passage in late modernist architectural thought – were widely circulated on the pages of *Casabella* and other magazines.[50] Despite both architects receiving equal praise in Italy, as proven by honorary degrees granted by the Politecnico di Milano in 1964, Tange's influence ultimately remained limited, as the organic metaphors associated with its metabolist follow-ups did not find as many supporters in Italy as Kahn's more abstract monumentalisation enjoyed. The gigantic park-and-ride silo structures that Kahn drew around the edge of central Philadelphia to mediate between the compact city and the city-territory were more in tune with the theses of Rossi, Aymonino, and Tafuri than were Tange's insistence on plug-in logics.

More generally, the victory of Kahn over Tange located the Italian large-scale architectural proposals of the 1960s in an intellectual zone different from much megastructural production of that time – at least, as far as Reyner Banham's definition of megastructure is concerned.[51] For Banham, megastructure rested on the two related pillars of augmented construction technologies and fixation with technical detailing, which resulted in a principle of a permanent structure with more temporary attachments – as manifested in the visions of the Japanese Metabolists and the British collective, Archigram. Conversely, the Italians did not generally insist on such technological concerns, but focused instead on the exemplary character that large-scale interventions – in particular, public ones – could play in relation to a general reordering of territories and as forces that

Figure 2.3 The new dimensions of a city-territory.
Source: Giorgio Piccinato, Vieri Quilici, and Manfredo Tafuri, 'La città territorio: verso una nuova dimensione', *Casabella* 270 (December 1962).

contrasted with private speculation. A gigantic *centro direzionale* was thus intended as a territorial dyke controlling the chaotic spilling out of the city onto the countryside, and it reclaimed a directional role for the public authority, while also allowing possible partnerships with private urban actors, though always in ways that subordinated the private to the public.[52]

Given this widely shared objective, whether formal finiteness was to be the final answer remained an issue of debate among Italian architects. One of the initiators of the debate, Giuseppe Samonà, opposed the prospect of universal formal recipes. Speaking at a roundtable on the design course led by Greco and Aymonino in Rome, Samonà insisted that no model solutions existed and that the worst possible choice would be a reduction of a *centro direzionale* to a codified building type.[53] His son Alberto elaborated on the related risk of importing solutions from abroad. In another *Casabella* article that he wrote, 'Alla ricerca di un metodo per la nuova dimensione',[54] Alberto distanced himself from Tafuri's and Aymonino's elaborations of *città territorio*, warning that it was too early to verify them because they excessively relied on the definition of some fixed cardinal elements. What such elements could be still needed wider discussion and Alberto Samonà insisted that simply importing some from other contexts – such as the shopping centres and corporate office parks of North America – was risky:

> We should warn the Italian architects and urbanists against the risk of conforming to clichés derived from European or American models to grasp the new [urban] dimension. Conversely, we should encourage some original research on the Italian situation, as this is so differentiated from place to place, from case to case, that it hardly lends itself to a kind of thinking through 'models'.[55]

The inconsequential fate of the Turin competition contributed to a sense of disillusion that eventually dissipated the euphoria about *città territorio*. Alberto Samonà's article was the last piece of writing that still positively framed the new urban dimension as a possible object of design. Importantly, that article played the role of a hinge between a first phase of discussion that had centred on the reordering of tertiary activities and an upcoming new stage that would focus on education and the design of universities.

In fact, Samonà's text embedded a more general argument that *città territorio* meant more than mere tertiary functions and, instead, required that the country's educational infrastructure be rethought. In a crucial passage, he lamented the inadequacy of education for the growing masses of tertiary workers. Whereas the industrial worker had been shaped through the creation of specific schooling – secondary technical schools, in particular – similar educational pathways for the creation of a service worker were still to be defined. Samonà thus charged *centri direzionali* with an educational role as the possible environment for the cultivation of tertiary workers – professional figures who were becoming the majority among the working classes. Temporarily pausing the first phase of the city-territory discussion, his article hinted at its next chapter.

This new chapter was opened around 1967, when Italian architects joined the debate on a reform of the national higher education system. The implicit pedagogical charge of *centri direzionali* was thus unleashed in what became their heirs: *centri universitari*, as Giancarlo De Carlo named them in 1968.[56] With the *centri universitari*, the *città territorio* was brought back into the spotlight, along with the general attitude of refusing the importation of foreign solutions, as called for by Alberto Samonà. In accordance with this attitude, from the outset Italian university design declared war on the international campus phenomenon and aimed to define an alternative approach to higher education reform.

Notes

1 Paul Ginsborg, *Storia d'Italia dal dopoguerra a oggi* (Turin: Einaudi, 1989), 160–199.
2 Ibid., 173.
3 Italo Calvino, *La speculazione edilizia* (Milan: Mondadori, 1994), vi. First published as an essay in 1957 and republished in book form in 1963 by Einaudi.
4 Mario Ferrari, *Il progetto urbano in Italia: 1940–1990* (Florence: Alinea, 2005).
5 Giuseppe Samonà, *L'urbanistica e l'avvenire della città negli stati europei* (Bari: Laterza, 1959), 91. My translation.
6 Among many accounts, three useful references are Manfredo Tafuri, *Storia dell'architettura italiana, 1944–1985* (Turin: Einaudi, 1986); Cina Conforto et al., *Il dibattito architettonico in Italia, 1945–1975* (Rome: Bulzoni, 1977); and Ferrari, *Il progetto urbano in Italia*.
7 As early as 1964, Manfredo Tafuri signalled these three events as the markers of a fundamental shift in the architectural urbanistic discourse from the 1950s to the 1960s; see Manfredo Tafuri, 'Teoria e critica nella cultura urbanistica italiana del dopoguerra', in *La città territorio: Un esperimento didattico sul centro direzionale di centocelle in Roma*, ed. Carlo Aymonino (Bari: Leonardo da Vinci Editrice, 1964), 39–45.
8 The proceedings of the congress were published in *Urbanistica* 32 (1960).
9 Ludovico Quaroni et al., 'Tavola rotonda', *Urbanistica* 32 (1960): 7. My translation.
10 Jean Gottmann, *Megalopolis: The Urbanized Northeastern Seaboard of the United States* (New York: Twentieth Century Fund, 1961).
11 See Manfredo Tafuri, *Ludovico Quaroni e lo sviluppo dell'architettura moderna in Italia* (Milan: Edizioni di Comunita, 1946).
12 For an early review of many projects of new *quartieri* in Italy, see *Urbanistica* 7 (1951). For the projects developed under the auspices of INA Casa, see: Pier Giovanni Bardelli, Rinaldo Capomolla, and Rosalia Vittorini, eds., *L'architettura INA Casa 1949–1963: Aspetti e problemi di conservazione e recupero* (Rome: Gangemi, 2003). For a recent rereading of the Italian postwar housing projects, see Carlo Melograni, *Architetture nell'Italia della ricostruzione: Modernità versus modernizzazione 1945–1960* (Macerata: Quodlibet, 2015).
13 Ludovico Quaroni, 'Politica del quartiere', *La casa* 4 (1957). My translation.
14 Ludovico Quaroni, 'Il paese dei barocchi', *Casabella* 215 (1957), 24. My translation.
15 Quaroni et al., 'Tavola rotonda', 7.
16 Ibid.
17 Tafuri, *Storia dell'architettura italiana*, 96.
18 Ibid. My translation. The competition projects for Barene di San Giuliano were published in *Casabella* 242 (1960) and *Urbanistica* 31 (1960).
19 Ludovico Quaroni, review of Giuseppe Samonà's *L'urbanistica e l'avvenire della città negli stati europei* in *Casabella* 236 (1960). My translation.

20 Giuseppe Samonà, 'La nuova dimensione della città', *Urbanistica conversazioni* (May 1959).

21 Carlo Doglio, *L'equivoco della città giardino* (Naples: RL, 1953). Doglio's essay was published in a shorter form in *Urbanistica* 13 (1953). It has been republished as Carlo Doglio, *La città giardino* (Rome: Gangemi, 1985). The quotations used here are from the 1985 edition.

22 Lewis Mumford, *The Culture of Cities* (New York: Harcourt, Brace & World, 1966; first published in 1938), 397–398.

23 Doglio, *La città giardino*, 32.

24 Ibid., 34.

25 Samonà, *L'urbanistica e l'avvenire della città*, 12.

26 Ibid., 91. My translation.

27 Lewis Mumford, 'A New Regional Plan to Arrest Megalopolis', *Architectural Record* 137, no. 3 (1965): 153.

28 Mumford's ideas were popularised in Italy through the publication in *Comunità* of the articles 'L'unità di quartiere', *Comunità* 24 (1954), 'La nascita della città regionale', *Comunità* 55 (1957), and 'La via d'uscita umana', *Comunità* 83 (1960).

29 The Centro di Studi e Piani Economici was a not-for-profit association comprising planners, engineers, economists, sociologists, geographers, and other professional figures, whose aim was to develop an integrated approach to planning. Franco Archibugi, the Italian planner and coordinator of Centro Piani, has noted how a more holistic kind of planning was at the time being requested by the United Nations. Archibugi pointed out the absolute novelty of such an approach in Italy where, particularly at an academic level, different disciplinary contributions were still kept separate. For Centro Piani's work and its role in the formulation of studies and plans that led to the Second National Economic Plan (commonly known as Progetto '80), see Franco Archibugi, ed., *La città regione in Italia* (Turin: Boringhieri, 1966); and Cristina Renzoni, *Il Progetto '80: Un'idea di paese nell'Italia degli anni sessanta* (Florence: Alinea, 2012).

30 Archibugi, *La città regione*.

31 Quotation from A. Massé, *Prévision et prospective*, in Francesco Sirugo, 'Città e regione nello sviluppo storico della città industriale', in Archibugi, *La città regione*, 13.

32 Giancarlo De Carlo, 'Relazione conclusiva al seminario dell'ILSES sulla nuova dimensione e la città-regione' (Stresa, 1962), quoted in Aldo Rossi, 'Nuovi problemi', *Casabella* 264 (1962): 5. My translation.

33 Rossi, 'Nuovi problemi', 4. My translation.

34 Ibid., 6. My translation.

35 Vittorio Gregotti, 'Due concorsi', *Edilizia moderna* 82–83 (1964): 109. My translation.

36 Carlo Aymonino, 'Il sistema dei centri direzionali nella capitale', *Casabella* 264 (1962): 24. My translation. In 1967, Aymonino published a monograph on *centri direzionali* in the same series – which he also edited – as the 1964 book ,*La città territorio* (Bari: De Donato–Leonardo da Vinci Editore, 1964): see Carlo Aymonino, *I centri direzionali: La teoria e la practica, gli esempi italiani e stranieri, il sistema direzionale della città di Bologna* (Bari: De Donato, 1967).

37 See *Casabella* 278 (1963): 28. My translation.

38 The more faithful adherence of AUA's project to the international megastructural ideas of the 1960s did not escape Reyner Banham's radar, as is proved by the inclusion of the project in his 1976 book on megastructure: Reyner Banham, *Megastructure: Urban Futures of the Recent Past* (London: Thames and Hudson, 1976).

39 See *Casabella* 278 (1963): 48. My translation.

40 See Pier Vittorio Aureli, *The Project of Autonomy: Politics and Architecture Within and Against Capitalism* (New York: Princeton Architectural Press, 2008), 66–69.

41 Paolo Ceccarelli, 'Urbanistica opulenta', *Casabella* 278 (1963): 8. My translation.

42 Ibid., 6. My translation.

43 Ibid. My translation.

44 Aymonino, *La città territorio*.

45 Aymonino, 'Il sistema dei centri direzionali nella capitale', 24. My translation.

46 Rossi, 'Nuovi problemi', 4. My translation.

47 Ibid.

48 Manfredo Tafuri, 'Studi e ipotesi di lavoro per il sistema direzionale di Roma', *Casabella* 264 (1962): 32. My translation.

49 Luigi Piccinato, Vieri Quilici, and Manfredo Tafuri, 'La città-territorio: Verso una nuova dimensione', *Casabella* 270 (1962): 16–25.

50 Tange's Tokyo Bay plan was comprehensively presented to an Italian audience by Giorgio Grassi in *Casabella* 258 (1961). The Plan for the Center of Philadelphia was discussed in *Casabella* 260 (1962). Drawings of the two projects by Kahn and Tange were used by Aldo Rossi as the opening images for his 1962 article, 'Nuovi problemi'. See also Marcello Pazzaglini, 'Il dibattito sulla città e sul territorio', in Conforto *et al., Il dibattito architettonico*, 59–62.

51 See Banham, *Megastructure*.

52 I elaborate more on the relation between Italian mega-architecture of the 1960s and the phenomenon of megastructure in Francesco Zuddas, 'The Eccentric Outsider: Or, Why Reyner Banham Dismissed Giuseppe Samonà's Mega-project for the University of Cagliari', *Histories of Postwar Architecture* 1, no. 3 (2019): 50–71.

53 Giuseppe Samonà, 'Relazione e conclusione al seminario su città-territorio', in Aymonino, *La città territorio*, 90–9.

54 Alberto Samonà, 'Alla ricerca di un metodo per la nuova dimensione', *Casabella* 277 (1963): 50–54.

55 Ibid., 53. My translation.

56 As I will discuss later, the term *centro universitario* was used by Giancarlo De Carlo in 1968 as an alternative to *città universitaria* and *campus universitario*, with the intention of hinting at the definition of a new spatial and urbanistic model of university different from the predominant and traditional ones. See Giancarlo De Carlo, ed., *Pianificazione e disegno delle università* (Rome: Edizioni universitarie italiane, 1968).

3 Reform or revolution

The chimera of autonomy

Reclaiming autonomy for the university is as old as the academic institution itself. Historians have shown that the rise of the first medieval universities was a spontaneous phenomenon that defined them as one among the corporations making up the social fabric of the Middle Ages and implied the equivalence of the two notions of autonomy and freedom. In his study published in 1923, Charles Homer Haskins wrote: 'Historically, the word university has no connection with the universe or the universality of learning; it denotes only the totality of a group, whether of barbers, carpenters, or students did not matter.'[1]

The earliest universities enjoyed administrative autonomy, as students paid tuition fees directly to the professors, external funding did not exist, and the institution did not own any real estate so expenses were limited to individual salaries. Academic freedom was defined as the students' right to learn and the professors' right to teach freely, without programmes of study defined from the outside. Apart from philosophy and theology, in whose domains truth was 'something which has already been revealed to us by authority' and hence could only be 'expounded', 'men were normally free to lecture and dispute as they would'.[2]

In modern times, the striving for autonomy has been charged with anti-State sentiments. Yet the university has never constituted part of that 'public sphere' discussed by Jürgen Habermas as an arena of debate located outside both the private household and the public authority.[3] Unlike the literary circles and cafés described by Habermas as the places where a parallel discourse against the top-down decision-making of the State could be developed, the modern university has inextricably been imbricated with the State, to the point of acting as its brain and one of its major operative arms. This alliance was built on a conceptual separation of the notions of autonomy and freedom that had been one and the same thing in the Middle Ages.

It comes as no surprise, therefore, that in 1884 – that is, less than two decades since Italy had been defined as a unified, modern nation – a deputy to the Italian parliament, while discussing the institutions to be created to govern the new nation, openly attacked the prospect of a national university autonomous from State control, arguing that autonomy should not be confused with the freedom to cultivate knowledge. The latter, he claimed, would be possible only as long as the university was administratively anchored to State bureaucracy.[4] For years to come, the Italian university was structured precisely according to this terminological ambivalence, which made the term 'autonomy' the most ambiguous and frustrating recurrence in the laws and codes passed by the government, starting with the reform of education elaborated by Giovanni Gentile in 1923, a year after Benito Mussolini had taken power.[5] Providing the structural characteristics that Italian education would retain well into postwar democracy, Gentile's reform granted three types of autonomy to universities (administrative, pedagogical, and disciplinary) but at the same time tied the universities to the State for financial provision and for management of the relation between higher education and the job market – the latter was achieved by the establishment of State-run examinations (*esami di stato*) to test the eligibility of graduates to enter the professional world. However, despite the presence of some liberal intentions in the original text of the reform – such as granting freedom to students to define the curricula and to faculties for their organisation – the unfortunate timing of the reform occurring within the context of the rise of totalitarian fascism prevented the possibility of real academic autonomy. When Mussolini himself called Gentile's 'the most fascist of reforms', he was signalling the complete neutralisation of any liberal spirit. This anti-liberal approach was reinforced by new acts passed between 1933 and 1938 (also the year of the racial laws in Italy) that tightened State control over higher education.[6]

Not even the democratic turn after the war managed to fashion a clear conception of academic autonomy. Article 33 of the 1947 Italian Constitution stated: 'Arts and sciences and their teaching are free [and] institutions of high culture, universities and academies have the right to define their own autonomous statutes within the limits defined by the state.'[7] But in an essay in 1964, commenting on this constitutional declaration of autonomy, Salvatore Pugliatti complained: 'We know that something called university autonomy exists, but arguably no one could state exactly what that is.'[8] The mingling of freedom and autonomy in the wording of the Constitution shaped a slippery object, neither independent nor totally controlled. Ultimately, a widespread belief, shared across the political establishment and the Italian population alike, was that the university should remain a public institution. This tipped the balance towards the view that the State should have sovereign power over a higher education system, and that it should therefore grow as an array of public institutes, all very similar to one another and guaranteeing centrally controlled education throughout the country.

If anything, however, the Italian academic system became significantly unbalanced during the postwar years, and, by the 1960s, there was marked discrepancy between regions with small populations and numerous higher education institutions – such as Emilia Romagna, with three universities and an overall regional population of 3.5 million – and the southern areas of the country where only two universities, Naples and Bari, served a population of over 11 million. The debate on how to reform higher education to fuel the same level of development for Italy as that of other advanced economies thus gravitated towards a conception of changing the infrastructure of the country from the top down: it was supposed that by providing more, or at least renovated, institutions, the government would guarantee equal opportunities from north to south.

The restructuring hypothesis involved questioning the exclusively public nature of Italian higher education, prompted by foreign examples, particularly in the United States. The most overt embrace of an American dream positing a mixture of competition and collaboration among public and private institutions came from Adriano Buzzati-Traverso, a geneticist who, in the 1950s, spent a few years as a visiting professor at the University of California. On returning to his academic base at the University of Pavia, Traverso began commenting on the condition of the Italian university in a series of newspaper articles, subsequently collected in the polemically entitled book *Il fossile denutrito: L'università italiana* (*The Undernourished Fossil: The Italian University*), in which he asked his readers to dream of a different future for universities:

> Imagine a different university in which nothing was ruled, but everything always under experimentation; a university without faculties as we understand them today; governed by temporary committees of professors; imagine a university in which industrialists, farmers, bankers, professors and students took an active part in its administration; in which professors were obliged to live and spend the whole day in classrooms and laboratories; imagine a different university in which professors did not have any side job, and received salaries similar to an industrialist; a university in which students were obliged to live in colleges, with scholarships for at least one third of the student body; ... imagine a university whose life happened in a beautiful campus, among trees, flowers, good libraries and laboratories far from the noise and the distractions of a big city.[9]

A mediocre level of teaching, a high degree of absenteeism by students and professors, a lack of proper university life, old-fashioned curricula, and archaic forms of academic government were the main failures of Italian higher education, which Traverso contrasted to the American system whose superiority, he claimed, stemmed from the rivalry between academic institutions. However, ambiguity runs through his words, which contain the contradictions of what Clark Kerr had named a multiversity[10] – and not coincidentally, given that Kerr's own University of California had been the gateway to America for Traverso. His commentary orchestrated an impossible reconciliation of opposites that is evidenced by the concomitant calls for freedom – a university where nothing is ruled, and one that is governed by temporary associations – and top-down control – a university where students and professors are obliged to live.

Focusing on all the critical aspects touched on by Traverso, the reform proposals for Italian higher education that came under discussion in the early 1960s absorbed this contradictory attitude of advocating change from within a substantial confirmation of the status quo.

Minimalist reformism

The American-influenced ideas of Traverso, and of others who began equating universities to business enterprises – as stated in the 1967 book, *L'università come impresa* [11] – suggested that different institutions, including those of a private nature, were needed both to complement and to disrupt the homogeneity of a system that would otherwise be unable to survive in what was increasingly perceived as an inevitable marketisation of knowledge in consumer capitalist societies. Faced by such a revolutionary scenario for a system that was kept under control because it was totally public and mostly made up of small to medium-sized institutions, the defensive strategy of administrators and politicians was from the outset disguised as praise for an existing intelligence of the system:

> We believe in the unique and precious role of small universities. For this reason, we claim that before building new, petty, incomplete, isolated universities, it is necessary to pay as much attention and care as possible to the existing ones whose roots lie deep in our history and traditions. [12]

The dream of smallness, however, did not last long. An act of parliament in 1961, [13] which granted university access to students coming from any type of high school, officially marked the birth of a mass higher education system whose impact was massive: a student population of 231,000 in 1950 escalated to 314,000 in 1963, to 682,000 in 1970, and to over one million in 1980. [14] In the face of such self-inflicted growth, the urgency of achieving agreement about a reform of higher education became paramount.

Attempts to reform education had already been under way since 1957, when the then Minister of Education, Aldo Moro, presented a proposal that included setting up multidisciplinary university departments and flexible curricula tailored to the individual student. [15] Then, in July 1963, the new Minister of Public Education, Luigi Gui, was presented with a report on the condition of Italian education – a sort of Italian equivalent of the Robbins Report, published a few months before the British document. [16] A few months later, on 4 December 1963, Moro led the instauration of a centre-left government, officially inaugurating a new reformist period that historians have dubbed 'minimalist reformism' to reflect the Christian Democratic Party's prioritisation of taming their socialist coalition partners over profoundly altering the country's status quo. [17] Consequently, the higher education reform proposal that followed carefully balanced change and preservation. Based on the recommendations of the 1963 report, a formal reform proposal was elaborated by the Ministry of Education and presented to parliament on 4 May 1965. [18] Introduced as the necessary innovations to align Italian higher education both with international standards and with a changing national labour structure, the main novelties included the creation of multidisciplinary departments to complement the existing faculties, and a three-tier degree system, comprising a university diploma, a full degree, and a research doctorate, that aimed to depart from the single title (*Laurea*) traditionally granted by Italian universities.

This proposed diversification of academic titles emerged as a double-edged strategy that signalled the adoption of democratic education for all but, like anything in welfare state democracies, also implied the simultaneous neutralisation of this adoption. The recommended hierarchy of degrees did not really break with the concept of classes; rather, it redefined them in the service of a better performing State economy. In the new system, a first-level degree would give speedy access to lower jobs; the second level equated to the old *Laurea* and catered for the higher professions; and the third level opened up the path to academic careers. This restructuring confirmed and codified the status quo: ruling classes with a proper academic certificate hovering over a more competitive working class (because it now needed its own certificate), and an academic caste safely preserved as a special category.

By the mid-1960s, the cosmetic democracy of the reform was brought to light by university students who, influenced by the international climate of social protest against authority and paternalism, claimed direct control over the academic institutions in order to experiment with alternative forms of direct democracy.

Revolution and restoration

> In the current system, the university is a production institute that has as its objective the reproduction of the system itself.[19]

A few months into the 1963/64 academic year, the students at the Politecnico di Milano occupied the School of Architecture and asked for direct involvement in academic governance in order to change a university that, in their view, was little more than an exam factory (*esamificio*). Quickly followed by colleagues in Rome and Turin, and taking inspiration from the sociology students at the University of Trento, they organised into a Student Movement (*Movimento Studentesco*) and created assemblies to self-run the universities.[20]

Besides sharing the main intellectual references of other students in revolt around the world – especially Mao Tse-tung's *Little Red Book* and Herbert Marcuse's *One-Dimensional Man* (1964)[21] – their experiments with direct democracy were influenced by the ideas of some radical Italian figures of the time, such as psychiatrist Franco Basaglia and the dissident Catholic priest, Lorenzo Milani. Basaglia's revolutionary psychiatric work, which eventually led to the abolition of asylums in 1978,[22] provided a general framework for criticising the fake democratic institutions of an ultimately authoritarian state. Rephrasing Basaglia's ideas, a document produced by students at the School of Sociology in Trento in 1968 (entitled 'Power and Society') claimed:

It is evident that in order to hinder awareness of people's impotency the system must convince them that its planning activity is intended to redistribute power to the advantage of those without it. This is a very subtle and astute way to strip contradictions of their disruptive power and integrate ever growing masses within the logics of the system.[23]

This argument was similar to the thesis proposed by Marcuse, who had highlighted the double-edged nature of government in advanced technological societies. In a Marcusian vein, the Italian students attacked welfare as a strategy carefully devised to keep people docile because 'with a full belly one does not feel like making a revolution'.[24]

If Basaglia provided a valid intellectual framework, Lorenzo Milani offered an operative example of an alternative to the system. 'There is nothing more unjust than making equals among the unequal', he wrote in *Lettera a una professoressa*, a book collectively written by eight young students at the idiosyncratic school Milani had created at Barbiana, the isolated hamlet on the hills of Tuscany where the Vatican exiled him in 1954 because of his progressive views.[25] Barbiana provided a practical example of alternative education that influenced the Student Movement, as its pedagogic approach rejected all established norms and conventions: no fixed timetable or calendar, no graded assessment, no formal exams, no differentiation of classes according to age, and no univocal distinction of teachers and students. In Barbiana, students ranged between the ages of 7 and 18, older students taught the younger students, and school time was 365 days a year, 12 hours a day. As such, Milani's school epitomised an idea of learning that opposed top-down instruction and aligned with the anti-schooling ideas of other radical thinkers of the time like Ivan Illich,[26] Paulo Freire,[27] and, from within the domain of architecture, Cedric Price.[28]

In an attempt to replicate Barbiana as a model for higher education, the Student Movement demanded that exams, grading, and distinct and hierarchical years of study be abolished. However, the translation from small hamlet to mass university was not an easy one. In fact, Milani's school was not mere anarchy, since it was dependent on the overarching figure of Milani himself as the personification of the maieutic teacher. Scaling up his school to a model of self-governance for a large institution like a university required answering the difficult question of who would play the maieutic, supervisory role – and even whether there should be such a role. Moreover, direct democracy inside universities clashed with a still one-dimensional academic social fabric. The Student Movement was still very much the expression of a middle class that was protesting against their parents' bourgeois values but which was unable or willing to completely emancipate themselves from those values. Pier Paolo Pasolini's poem 'Il PCI ai giovani', written in March 1968 in the wake of a fight between students and police in front of the School of Architecture of Valle Giulia in Rome, offered the harshest critique of the bourgeois false consciousness of the Student Movement. To their slogans of fighting against 'the school of the masters' – as a song commemorating that occasion reiterated[29] – Pasolini replied:

> You have daddy's boys' faces.
> I hate you as I hate your daddies.
> Chip off the old block.
> ...
> When yesterday at Valle Giulia you fought the police,
> I sympathised with the policemen.
> Because the policemen are sons of the poor
>
> They come from subtopias, whether peasant or urban.[30]

The Battle of Valle Giulia, as it became known (Figure 3.1), marked the switch from an earlier intellectual stage of the Student Movement to a violent one to be fought on the streets alongside the factory workers.

But it was not only violence that gave legitimation to the top-down military oppression by the State. As the student assemblies became larger, their original good intentions of experimenting with direct ways of governance were corrupted by concomitant forces of idleness. This is what happened at Politecnico di Milano, where a 'cautious teaching experimentation' that had been granted by the Ministry of Education in 1967, and which had generated an innovative renovation of teaching and research methodologies, degenerated towards the attractive prospect of getting a degree without being formally tested. The restoration imposed in 1971 by the government through the appointment of an external technical committee to reorder the university put a repressive end to the hope of a self-run university.[31]

Despite the failure to sustain a complete bottom-up reform, the student protests managed to strike the final blow to the 1965 reform proposal, which ultimately never received parliamentary approval. The students' activism and intellectual elaboration also influenced the architectural community, as demonstrated by excerpts published in *Casabella* [32] and by Giancarlo De Carlo's 1968 essay, *La piramide rovesciata*, which stemmed from direct observation and discussion with the occupying students, whose experiments of self-governance he praised as tangible examples of an alternative form of democracy.[33] It was around the same time as the worsening of the student protests that the Italian architectural community began considering more seriously the prospect of redesigning the country's universities, commencing a search for possible references and precedents.

A precedent to reject

To add further self-inflicted chaos to the disagreements about educational reform, between 1967 and 1969, the Italian parliament passed two Acts that expanded the liberalisation of access to higher education and granted money for

Figure 3.1 The battle of Valle Giulia, Rome (1 March 1968).
Source: Courtesy of *L'Unità*.

the physical expansion of universities.[34] Politicians were thus handing over
responsibility for reform to the individual universities, which in turn abruptly
called into action an Italian architectural community with no previous experience of designing academic space. The only precedents of properly designed

universities in Italy dated back to the 1930s, with the Città Universitaria in Rome the most conspicuous example (Figure 3.2). Master-planned by Marcello Piacentini, it had been opened by Mussolini in 1935 with the ostentatious statement that only the fascist regime was capable of creating such a magnificent concentration of university buildings.[35] Unsurprisingly, the predominantly left-oriented architectural community of the 1960s could hardly accept this project as a workable precedent.[36]

The ideological contrast also had an important implication for the urbanistic idea of a university, which, as an example emerging from a fascist regime, aroused suspicion of the concept of spatial concentration of an academic institution. More generally, however, spatial concentration was a common characteristic of new university complexes built across European capital cities in the 1930s. Discussing some of these projects, the June 1936 issue of *L'architecture d'aujourd'hui* framed them within the claim that concentration was the general underlying logic of the modern city and that universities naturally followed such a principle.[37] Among examples chosen to illustrate this claim, the 320-hectare Ciudad Universitaria in Madrid represented most clearly the nation-state ambitions in the 1930s.[38] Planned in 1929 in the form of buildings scattered in clusters over a vast landscaped area in isolation from the city, the Madrid university has rightly been described as the first 'American-style campus' ever built in Europe.[39] At the time of its construction, the enthusiastic reception of such a large out-of-town campus was attributed to anti-urban sentiments that argued for its superiority to inner-city universities that produced 'full brains, empty souls'.[40]

Conversely, Piacentini refused the campus ideology, claiming instead an 'urban intention' for the University of Rome. While he grounded the project on a study of American and European precedents that included the Madrid campus,[41] these were not taken as formal models but were used merely for the technical purpose of learning about 'construction techniques, plan organisation of buildings, exterior finishes and technical installations'.[42] On a formal level, the Città Universitaria distanced itself from the idyllic image of Madrid and its American influences, and opted instead for an environment with urban density and materiality where hard surfaces replaced the landscaped grounds of a canonical campus. In this material substitution stood an idea of the university that differed from the total life experience promoted by the American campus. The latter's identity as a social condenser gave as much emphasis to the space between buildings as to the single built structures. In contrast, the space between buildings at Rome simply pursued representational intentions that could best serve an image of order regulated by the fascist regime. In 1930s Rome, higher education was declared an activity to be consumed within interiors, and this included extra-curricular activities, which were kept to a minimum and were architecturally represented as interior spaces – as the buildings of *dopolavoro* and *quadriportico* indicated.

An academic ritual corresponded to this interiorised, specialist conception of higher education, according to which an individual became a student each time

Figure 3.2 Planning the modern Italian university. Città Universitaria, Rome (master
  planner: Marcello Piacentini, 1932–35).
Source: *Architettura* 14 (1935).

he or she crossed the threshold of an institute or faculty building. Affirming that the Italian university student was first and foremost an urban dweller, Città Universitaria also made an implicit urbanistic claim that, unlike the Madrid example, its isolation from the city would be just a temporary phase; indeed, it declared that a university needed to be embedded in the city fabric. The aerial pictures taken at the time of its completion back up this vision by their depiction of a complex located between the historic areas of Rome and the peripheries that had grown since the beginning of the century. Rather than launching a different condition, the perfect package of order planned by Piacentini could not – and did not want to – escape from being digested by the mutual growth of core and periphery. Without claiming any preservation of the areas around it, the university accepted its role of stimulating privately driven urban growth.

This type of encounter between architecture and politics was the opposite of what the architects/urbanists of the 1960s were looking for. In his 1965 book, *Origini e sviluppo della città moderna*, Carlo Aymonino maintained that on only very few occasions during the twentieth century had there been a positive encounter between architecture and politics. In keeping with his own political views, the positive examples he gave all involved variations on a possible form for the socialist city, such as Red Vienna and Soviet urbanism from the 1920s.[43] Conversely, he located the fascist university complex within a wider planning ideology of creating 'ghettos' of specialised functions 'with no relation to their urban areas'.[44] As discussed in the Chapter 2, in the early 1960s, Aymonino was among the advocates of a city territory that could interpret the new urban dimension of postwar Italy in architectural terms. He argued for the need to 'call again into question the whole city as structure and form' and to define new 'reference points'[45] that had to be closer – both spatially and intellectually – to the large complexes of popular housing represented by the Viennese *hofs* than to the ostentatious power of a fascist autocratic complex.

In 1967, the prospect of designing new universities offered new opportunities for the definition of city territories advocated by Aymonino and others, in turn bringing back to the fore a debate that had fallen into oblivion due to the inconsequentiality of the early 1960s ideas and their implementation. Determined to overcome the ideology behind Città Universitaria, and to question its principle of academic spatial concentration, the Italian architectural community set off to study what a university for an open society could be. The only aspect they kept of Piacentini's precedent was the refusal to relocate higher education to out-of-town and supposedly idyllic campuses.

The university in academe

As the universities started preparing their expansion and restructuring plans in 1967, a number of research studies and design studios on the topics of university planning and design were launched at the major schools of architecture across the country. Admitting their lack of competence on the subject,[46] Italian academics sounded out the contemporary production of higher education environments in search of specific knowledge on university planning and design. It is important to emphasise that these studies were undertaken by academic-practitioners, such as Guido Canella in Milan, Fernando Clemente in Bologna,[47] Paola Coppola Pignatelli in Rome,[48] and Giancarlo De Carlo in Venice.[49] The university was thus researched from within itself, but always with an eye on the most operative aspects, and it is no coincidence that those same names would also be among the authors of real projects for universities.

De Carlo's research coagulated in the book that provided the most complete collection of recent architectural examples: *Pianificazione e disegno delle università* (1968).[50] Looking at the selection of projects, a clear rejection of the isolated idyllic campus emerges, as the attention was directed towards the large-scale relations of universities and territories. The switch from the design of finite forms to the definition of relations – which, as discussed in Chapter 2, had characterised a new phase of urban thinking in Italy since 1959 and which De Carlo himself had been among the first to discuss at the urbanists' congress in Lecce[51] – found representation in De Carlo's book through the inclusion of the drawings of Candilis, Josic and Wood's Berlin Free University, some of the entries to the competition for Bochum University (the nearest counterpart to the Italian competitions of the early 1970s), and Cedric Price's Potteries Thinkbelt. These projects offered different interpretations of a university as a motive force for territorial restructuring. Besides them, the inclusion of SOM's University of Illinois at Chicago Circle – the first important commuter campus in the US[52] – further signalled a clear intention: the university was to be treated as an open urban service rather than a finite sub-community.

De Carlo claimed that a university for the open society was a 'state of permanent fluidity allowing the continuous, multidirectional, and capillary circulation of information and experiences'[53] – words that clearly echoed his own 1962 definition of *città regione* as a dynamic condition opposed to the static traditional city.[54] None of the existing university models – the British colleges, the American campuses, and the European urban university complexes, including the Italian models, which De Carlo described as a 'disaggregate model' of academic feuds set one against the other – corresponded to this definition.

Besides studying the international architectural production, towards the end of the 1960s, Italian architects and urbanists also started debating possible scenarios for a reorganisation and expansion of higher education in their country, as was done at a conference on university design held in Rome in October 1970. Trying to fill the gaps of a 'university without reforms' – as the situation was later apostrophised by some of the participants in the architectural competitions of the early 1970s[55] – the conference was organised by the Istituto per lo Sviluppo dell'Edilizia Sociale (ISES) – a public agency for housing policy – and approached university design by stressing the institution's crucial public role. (The full list of participants in the conference, according to the thematic sessions is shown in Appendix 1.) Four panels – 'typology and technology', 'urbanistic problems', 'quantitative problems', and 'legislative problems'[56] – were populated by architects and urbanists who were mostly clustered at three institutions: the La Sapienza University in Rome (including Ludovico Quaroni, Paola Coppola Pignatelli, and Piero Sartogo), the Politecnico di Milan (Guido Canella and Lucio Stellaro D'Angiolini), and the University of Bologna (Fernando Clemente). Several of these names would later take part in the architectural competitions for Italian universities of the early 1970s, the first of which, for the University of Florence,[57] had been launched a few months before the conference, with the result that some participants were trying simultaneously to advance both the theory and the practice of university design.[58] Many of the conference papers dealt with redefining the quantitative aspects of the problem and built on the indications given by the second National Economic Plan – also known as *Progetto '80* – which was authored by Centro Piani and published in 1969.[59] Among other proposals, the Plan prescribed that 'at least 20 new university centres are needed – each with a population of 15–20,000'.[60] These new universities would act as major 'poles of development'[61] around which the planners envisaged a thorough restructuring of the whole built substance of Italy towards the prospect of vast city territories discussed in their theoretical work. With this quantitative indication, *Progetto '80* pushed the ambition of the 1965 reform proposal, which had timidly identified the need to create only two new universities while treating the reform and expansion of higher education mostly in terms of restructuring of the existing institutions. Faced with this challenge, the architects participating in the 1970 conference lamented the lack of State guidance,[62] although this complaint concealed a deeper satisfaction about the possibility of acting autonomously to define a future for Italian higher education. Moreover, the delay with which Italy approached university design in comparison with other countries could also have a positive impact because it enabled the independence and originality of methods that had been advocated in the first stage of discussion among the city territorialists – as was done in 1963 by Alberto Samonà, who called on Italian architects to reject the importation of models from abroad.[63] By 1970, originality of approach was charged with novel significance in the context of the critical condition of Italian higher education, which was considered so dramatically lagging behind other countries that no solutions could be imported; only 'an autonomous and totally original approach', it was claimed at the conference, could provide answers.[64]

Calling for originality and defining it, however, were very different things. The earlier phases of the architectural debate on the new urban dimension had stopped before any encounter with reality, and the ideas had remained on paper. What had emerged from the short-lived experience of *centri direzionali* was a rejection of their normalisation as model solutions – that is, as codifiable building types. Consequently, the conference panel that discussed the typological aspects of higher education claimed that universities, like any service, could not be reduced to a specific architectural configuration. Their words, however, did not eradicate ambiguity and tentativeness:

> What has been discussed up to this point allows clarification of what we mean by university typology. This does not refer to a complex that is

different from the urban and territorial structure, detached from it, and defined solely by its functional needs. Conversely, university typology means an aggregate of built academic space capable of allowing the maximum of exchange and interaction among study, research, work, dwelling, and nature.[65]

How these words departed from the notion of the normalised university campus defined by Richard Dober in 1963 was not easy to discern (see Chapter 1).

To try to eradicate ambiguity, it was necessary to directly confront the campus in its birthplace. This was attempted by Piero Sartogo, one of the conference participants, who endeavoured to build an alternative idea of university space on his own experience of American higher education and campus life. In 1967/68, Sartogo had been a visiting professor in architecture at the University of Virginia, where his design studio had focused on a reconceptualisation of the notion of the campus in relation to a society increasingly connected by communication infrastructure and technology.[66] In a series of articles on 'Campus Design' that he published in *Casabella*, [67] he wrote of learning as 'an unlimited time frame', a description that clashed with the common definition of a campus as 'closed towards the outside world [thus] only allowing limited experience'.[68] The relation between city and university had to be turned into a 'state of mind'[69] in which, quoting Clark Kerr, 'the boundaries of the university are stretched to embrace all society. The student becomes alumnus and the alumnus continues as student: the graduate enters the outside world and the public enters the classroom and the laboratory.'[70]

Sartogo's articles signalled a new phase at *Casabella* after the ten-year tenure of Ernesto Nathan Rogers as the magazine's editor. By the later 1960s, new alliances were sought within the international debate to finally get out of the impasse started by the famous dispute that, in the mid-1950s, had opposed Rogers's interpretations of high modernism to those of Reyner Banham.[71] Evidence of this attempted relaxation of Italy-UK relations was that some of Banham's own friends and colleagues started being published and debated in Italy, while *Casabella* built bridges with *Architectural Design* and its protagonists from Archigram to Cedric Price.

Those very names – Archigram, Price, and so forth – advocating an open society that reclaimed rights of freedom and playfulness represented the opposition to the status quo, and they attracted increasing interest from the Italian architectural community. At the same time as finding some Italian equivalents – albeit from different ideological standpoints – in the Florentine Radical movement, Sartogo's articles introduced their ideas to an Italian audience through projects like Peter Cook's *Ideas Circus*, David Greene's living pods, and Price's *Atom* – all proposals that shared a notion of learning characterised by a 'high degree of anonymity' and generality.[72] This conception of learning informed *Academity*, [73] a project developed by Sartogo's students in the US as an alternative to the self-contained campus. The project envisioned the North American East Coast as a large informational territory regulated by a horizontal grid that would organise educational functions at the lower levels (from primary to secondary education), with the university emerging as vertical towers allocated to more specialised uses. Rampant optimism in the technological society marked *Academity*'s continuous informational territory; like Adriano Buzzati-Traverso, Sartogo was also struck by an American dream. The flipside of this dream would soon be elaborated by Archizoom at the architectural competition for the University of Florence in 1970 where they inverted the positive connotation of the term 'continuity' to unveil the ambiguous condition of an advanced industrial consumerist society doomed to accept its own crisis.[74]

What Sartogo and Archizoom expressed from their opposite standpoints was that there could only be one way out of the dead end of the anti-campus rhetoric that was being repeated as a mantra in the oral and written discussions among architects. This way out was the drawing board. Between 1970 and 1973, the architectural competitions for the universities of Florence, Cagliari, Calabria, and Salerno moved the discussion from theoretical diagnosis to design proposal. After having been handed the steering wheel by the government as a result of the latter's political failure, the Italian universities now handed it over to the architects.

Notes

1 Charles Homer Haskins, *The Rise of Universities* (New York: H. Holt and Company, 1923), 8–9.
2 Ibid., 51.
3 Jürgen Habermas, *The Structural Transformation of the Public Sphere: An Inquiry into a Category of Bourgeois Society* (Cambridge: Polity, 1992).
4 See Silvio Spaventa, 'L'autonomia universitaria' (1884), in *Il resistibile declino dell'università*, ed. Gerardo Marotta and Livio Sichirollo (Naples: Guerini e Associati, 1999), 123–170. For a history of the Italian university, see Gian Paolo Brizzi, Piero Del Negro, and Andrea Romano, eds., *Storia delle università d'Italia*, 3 vols (Messina: SICANIA by GEM s.r.l., 2007).
5 The educational reform elaborated by Giovanni Gentile (1875–1944), and generally known as the 'Riforma Gentile', comprised a number of decrees passed by the Italian parliament in 1922–23: Regio Decreto no. 1679 (1922); Regio Decreto no. 1054 (1923); Regio Decreto no. 1753 (1923); Regio Decreto no. 2102 (1923) (specifically on the university); Regio Decreto no. 2185 (1923); and Regio Decreto no. 3120 (1923).
6 The main Acts that 'corrected' the reform proposal of 1923 were Regio Decreto no. 1592 (1933); Regio Decreto no. 1071 (1935); and Regio Decreto no. 1269 (1938).
7 Costituzione della Repubblica Italiana, Art. 33, 1947. My translation.
8 Salvatore Pugliatti, 'Relazione sull'autonomia universitaria', in Salvatore Pugliatti, *L'università italiana* (1964), quoted in Andrea Romano, 'A trent'anni dal '68: "Questione Universitaria" e "Riforma Universitaria"', *Annali di storia delle università italiane* 2 (1998). My translation.
9 Adriano Buzzati-Traverso, *Un fossile denutrito: L'università italiana* (Milan: Il saggiatore, 1969), 66–77. My translation. The book collected articles written between 1956 and 1969 for the newspaper *Il giorno*.
10 Clark Kerr, *The Uses of the University* (Cambridge, MA: Harvard University Press, 1963). For a discussion of Kerr's ideas, see Chapter 1. Kerr's book was published in Italian in 1969 by Armando Editore with the title, *A che serve l'università*.

11 Gino Martinoli, *L'università come impresa* (Florence: La nuova Italia, 1967).

12 Luigi Amirante, in Comitato di studio dei problemi dell'università italiana, *Studi sull'università italiana*, vol. 5 (Bologna: Società editrice Il Mulino, 1960), 37. My translation. These words were uttered at a conference held on 2–4 April 1960 with the title, 'Una politica per l'università'. The conference was organised by the Committee for the Study of the Problems of the Italian University, a volunteer association established in 1956 and composed for the most part of university professors and some other Italian intellectuals. In 1958, the committee applied to the Ford Foundation for funding for a study on the condition of the Italian university, eventually receiving a grant of $25,000. The study was developed between 1958 and 1960, discussed at the conference in Bologna and published by the Società Editrice Il Mulino as a five-volume report on the condition of the Italian university.

13 Law no. 685, 21 July 1961, 'Ammissione dei diplomati degli Istituti tecnici alle Facoltà universitarie'.

14 See Romano, 'A trent'anni dal '68'.

15 The Piano Decennale della Scuola was presented to parliament in 1958 by Prime Minister Amintore Fanfani and the Minister of Public Education, Aldo Moro. See Redi Sante Di Pol, *La scuola per tutti gli italiani: L'istruzione di base tra stato e società dal primo ottocento ad oggi* (Milan: Mondadori Università, 2016), 147.

16 The Commissione di indagine sulla scuola italiana was set up by National Act in 1962 (Law no. 1073, 24 July 1962). It was headed by Giuseppe Ermini and comprised thirty-one members: sixteen members of parliament, eight experts on education, and seven experts on economics and social studies. The report entitled 'Relazione sullo stato della pubblica istruzione in Italia' was presented to the Minister of Public Education, Luigi Gui, on 24 July 1963.

17 Paul Ginsborg, *Storia d'Italia dal dopoguerra a oggi* (Turin: Einaudi, 1989), 210.

18 Proposed law no. 2314, 4 May 1965, 'Modifiche all'ordinamento universitario'. The law had been preceded by a preliminary document entitled 'Linee direttive del piano di sviluppo pluriennale della scuola per il periodo successivo al 30 giugno 1965'.

19 Mauro Rostagno, 'Università come istituto produttivo', quoted in Marco Boato, 'La lotta a Trento', in *Contro l'università: I principali documenti della critica radicale alle istituzioni accademiche del sessantotto* (Milan: Mimesis, 2008), 41.

20 A collection of the main documents produced by the protesting students in Italy was published in 1968 as *Università: L'ipotesi rivoluzionaria. Documenti delle lotte studentesche. Trento, Torino, Napoli, Pisa, Milano, Roma* (Padua: Marsilio, 1968).

21 Herbert Marcuse, *One-Dimensional Man: Studies in the Ideology of Advanced Industrial Society* (Boston: Beacon Press, 1966; first published in 1964).

22 The abolition of asylums and a whole new regulation for the treatment of psychiatric patients came with the Law no. 180, 13 May 1978, 'Accertamenti e trattamenti sanitari volontari e obbligatori'. This law was commonly known as Legge Basaglia because it was essentially shaped by the work and ideas of Franco Basaglia (1924–80) against institutionalised confinement. Basaglia's work aligned with the anti-institutional theses of other international thinkers, many of whom contributed to a book edited by Basaglia and his wife, Franca Basaglia Ongaro, which discussed what they described as forms of 'institutionalised violence'. The contributors included Michel Foucault, Noam Chomsky, and Erving Goffman: Franco Basaglia and Franca Basaglia Ongaro, eds., *Crimini di pace: Ricerche sugli intellettuali e sui tecnici come addetti all'oppressione* (Turin: Einaudi, 1975). For a collection of Basaglia's main texts, see Franco Basaglia, *L'utopia della realtà* (Turin: Einaudi, 2005).

23 Davide Bernardi, 'Potere e società', quoted in Marco Boato, 'La lotta a Trento', in *Contro l'università*, 63. My translation.

24 Ibid.

25 In Barbiana, Don Lorenzo Milani (1923–67) defined his mission as the alphabetisation of the countryside at a time when the levels of illiteracy were dramatically high

throughout the country. While Italy had been politically united for almost a century, the developmental gap between north and south had continued widening. Don Milani criticised the claims of a possibly achievable balance by means of schooling, as he saw them as fake statements of equality masking the will of the national sovereign authority to reinforce disparity among classes. He considered the school to be the most extreme case of false consciousness disguised under a cloak of alleged inter-classism. Against the traditional school, he set up the educational experiment at Barbiana. For the school of Barbiana, see the documentary produced by Radio-Televisione della Svizzera Italiana in 1979, 'Don Lorenzo Milani e la sua scuola', available at: www.arcoiris.tv/scheda/it/1037/.

26 Ivan Illich, *Deschooling Society* (London: Marion Boyars, 1970). For a discussion of Illich, see Chapter 6.

27 Paulo Freire, *Pedagogy of the Oppressed* (New York: Herder and Herder, 1970).

28 For a discussion of Cedric Price's ideas on education, see Chapter 1.

29 This was a verse of the song 'Valle Giulia', written by Paolo Pietrangeli in the aftermath of the events at the Roman university in 1968.

30 Pier Paolo Pasolini, 'Il PCI ai giovani', *L'espresso*, 16 June 1968. My translation.

31 For a discussion of the events at the Politecnico di Milano, see Chapter 8 and the related bibliography indicated therein.

32 See Carlo Guenzi, 'Università: Le assemblee propongono', *Casabella* 324 (1968): 58–63; Giovanni Klaus Koenig, 'La rivoluzione ad ottobre', *Casabella* 328 (1968): 4; 'Università: Altri documenti', *Casabella* 328 (1968): 58–61; 'Mini-riforma per l'università', *Casabella* 337 (1969): 51–54.

33 Giancarlo De Carlo, *La piramide rovesciata* (Bari: De Donato, 1968). See also Chapter 7.

34 See Law no. 641, 28 July 1967, 'Nuove norme per l'edilizia scolastica ed universitaria e piano finanziario per il quinquennio 1967–71'; and Law no. 910, 11 December 1969, 'Provvedimenti urgenti per l'Università' (also known as Legge Codignola, after Tristano Codignola, the socialist deputy who promoted it). The 1967 law was particularly important for triggering architectural and urbanistic debate around the reform of higher education. Asking universities to develop and submit a five-year expansion plan for approval by the Ministry of Public Education, the law allocated almost 210 billion Italian lira for university construction, which included whole new builds, expansions, and renovations. If the cost of construction of new complexes exceeded 500 million lira, universities were obliged to organise public architectural competitions. The law thus marked an important moment as it switched attention from an administrative and political debate to a spatial one.

35 See Marcello Piacentini, 'Metodi e caratteristiche', *Architettura* 14 (1935): 2.

36 The main bibliographic references for Città Universitaria in Rome are Renato Pacini, 'Cronache romane: Il grandioso progetto della Città Universitaria', *Emporium* 459 (1933): 177–182; Renato Pacini, 'La Città Universitaria di Roma', *Architettura* 8 (1933), 475-495; Mario Pisani, 'La Città Universitaria', in *Architetture di Marcello Piacentini* (Rome: CLEAR, 2004), 111–118; 'La Città Universitaria di Roma', *Rassegna di architettura* (1936), 8, no. 14–15: 181–194; 'La Città Universitaria di Roma', *Architettura* 14 (1935); Michele Brescia, 'I viaggi all'estero degli architetti della Città Universitaria', in *Sapienza razionalista: L'architettura degli anni '30 nella Città Universitaria*, ed. Manuel Carrera (Rome: Nuova cultura, 2013), 93–99; and *1935/1985 La 'Sapienza' nella Città Universitaria: Catalogo della mostra* (Rome: Multigrafica Editrice, 1985).

37 See Alexandre Persitz, 'Les Cités Universitaires', *L'architecture d'aujourd'hui* 6 (1936): 8–11. The cases presented in the issue were Rome, Madrid, Athens, Oslo, Paris and, outside Europe, Montreal.

38 'La Cité Universitaire de Madrid', *L'architecture d'aujourd'hui* 6 (1936): 26.

39 See Pablo Campos Calvo-Sotelo, *The Journey of Utopia: The Story of the First American Style Campus in Europe* (New York: Nova Science Publishers, 2006). Campos

Calvo-Sotelo discusses the trips to some of the most prestigious American universities and their campuses made by a Spanish delegation with the aim of studying the American tradition of university planning in order to import it to Europe.

40 'La Cité Universitaire de Madrid', 26.

41 In the early stages of the project, Piacentini set up a team of collaborators to study examples of international universities, which included Madrid, Paris, Zurich, Brussels, The Hague, Amsterdam, Hannover, Leipzig, and Munich in Europe, and Harvard, Virginia, Columbia, Pennsylvania, Colorado, and Berkeley in the United States. Similar to the planning of the university of Madrid, one of Piacentini's collaborators, Gaetano Minnucci, was sent on a trip to visit the European cases, which resulted in a report presented in 1932. See Gaetano Minnucci, *Degli edifici per l'istruzione superiore: Relazione redatta per l'ufficio tecnico per la costruzione della Città Universitaria di Roma* (Rome, 1932); Brescia, 'I viaggi all'estero degli architetti della Città Universitaria'. The Madrid university, in particular, was considered by Piacentini who, as the director of *Architettura* – the main architectural press organ of the fascist regime – published the project in the journal in 1934: 'La Città Universitaria di Madrid', *Architettura* 10 (1934): 581–596.

42 Minnucci, *Degli edifici per l'istruzione superiore*, 1–2. My translation.

43 Carlo Aymonino, *Origini e sviluppo della città moderna* (Padua: Marsilio, 1965), 6.

44 Ibid., 67. My translation. In a sketch of the plan of Rome, Aymonino included the modern health and higher education complexes as instances of what he considered the wrong way of understanding the city as a collection of autonomous pieces rather than as a whole.

45 Ibid., 80.

46 See Paola Coppola Pignatelli, *L'università in espansione: Orientamenti dell'edilizia universitaria* (Milan: Etas Kompass, 1969), 237.

47 See Ferdinando Clemente, ed., *Università e territorio* (Bologna: S.T.E.B., 1969).

48 See Coppola Pignatelli, *L'università in espansione*. Paola Coppola Pignatelli delivered a lecture series on 'University typology' ('Tipologia dell'organismo universitario') at the University of Rome in the academic years 1966/67 and 1967/68.

49 See Giancarlo De Carlo, ed., *Pianificazione e disegno delle università* (Rome: Edizioni universitarie italiane, 1968).

50 The book was the outcome of research funded by the Ministry of Public Education and linked to the courses on urban planning that De Carlo had delivered at IUAV in Venice between 1963 and 1967. See Filippo De Pieri, 'Il breve e il lungo '68 di Giancarlo De Carlo', in *La piramide rovesciata: Architettura oltre il '68*, ed. Filippo De Pieri (Macerata: Quodlibet, 2018), 29–30.

51 For the congress in Lecce, see Chapter 2.

52 See Sharon Haar, *The City as Campus: Urbanism and Higher Education in Chicago* (Minneapolis, MN: University of Minnesota Press, 2011).

53 De Carlo, *Pianificazione e disegno delle università*, 14. My translation.

54 See the discussion on the city region by De Carlo in Chapter 2.

55 Giovanni Maria Campus and Paolo Casella, 'Università senza pianificazione e senza riforme', *Casabella* 367 (1972).

56 *Atti del convegno di studio sull'edilizia universitaria* (Rome: ISES, Istituto per lo Sviluppo dell'Edilizia Sociale, 1970). The proceedings of the conference were held at the Archivio Bottoni in Milan.

57 An earlier, less ambitious competition was launched in 1966 for the design of the Free University of Abruzzo Gabriele D'Annunzio at Chieti. The competition was by invitation-only and was won by BBPR (Banfi, Belgioioso, Peressuti, Rogers). See Piero Sartogo, 'Campus Design 6: Modelli di sviluppo territoriale urbanistico ed architettonico della istruzione superiore in Italia', *Casabella* 333 (1969): 16–21; Piero Sartogo, 'Campus Design 7: Concorso per la Libera Università abruzzese "Gabriele D'Annunzio" a Chieti', *Casabella* 334 (1969): 20–25; Romano Chirivi, *Università Abruzzese, Chieti: Progetto di larga massima per la Città Universitaria di Chieti*,

concorso ad inviti, anno 1966 (Venice: Istituto Universitario di Architettura, Istituto di Urbanistica, 1967); and Maristella Casciato, *Il campus universitario di Chieti* (Milan: Electa, 1997).

58 Among the conference participants who entered the University of Florence competition as a team were Ludovico Quaroni, Luigi Spadolini, and Fernando Clemente; they eventually won the third prize. Quaroni and Spadolini subsequently entered the competition for the University of Calabria in 1972, and Quaroni alone developed private commissions for the University of Lecce and the University of Somalia in 1973–75. Another speaker at the conference, Giuseppe Rebecchini, also submitted a project at Florence and subsequently was part of the winning team at the competition for the University of Cagliari in 1971–72; he was also a participant in Calabria. Other speakers who entered the Calabria competition were Piero Sartogo (who received the sixth prize with a project developed in collaboration with Ove Arup) and Guido Canella (who took part with some of his former students at the Politecnico di Milano). See Chapter 4 for a discussion of the competitions.

59 Ministero del Bilancio e della Programmazione Economica, *Progetto '80: Rapporto preliminare al Programma Economico Nazionale 1971–75* (Milan: Feltrinelli, 1969). See also Cristina Renzoni, *Il Progetto '80: Un'idea di paese nell'Italia degli anni sessanta* (Florence: Alinea, 2012). For a brief discussion of Centro Piani, see Chapter 2.

60 Ministero del Bilancio e della Programmazione Economica, *Progetto '80*, 126. My translation.

61 Ibid., 103. My translation.

62 See Michele Achilli, 'Nuovi centri universitari: Rapporto sugli aspetti legislativi', in *Atti del convegno di studio sull'edilizia universitaria*.

63 Alberto Samonà, 'Alla ricerca di un metodo per la nuova dimensione', *Casabella* 277 (1963): 50–4. See Chapter 2.

64 Romano Chirivi *et al.*, 'Rapporto sui problemi dell'edilizia universitaria nei riguardi delle tipologie e delle tecnologie', in *Atti del convegno di studio sull'edilizia universitaria*, 4–5. My translation.

65 Ibid., 22. My translation.

66 See Piero Sartogo and Carlo Pelliccia, 'A Study of Higher Education Environment', *Modulos* 67 (1968).

67 Sartogo's articles, some of which were co-authored with Carlo Pelliccia, appeared in 1968–69 in the *Casabella* issues 322, 323, 326, 332, 333, and 334. The series started with a general discussion of the notion of campus and the contemporary state of campus design, then investigated the specific challenges of university planning in the United States, and subsequently switched attention to Italy and to the ways in which models of territorial development of universities could be defined.

68 Piero Sartogo and Carlo Pelliccia, 'Campus Design 3', *Casabella* 325 (1968): 35. My translation. Sartogo's experience with campus design dated back to his work with Walter Gropius's Architects Collaborative in the design of the University of Baghdad in 1960.

69 Piero Sartogo and Carlo Pelliccia, 'Campus Design', *Casabella* 322 (1968): 21.

70 Clark Kerr, *The Uses of the University*, quoted in Piero Sartogo and Carlo Pelliccia, 'Campus Design 2', *Casabella* 323 (1968): 11.

71 See Reyner Banham, 'Neoliberty: The Italian Retreat from Modern Architecture', *The Architectural Review* 125 (1959): 230–235; and Ernesto Nathan Rogers, 'L'evoluzione dell'architettura: Risposta al custode dei frigidaires', *Casabella-Continuità* 228 (1959): 2–4.

72 Sartogo and Pelliccia, 'Campus Design 2', 14–15.

73 Ibid.

74 For a discussion of Archizoom's entry in the University of Florence competition, see Chapter 6.

4 Architecture or system
A parable in four episodes

The controversy of competitions

Between 1967 and 1970, Italian architecture tried to come to terms with higher education as a new architectural brief. The 1970 conference in Rome on university design discussed in Chapter 3 summed up three years of research undertaken at various Italian schools of architecture and marked the passage to an operative stage facilitated by four consecutive architectural competitions, one per year, for the universities of Florence, Cagliari, Calabria, and Salerno (see Appendix 2 for the specifics about the four competitions).

Not all voices were represented in the conference and the competitions. A notable absentee was Giancarlo De Carlo, who at the time could rightly claim to be the only expert on university design in Italy, given his work since the mid-1950s on commissions from the Universities of Urbino and Pavia, which in 1970 asked him to develop an urbanistic plan for the expansion of the institution inside the city.[1] Because of these commissions, De Carlo had no need to participate in competitions to get work and his name is not only absent in the conference's proceedings but also among the entrants to the Italian competitions for universities of the 1970s. Other missing names at the conference were some of the leading Italian city-territorialists who skipped this discussion stage to jump directly to an operative mode, making the story of the four competitions one that stars some recurring protagonists whom we have encountered in Chapter 2: Vittorio Gregotti (winner in Florence and Calabria), Giuseppe Samonà (second prize in Cagliari and participant in Calabria), Carlo Aymonino with Costantino Dardi (honourable mention in Florence, third in Cagliari, and participants in Calabria; Aymonino was also a member of the jury in Salerno), Ludovico Quaroni (third prize in Florence and a participant in Calabria), and Guido Canella (participant in Calabria and a member of the jury in Cagliari).

Despite the enthusiastic reception by the leading names of Italian architecture who saw in the competitions the opportunity to revive a debate that had been interrupted around 1963, the very nature and premises of architectural competitions ended up being the object of diffused criticism. While it was a legal prescription that big-budget public works be commissioned through open competition calls,[2] scepticism about the use of architectural competitions was widespread and possibly triggered by the inconsequential fate of early 1960s' cases, such as the competition for Turin's *centro direzionale* that had already generated critical comments:

> The inadequacy of technical agencies, which in other states with more efficient management capabilities formulate structural and morphological solutions for the city, compels in our country the use of design competitions also to cope with very complex problems.[3]

Eight years later, these words of Gregotti and Eugenio Battisti echoed in the text submitted by Carlo Aymonino and Costantino Dardi alongside their design proposal for the University of Cagliari:

> Given the lack of a national plan providing a clear correspondence between political decisions about the role of the university in our country and strategies of size and location, design competitions inevitably risk becoming a means of giving cultural authority to invention without any relation to a real context. They also free the institutions that commission the projects from any responsibility for actual implementation.[4]

The subtler aspects behind this washing of hands was formulated in a much more conspiratorial way by Massimo Scolari, who attacked competitions as perfect instances of authoritarianism. Scolari's argument was that posing overly complex questions – which, as we will see, the competition briefs for the Italian universities ended up doing – was a way to ultimately guarantee the maintenance of top-down control because architects could give only partial answers that would require the subsequent intervention of the institution, which, more often than not, would result in drastic alterations especially capable of neutralising the most subversive ideas. In other words, competitions were accused of maintaining the status quo from behind an apparent acceptance of innovation.

In hindsight, Scolari was proved right, as the most innovative outputs of the four competitions were massively manipulated during subsequent implementation phases. The projects built in Florence and Cagliari ended up being very different from the ambitious winning entries: diametrically opposite, in the case of Florence, where the university complex was transformed from a podium-and-slabs design to a more conventional series of block-buildings surrounding a lawn; and substantially scaled down and spatially reconfigured by a different architectural practice to that of the winning team in Cagliari. Despite being shorter than originally conceived, Gregotti's first-prize-winning entry in Calabria was built mostly faithfully to its first scheme, although its author would later criticise the way the university handled the wider urbanistic reasoning behind the project, which resulted in a washing away of the vast preserved agricultural land around an academic complex that Gregotti and his collaborators had conceived as a dyke controlling its surrounding territory. For reasons that I will describe later in this chapter, which relate to an important switch of prerogatives from the earlier competitions that, in turn, signalled a new phase in architectural discourse, the last competition, for Salerno, was the most successful in terms of the smooth translation from drawing to building of a not too ambitious or innovative project.

While the vicissitudes of the aftermaths of the four competitions allow important considerations on the workings of the building industry and the relations between thinking and making architecture, assessing them merely on the basis of their actual implementation or, for that matter, in terms of their technical contribution to university architecture, misses the point of this episode of postwar higher education design. Their real importance lies in the way they – perhaps pushed by the diffused feeling of suspicion floating among the participants and the related disillusionment about actually getting their visions built – were instrumentally seized upon more as opportunities to continue a discussion on large-scale territories than as technical responses to the brief of designing new academic complexes.

Florence, 1970: inside, outside, or neither

On 4 May 1970, the Ministry of Public Education published the call of the 'International Competition for the Re-arrangement of the University of Florence'.[5] The brief asked for a 'total reorganisation' [6] to impose order on the territorial distribution of a university scattered throughout the historic urban fabric.[7] Crucial for the reorganisation was the availability of a 600-hectare site located on rural land owned by the city and three smaller towns west of Florence,[8] which the 1962 metropolitan master plan, authored by Edoardo Detti, an urbanist and professor at the University of Florence, had allocated for university use and the creation of a *centro direzionale*. Yet the brief aimed to prevent the prospect of a mere suburban exile of the university. A design *tour de force* from the scale of 1:25,000 to 1:10 was requested of the competitors who had to combine new peripheral university settlements (in the plural) 'with an urban structure that should have a directional character at a metropolitan and regional scale',[9] alongside proposals for the renewal of the city's historic centre.[10]

A team headed by Vittorio Gregotti and Edoardo Detti won the competition with a project entitled *Amalassunta*. [11] Surely, Detti, as the author of the metropolitan master plan, benefited from a crucial pool of knowledge about the territory that other participants did not have. In fact, the project was conceived along the lines drawn by Detti in his master plan for the westward expansion of Florence, where he conceived of the new academic complex not only as a hinge between city and city-territory but also as one element of a wider system of interventions. *Amalassunta* stretched as far as it could to conquer a vast territory where a dense core of academic, tertiary and leisure activities, designed in the form of a horizontal podium connecting five slabs for the university departments, were complemented by smaller clusters of housing and services on the edges of existing towns and, in a clear quotation from Louis Kahn's plan for the centre of Philadelphia, by a series of large park-and-ride structures and railway terminals placed along the edges of Florence's historic core to mark the interface between the old city and the new urban dimension.

Detti's presence as one of the competitors could easily have attracted complaints, but this potential controversy dissipated within the much wider polemical climate that surrounded the competition. Complaints came from different directions, starting with Oriol Bohigas, one of the jury members,[12] who criticised the planning chaos of the area in which competitors were called to operate and insisted on the arbitrariness of architectural solutions to a brief that had not been clarified at a political level.[13] Bohigas's polemic was echoed in a more ostentatious form by the decision of fellow jury member, James Gowan, lamenting the inadequacy of the brief and the mediocre level of the proposals, to resign his role after the first meeting.

Gowan's criticism is a crucial moment in the story of Italian university design because it reveals the fundamental difference in approaches and ideas between the Italian and the British responses to higher education reform. It ignited a debate mediated by the main architectural magazines of the two countries. Accused of having an infantile attitude by Massimo Scolari in *Controspazio*,[14] Gowan, replying in *Casabella*,[15] defended his criticism of the brief's proposal to exile the university to a peripheral site. *The Architectural Review* took Gowan's side in a piece entitled 'A Florentine Fiasco' (Figure 4.1), in which the editors clarified how the British experience of new university building had provided enough evidence that 'a campus of culture, learning and athleticism, sitting in 200 acres of playing fields and parkland two miles from town' was a bad idea, and suggested that 'the sooner the university is back in town and making its unique contribution to the quality of life of the town, the better for all concerned'.[16] On the Italian side, the *Amalassunta* team responded in a letter to the British magazine in which they tried to reposition their project where it belonged: inside the ten-year-old Italian debate on the new urban dimension.[17] *Amalassunta*, they explained, aimed beyond the perfection of an academic settlement, and for this reason it took the crucial decision of keeping housing separate from teaching and research facilities. For them, if a campus had to exist, then it would have to coincide with the whole western territory of Florence.

Compromise was concealed in the defence of the winners who knew all too well that to take on the role of an open service in a vast territory the university had to sacrifice its identity as a pure domain of intellectual and scientific enquiry and to accept a degree of corruption to satisfy the desires of an open society. Combining university activities with a number of leisure and commercial facilities, including a regional shopping mall, the academic core proposed in *Amalassunta* embodied the character of a radical consumer version of the multiversity discussed in America, shaping a knowledge retail centre. Yet there was a key postulate to the corruption of the academic ideal: no matter how compromised by leisure and commercial services, a university still maintained its role as a public agent. In line with the urbanistic discussions of the 1960s, *Amalassunta* was an ode to public planning and architecture that aimed to orchestrate a large-scale system within which private intervention could happen only according to strictly prescribed rules. The extensive preserved parkland that would form a continuous ground around the proposed built complexes worked precisely to keep under control the improvisation of private development.

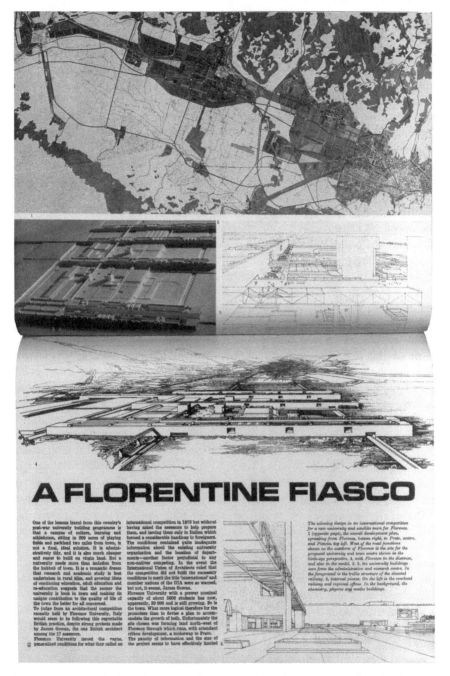

Figure 4.1 The Italy-UK diatribe on the international design competition for the University of Florence (1970–71).
Source: *The Architectural Review* 900 (February 1972).

Overall, the project expressed a twofold vote of confidence, on the one hand, in the planning and implementation capacities of public authorities, and, on the other, in the autonomous power of the drawing that envisioned large-scale reordering. To this twofold trust, the project that received the second prize married only the argument about public planning, but it fiercely opposed the idea of autonomous formal gestures, claiming that 'architecture doesn't matter'.[18] Entitled *Aquarius*, the entry by Pier Luigi Cervellati and Italo Insolera argued that no formal solution could be provided for something that had not yet been defined (Figure 4.2). Their polemic did not stop at formalism, but more generally attacked the very discourse on city-territories by taking sides with Gowan's opposition to an out-of-town academic relocation. Declaring 'No to the concentration campus',[19] Cervellati and Insolera steered attention away from the positivist scenarios of vast urban territories and towards the urgency of resolving the problems of Italian old cities, because 'only when we will know what will remain in the centre will we be able to decide what to build in the periphery'.[20]

Consequently, *Aquarius* questioned the value of the peripheral site, and looked instead at the centre of Florence where it made a radical proposal: making a *tabula rasa* of a vast area that had been generated by private speculation since the nineteenth century, and building in its place a large canopy that epitomised an idea of the university as a *Forum* – as the architects called it – which would act as a place of debate, protest and contradiction right at the heart of the city. Unashamedly imbued in ideology – a red flag waved over Florence in the submitted drawings – *Aquarius* was making an important point: since, as Italian architects, they were not technically prepared to design a university, rather than learn how to do it they should instead focus on more general arguments about the city, a topic they felt more comfortable discussing.

Dissent in the Florence competition was not so much about different ideas of the university; rather, it mirrored a wider crisis in architectural discourse. As the prospect of vast urbanisation became a daily reality, architects, sensing that time was running out, felt more anxiety in comparison to their somewhat calmer approach a decade earlier to the notion of a new urban dimension. Perhaps also prompted by their experience that implementation would not follow the new wave of competitions, as had been the case with the competitions of the 1960s, they retreated into a more general discourse about architecture and urbanism, which was also enabled by the generous – or generic – ambition of the brief that asked for arguments about the city rather than specifically about a university complex.

Five main positions on the city emerge from a reading of the competition entries in Florence. The first posited that a new urban dimension could be drawn and that the drawing should be composed of clear pockets of order arranged along enhanced infrastructural lines and within a vast preserved natural and rural landscape. Besides the winning entry, the project by Carlo Aymonino and Costantino Dardi[21] was the one that most clearly expressed such an archipelago of unmistakable figure-ground relations.

Figure 4.2 Competition panels for the University of Florence, 1970–71. Project: *Aquarius*. Architects: Pier Luigi Cervellati and Italo Insolera (second prize).
Source: Courtesy Studio Cervellati, Bologna.

A second argument also trusted the power of drawing but lowered its supremacy to the advantage of a general intention for continuity. Unequivocally entitled *Continuum*, [22] one of the schemes envisaged the westward projection of Florence literally as a continuous built structure. The main difference with the archipelago was that, whereas in the latter the drawing was prescriptive – the islands had to take on the formal characteristics depicted in the drawings – *Continuum*'s hypothesis was indicative, as what mattered was continuity of development. Thus, whereas the archipelago prevented private improvisation and declared absolutist public sovereignty, this second argument could potentially accept multiple scenarios of implementation and could also encompass public–private partnerships.

Third, there was an opposite statement of distrust in architectural drawing, manifested by the third-prize-winning entry by Ludovico Quaroni,[23] which brought to an extreme consequence the resolution he had proposed at the ISES conference in 1970 where he had claimed that a university could not be reduced to a building typology.[24] Rather than using traditional architectural drawings, his entry was presented in seven written chapters, charts describing a decision-making process, and a set of abstract plans populated with arrows and symbols that aimed to define a methodology rather than a final product (Figure 4.3). Attacked as 'formal aboulia' by Massimo Scolari in the pages of *Controspazio* [25] – a magazine that defended architecture as a formal discipline – Quaroni's *metaprogetto* – 'the project of the project'[26] – represented a shocking final destination for the path towards indeterminateness that he had started with the project for Barene di San Giuliano in 1959.[27] The main difference from the earlier project was that, now, formal gestures had disappeared altogether.

A fourth position was represented by Cervellati and Insolera's entry that added a wider declaration of suspicion towards the prospect of controllable vast urbanisation to the scepticism about the autonomy of the architectural drawing, thus shaking the premises of many postwar beliefs.

It was the fifth and final position, however, that most polemically expressed a wholesale rejection of the values and beliefs of the city-territory debate. The entry submitted by Archizoom swept away all other arguments in a declaration of distrust, *tout court*, of any possible project – whether it was a renewal of a historical centre or a plan for a large-scale urban territory. Influenced by the critique of advanced industrial capitalism set out by the Operaist movement in 1960s' Italy, Archizoom conceptualised the city as a vast machinery of production: a city-factory that absorbed and neutralised architecture's traditional goal of representing a social system.[28] As they wrote in relation to their entry, in advanced capitalism, 'architecture no longer "represents" the System; rather it "is" the System. The city is no longer a "place"; it is a market "condition".'[29] Accordingly, Archizoom maintained that it no longer made sense to define the architectural project in terms of a correspondence of means and ends, since no particular formal invention – no 'project of roofs' [30] – could be claimed as a 'solution'. Whereas Quaroni's *metaprogetto* abandoned the product in order to design the process, Archizoom abandoned both. What they were left with was a

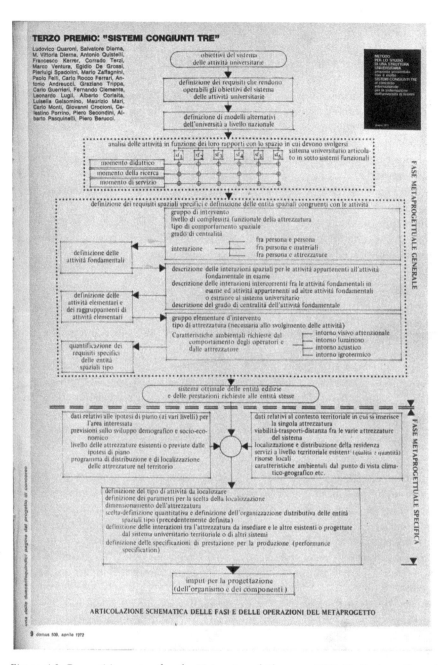

Figure 4.3 Competition entry for the University of Florence, 1970–71. Project: *Sistemi Congiunti Tre*. Architects: Ludovico Quaroni *et al*. (third prize).
Source: *Domus* 509 (April 1972).

representation of reality as it stood, which is what their competition panels proposed through the depiction of a continuous landscape in which information was produced and exchanged like any other commodity in a consumer society.

Despite breaking all conventions – or perhaps precisely because of this – Archizoom's entry was the only one that really reflected on the competition's topic – higher education and knowledge in the late twentieth century. All the other entries seized the topic to repeat established arguments and defend partisan positions on large-scale urbanisation. For better or worse, this is what characterised the competition as inextricably Italian, an occurrence reinforced by the fact that, despite the international outlook of the brief, all the entries came from Italian architects.[31] An intuition that this 'had to be' an Italian debate informed the brief of the follow-up competition for the University of Cagliari, an almost exact replica of the Florence brief that extended the confrontation between ideas on the city – with university design, once again, acting as just a pretext.

Cagliari, 1971: University workplace

Sardinia, July 1971:[32] history was repeating itself. The substitution of a city's name – Cagliari for Florence – was one of the only two real changes in a new competition brief that again put on the table the image of a regional territory reorganised in its services and infrastructure to embody 'the new dimension of the city'. The other alteration was a more sustained argument about the total relocation of the local university to a 400-hectare peripheral site, which was proposed as a reasonable strategy for a smaller institution that would benefit from clustering on a single site.[33]

A less polemical climate than the previous year made the competition pass rather unnoticed, as evidenced by limited commentary in the architectural press, which might have been related to the narrower range of entries compared to the cacophony of ideas in Florence.[34] The competition produced two major opposing approaches, one arguing for an archipelago strategy even more radical than in Florence, the other for a single, gigantic architectural gesture. The first was authored by the Roman architect, Luisa Anversa Ferretti, the second by Giuseppe and Alberto Samonà, in their first participation in a competition on university design.

Anversa Ferretti received the first prize with a scheme intended, in her words, to define the framework for a 'diffused urban condition'[35] in which value was redistributed more equally across a vast territory, in contrast to the centripetal logics governing the area at the time (Figure 4.4). Crucial to this accomplishment was the creation of an extensive tertiary armature for the metropolitan area that would constitute the connective tissue of a complete reshuffling and systematisation of agriculture and industry. Compared to Gregotti's scheme in Florence, Anversa Ferretti's archipelago strategy showed an even more emphatic 'rationalising will' (as she called it),[36] represented in the abstractness of an

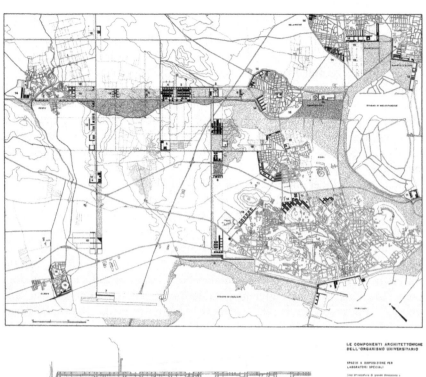

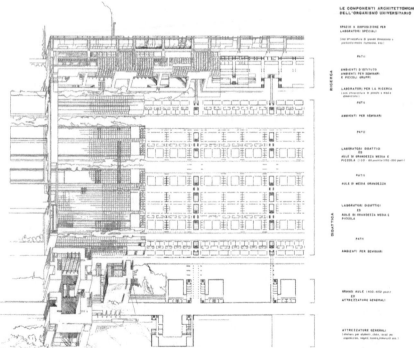

Figure 4.4 Competition entry for the University of Cagliari, 1971–73. Architects: Luisa Anversa Ferretti *et al.* (first prize). Territorial plan and project of the university node.

Source: Courtesy Luisa Anversa Ferretti, Rome.

orthogonal grid of roads overlaid on the metropolitan area to orchestrate the disposition of major regional services, which included an international airport, a new railway terminal, an expo centre, hotels, sports facilities, schools, a regional medical centre and the new academic complex. The latter was designed in the form of juxtaposed linear bands, with the outermost one hosting public facilities (shops, clubs, ateliers, art galleries, museums and restaurants), followed by a teaching podium with classrooms and seminar rooms of varying sizes alternated with outdoor patios, and a final zone of research laboratories and offices for professors.

Compared to other international projects of the time, this spatial diagram provided a different representation of the interrelation between generic and specialised areas of a university. Most recurrent solutions ranged between the modular repetition of a basic cell (for example, ARUP's Loughborough Technical University), a ladder scheme with rooms attached along a central spine (such as the University of Essex, or De Carlo's competition project for the University of Dublin), and a horizontal concatenation of indoor and outdoor rooms (such as the mat-building diagram pioneered in Candilis, Josic and Wood's Berlin Free University).[37] Anversa Ferretti also made use of modularity (considered paramount for speedy, prefabricated construction), but whereas those other diagrams were claimed to have derived from the spatial organisation of urban environments (explicit in this respect was Shadrach Woods' reference to an 'educational bazaar'),[38] the project for Cagliari displayed a closer affinity to a project such as the Soviet model school by Aleksander Nikolskij of 1928, which had itself blurred the boundary between an educational environment and a production plant. If a close-up of the Berlin Free University would have revealed its status as a casbah, a similar zoom into Anversa Ferretti's unbiased repetitive plan could easily have confused it for a portion of the city-factory depicted by Archizoom on the Florentine area. In common with Archizoom's argument, the winning entry in Cagliari declared that the project of a university complex could not be separated from the wider territory to which it belonged, and the university's configuration as a specialised knowledge-based production facility depended on its coexistence with other production poles rationally scattered across a vast territory.

Yet the archipelago was not the only possible configuration of a territory of production that indissolubly linked the architectural and urban scales. It took the architect who vehemently waved the flag of a 'unity of architecture and urbanism' – the title of his 1971 book[39] – to prove this point with one of the most prodigious products of the entire Italian production of university designs, and one that was surely not inferior to the first-prize winner in terms of territorial-ordering ambitions. Giuseppe Samonà, the competition runner-up, answered the brief through a single, gigantic architectural gesture filling the entire 400-hectare site: a 'disegno sul territorio' ('a drawing over the territory') [40] conceived as a 3-kilometre-long, 300-metre-wide linear settlement almost completely dug under the ground level. Like the first-prize entry, Samonà's huge bas-relief posited the idea of the university as a workplace. A single cross-section extruding along a line defined a work-and-service settlement in which the university would co-inhabit along with other tertiary offices, complementing them with an experimental, scientific mentality and, eventually, disappearing as an identifiable institution to become part of a general 'professional culture'.[41]

Produced in collaboration with his son, Alberto, the project reconnected with the *città territorio* discussion that had been put on hold with the latter's article in 1963.[42] As seen in Chapter 2, Alberto Samonà had claimed that giving formal characterisation to an advanced tertiary society created a pedagogic challenge. For him, the real problem was to understand the type of education necessary to define the figure of a tertiary worker, which would involve a similar endeavour to the way that technical education had been implemented to shape an industrial worker, but would take into consideration the differences between the two figures. More than the industrial worker, a service worker required generic intellectual capabilities that, in the text submitted to the competition in Cagliari, the Samonàs called 'professionalism', which they defined as the ability to solve problems of an administrative rather than a merely technical nature. A university should thus aim to provide generic skills, breaking from the fixation with specialisms appropriate to the industrial sector in order to shape a flexible worker. To achieve this educational task, the Samonàs' project posited that the most sensible thing was to embed university students within a tertiary work environment as workers among other workers.

Sharing this recognition, the Samonàs' and Anversa Ferretti's projects not only added a level of specification to an idea of *centri direzionali* that had been left open seven years before, but they also proposed an idea of the university that had been left undefined in Florence, thus advancing a step from the generality of the previous competition. Additional specification would have been necessary, and this required some new opportunities to confront ideas along the lines of the Florence–Cagliari trajectory. This opportunity did not, however, materialise. Two more competitions for Italian universities were ready to be launched but neither of them would have allowed a proper continuation of the discussion initiated in Florence and Cagliari. Paradoxically – or perhaps logically – the reason for this must be found in the sharpening specificity of the two subsequent briefs, in which the universities in question were more clearly put into focus to the detriment of that generality – as chaotic as it was liberating – that had provided opportunities both to advance ideas of urbanism and to think instrumentally about higher education. Moreover, at the subsequent competition for the University of Calabria, the much-exorcised spectre of a university campus appeared as perhaps the only possible solution.

Calabria, 1972: The spectre of the campus

The third of the competitions for universities in Italy marked a turning point in many respects. It was the first to ask for a brand-new institution as opposed to the previous two restructuring projects. Moreover, the university declared its regional nature as opposed to an attachment to a specific city. In addition, sixty-seven international entries – against nineteen and seventeen respectively at Florence and Cagliari – made it the most successful competition of the season. A possible reason for this was the much more detailed brief, which depicted a clearer idea of a university structured according to departments and colleges and, most relevantly and perhaps worryingly, made the hypothesis of a self-contained campus all the more plausible. An additional novelty can be distilled with hindsight: for the first time, an Italian competition for a university moved beyond paper and landed on earth in a showcase of the impudent heroism proper to its generation. Authored by Vittorio Gregotti – his second competition victory and thus elevating him to the Italian champion of university design – the winning entry equalled in grandeur the Samonàs' scheme for Cagliari. It envisaged the university as a 3-kilometre-long bridge spanning valleys and hills – a proper piece of regional infrastructure in a territory that was desperately in need of it.

At the time of the competition, Calabria was one of the most socially and economically depressed areas in the whole of Europe. Its stagnation was linked to multiple problems, ranging from a lack of educational institutions and high illiteracy levels, to a hostile topography that hindered access to remote areas, and, not least, to archaic social habits compromised by widespread organised criminality. The Calabria of the 1960s still offered a tragic representation of that vast Italian southern territory that had been bypassed by history, let alone by modernisation, as Carlo Levi had described it in his 1945 novel, *Christ Stopped at Eboli*. Within the so-called southern question (*questione del Mezzogiorno*), defining strategies for socio-economic renewal had been central to the political agenda of the national government for a decade, and the idea of creating an academic pole in Calabria had been discussed as a main component of this agenda.

Eventually, the university was established by a national Act in 1968[43] and in July 1972 an international architectural competition call was announced.[44] The statute defined a university with 'a residential character'.[45] In a visible U-turn from the strong defence of anti-campus sentiments by Italian politicians, the institution would be provided with its own residential centre to accommodate the academic staff and the majority of the student body (12,000 students). Considering the territorial situation in which the institution was being created, the acceptance of a campus ideal was understandable. In the interpretation of the State, Calabria required some sort of proper colonisation that could only be initiated by a self-contained and integrated environment of studying and living.

As anticipated, the competition brief was substantially more detailed than in Florence and Cagliari in relation to the specification of the intended university. The brief and the statute on which it was based were already a project in its own right, showcasing a level of ambition that was certainly not inferior to the previous two competitions. On the contrary, heroism and utopianism were at their peak:[46]

> There comes to be created for Calabria and its population a centre of modern high culture comparable to the colossal Massachusetts Institute of Technology, the advanced Tecnion in Haifa and the Technological Institute

in Grenoble. Calabria is advancing today towards the twenty-first century with great ambitions and it could not be otherwise.[47]

The public authorities decided that 660 hectares were necessary to allow such prodigious advancement. Three sites, adding up to that overall size, were located at a territorial junction that would not only serve the Calabrese population but would also act as a barycentre for southern Italy.[48] Competitors were left free to choose among the sites, provided they matched the goal of creating a university 'completely different from the traditional ones'.[49]

Difference was to be enacted through two components: university departments and academic *quartieri*. The brief listed twenty-one departments,[50] with the intention of balancing the centralising power of four faculties[51] by blurring disciplinary boundaries and overcoming the traditional divide between teaching and research that had been among the main targets of the students' protests in the 1960s. A call for generality was embedded in this battle against the traditional dictatorship of faculties because, the brief explained, the university is a constantly changing entity by definition and hence could not be given excessive formal specificity.[52] Flexibility, one of the mantras of 1960s' university planning, thus made its official debut in Italy but less simplistically than the movable partitions or modifiable interior layouts, since the brief called for

> Space to be walked through, for typical and frequent activities, or for exceptional activities. Each part of the space will belong to more than one category, but not to all of them ... A system ... at the disposal of different human behaviours and responsive to constantly emerging new needs.[53]

This anything-can-happen attitude aimed to prove the permissiveness of an institution created in 1968, at a time when permissiveness and repression walked hand in hand, constantly shifting their position to confuse and neutralise the potential opponents. Unsurprisingly, just as the British 'new' universities had not managed to avoid moulding the ideal of liberal higher education around the most elitist possible form of university, Oxbridge also became Calabria's image of a paradise lost.

As described in the brief, academic *quartieri* with integrated communal services, dining facilities, study areas and libraries promised to dismantle the gigantic multitude of the Italian higher education community into smaller, more controllable groups within which – it was believed – a sense of belonging to the institution could more easily be instilled. Each student and teacher would have a double affiliation to one department and one *quartiere*, thus creating a more tightly knit collegiate environment that was traditional in British higher education but was unheard of in Italy.[54]

Further innovations confirmed that the object of the competition was a new pedagogic project for the country that was permeated with a dialectic between permissiveness and repression. Students would be kept under the control of a newly set up tutoring mechanism of a British type, which extended the sphere of the academic into the sphere of dwelling, blurring two traditionally separate parts of the Italian idea of the university. On the other hand, students would also be allowed more liberty in tailoring the curricula of studies to their particular interests, thus breaking away from the prescribed pathways of normal Italian universities. Such a mixture showed how the official approach of the government to higher education had not advanced much beyond the ambiguous minimalist reformism that had been attempted since the late 1950s.

In urbanistic terms, the written project for the University of Calabria walked the fine line between the self-contained/autonomous argument and the spread-out *città territorio* rhetoric. Gregotti's drawn project translated this controversial dialectic into an uncanny environment – a university 'deeply different from the traditional ones' indeed, as it broke with any established idea or image, either Italian or foreign.

Interpreting architecture's role as concomitantly diagnosis and modification of a given condition – an idea that Gregotti had been elaborating in his writing throughout the 1960s[55] – the bridge he designed 'commented' on and criticised the territory in which it operated, launching a message of hope for architecture's capacity of controlling it. If a university settlement was all that was required by the competition – as opposed to the briefs in Florence and Cagliari that asked for proper regional master plans – Gregotti's project responded that territorial reordering ambitions could be retained if the settlement itself extended as much as possible to provide an instance of absolute, rational order. With its repetitive, dehumanising generic cubes, the university was also a metaphorical bridge suspended between an intention of enabling the flexible formation of a new, liberal individual and a totalising ambition of control pushed much beyond its interior community.

Based on the polemics that had tormented the competition in Florence, the jury – which included George Candilis, Michael Brawne, and Joseph Rykwert as international experts[56] – cautiously claimed that 'the problems of building a new university are not solved by holding an architectural competition for its design whatever the outcome of such a competition'.[57] Instead of choosing a winner in the first round, six schemes were selected for further assessment according to the criteria of response to landscape and topography, connections with existing infrastructure, provision of 'publicly accessible space' and avoidance of separating the sciences and the humanities. The final results, announced in June 1974, ranked Gregotti's proposal first,[58] followed by Tarquini Martensson from Denmark, Jerzy Josefowicz from Poland, Robert Smart from Scotland, Riccardo Dalisi from Italy, and Piero Sartogo in partnership with ARUP.

Despite the qualities of each of the runners-up, it was a number of entries by other Italian architects that provided an ideal continuation of the discourse established by the Florence competition in 1970. For their third participation in a row, Carlo Aymonino and Costantino Dardi unashamedly re-proposed the same scheme of large juxtaposed 'amphitheatres' they had submitted at Florence and Cagliari (Figure 4.5).[59] Over their three competition entries, a

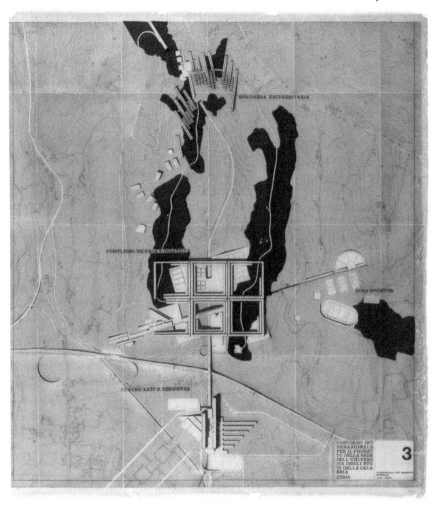

Figure 4.5 Competition entry for the University of Calabria, 1972–74. Architects: Carlo
Aymonino, Costantino Dardi *et al*. General plan.
Source: Università IUAV di Venezia, Archivio Progetti. Fondo Costantino Dardi.

trajectory can be identified from the first iteration of a composition of typological solutions (Florence), through an elaboration of the main element of that
composition (the proper university building in Cagliari), to its refinement in the
form of a figure suspended between openness and closure, finiteness and indeterminacy (Calabria). To be sure, the trajectory did not end there but pointed
towards a final representation that, predictably, was a proper project for the
city. This culminating outcome was the *Proposta architettonica per Roma Est*,
a collage-city presented at the Fifteenth Milan Triennale in 1973 that put together some of the projects of its authors and other Italian and international
pieces of publicly (mostly socialist) architecture.[60] Closing a loop that

Aymonino himself had initiated with the design course at the School of Architecture in Rome in 1961,[61] this final vision of a *città territorio* of formally contrasting parts unequivocally confirmed that the only possibility left to architecture for avoiding the triumph of privately driven urbanisation was to claim its self-referential nature at a monumental scale.

Following the second prize at Cagliari, Giuseppe and Alberto Samonà submitted a scheme that apparently marked a strong change of direction from the magnificent single gesture of their territorial bas-relief.[62] Their Calabrese proposal, conversely, took advantage of the three sites indicated in the competition brief to devise parts with different morphologies. Indubitably losing the clarity of the project for Cagliari, the scheme nonetheless manifested a consistency of argument about how a university could enable a city-territory. Keeping residences and academic services clearly separate, the Samonàs' project interpreted the commission of a large university-led development as the opportunity to provide an exemplary case of public housing. As such, the scheme is more relevant as a continuation of the 1950s' *quartieri* discourse than as a contribution to university design.

Aymonino's and the Samonàs' projects demonstrate that, despite the spectre of a campus haunting the Calabrese competition, a sudden retreat from the anti-campus ideology so euphorically sustained in the immediately preceding years could only be an improbable occurrence before the Italian architectural community's pride. Further proof came from the project submitted by Guido Canella (Figure 4.6),[63] whose participation in the competition was obviously anticipated, given that he had devoted two academic years with his students at the Politecnico di Milano studying the Calabrese territory and testing design hypotheses for a learning territory.[64] Canella had defended the idea that imagining a university in southern Italy required holistic thinking in which would be combined an understanding of rural traditions, intelligent industrial policy and a thorough modification of the learning system across primary, secondary and higher education. This idea had resulted in proposals for a peripatetic academic population studying and working both inside the proper university halls and in other institutions and industries, with university students acting as primary and secondary school teachers and industries offering training to complement formal academic teaching. However, Canella's argument that a university had to be 'everywhere' received a deathblow when the authorities opted instead for a conventional academic complex – 'a bit of university, no matter what' as he commented on the competition brief.[65] Logically, his participation in the competition could only be an oppositional one, as he openly declared by relocating part of the proposed new facilities to sites outside the competition boundary in a desperate attempt to reach out to a wider industrial territory.

Through its more detailed brief, the Calabria competition had offered a defined object that could be more easily translated into a project thanks to the advances in building technologies. Commenting on Gregotti's project a few years after the competition, Kenneth Frampton praised it precisely for its

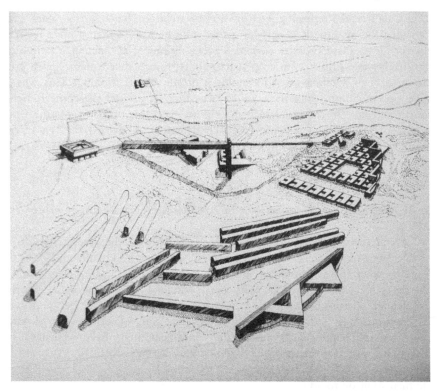

Figure 4.6 Competition entry for the University of Calabria, 1972–74. Architects: Guido
Canella *et al.* Bird's-eye view with the student residencies (foreground),
research and teaching centre (middle ground, right), office for regional consultancy (middle ground, centre), cultural and social centre (middle ground,
left), and laboratories and sports complex (background).
Source: Courtesy Studio Canella, Milan.

capacity not to succumb to technological rationalisation and for proving still
'able to turn productive logic to an architectural syntax that is open to
inflection and variation at many different scales while still maintaining the
tectonic integrity and cultural legitimacy of the elements involved'.[66] While
it cannot be known whether Aymonino, Samonà, Canella, or the other Italian participants[67] would have accomplished the same result had their project been built, it is nonetheless a truism that their interests lay much more
in formal morphology than in technological specification. Indeed, it was
exactly this difference of priorities that made the 'mega' ambitions of the
Italian city-territorialists depart from those of the international mega-
structuralists of the 1960s. Reyner Banham himself, in his attempted histor-
icisation of megastructure, highlighted a key distance between Archigram's
fixation on technology and detail and the Italian obsession with ideology.[68]

In Calabria, the returning participation of architects who, for ten years, had defended the hypothesis of city-territories indicated more than a mere reiteration of ideas. Their projects were also premonitions of an upcoming switch of approaches and priorities in large-scale public projects that would happen precisely through a takeover of technologist-productivist reasoning. This was a timely premonition, since the takeover was literally around the corner: in the fourth and final in the series of competitions – on this occasion, for the University of Salerno – a systems approach defeated and buried the last tragic attempts of a defence of architectural and formal autonomy.

Salerno, 1973: the triumph of system

In *Architecture, Cities and the Systems Approach*, Francis Ferguson wrote:

> Architecture has traditionally been produced by the interaction of a designer's experience, intellect, aesthetic sensitivity, and common sense. A city, when it was consciously planned or designed at all, drew largely upon the same creative sources, with correspondingly larger but more poorly defined sets of objectives and constrains. Within the last decade, questions have arisen as to the adequacy of this historic mode of form-giving for both cities and buildings. Critics of the traditional mode have argued for a greater systematization of the planning and design process.[69]

He then went on to add:

> In traditional architecture one was usually dealing with a single client and in many instances an autocratic one. In that context, decisions needed no justification. For example, if Louis XIV was shown a drawing by Le Nôtre, the issue was simply whether he liked it or not ... Questions of design process, cost-benefit analysis, rationality of the solution, and so forth would have been both irrelevant and tedious. Such is not the case today when the client is very likely to be a corporate body, a community, a building committee, or some other potentially divisive group having diverse objectives and interests in the particular urban and architectural problem.[70]

These words were written in 1975 to introduce – 'as objectively as possible'[71] – the growing interest of architects at that time in the systems approach. Ferguson's aim at objectivity recognised existing criticism of an idea that was received by some as 'a tacit acknowledgment of lack of imagination', 'a technocratic diversion from a more fundamental and searching analysis of society's problems', or even 'an attempt to institutionalize simplemindedness in urban and architectural problem-solving'.[72]

Indubitably, the competition for the University of Salerno, launched in June 1973,[73] posed these issues in a way that closed the short-lived Italian season of university design with an abrupt change of preoccupations. The wider objective of the competition was to expand an existing school of education[74] into a complete academic institution so as to alleviate pressure on the overcrowded University of Naples and enhance higher education in southern Italy in conjunction with the parallel establishment of the University of Calabria. The competition brief included a territorial study produced by urbanists Corrado Beguinot and Giulio De Luca which had been commissioned by the School of Education in 1968. The following year, Beguinot was asked to coordinate a committee for the choice of a site for the new university. Following a conference held on 26 January 1970 to discuss locational options ('Convegno di studio sulle strutture del sapere in Campania'), the choice fell on a 650-hectare area across the municipal territories of Fisciano, Mercato San Severino, and Baronissi, which was approved by the university officials on 17 May 1971.[75] This territorial goal, however, did not replicate the types of requests made to the competitors in Florence and Cagliari – and, to a much lesser degree, in Calabria. Now the brief hinted at how it was no longer necessary to draw extensive territorial master plans covering a regional or metropolitan dimension in order to define a new university. Multi-scalar thinking, it is true, was still present but in a very different way. It was not only that the scalar range spanned from the construction joint to the academic complex, thus ignoring any dimension beyond the latter; what also changed, most relevantly, was the prescribed approach to keep together that more limited scalar range.

The competition's rationale was imbued with enthusiasm for the systems approach, as demonstrated most plainly by the jargon used in the brief, which encompassed all the keywords discussed by Ferguson: problem-solving, procedure, cost-benefit ratio, component, and organisation. Linked to this terminology was a way of representing ideas through graphs, charts, flowcharts and matrixes. All of these populated the competition brief and reappeared in the entries of those competitors who adhered to the systematic philosophy that the Salerno competition contributed to introducing in Italy.

The maximisation of a rationalising will for arguably the most irrational institution – the university – was the competition's main objective: an attempt to turn the academic institution into an 'organisation' of logically related parts. The twofold rationalising endeavour of the previous competitions and their entries suddenly lost one of its referents: now, the outward impact of the university was overshadowed by an interest solely concentrated on the interior functioning of the academic complex. This interest stemmed from a productivist mentality apparent from the presentation of the Salerno competition as an unashamedly totalising, technocratic endeavour. The still timid attempt at systematising the university in Calabria paled in front of the clockwork clarity of intentions of the Salerno brief, which dissected with microsurgical precision the academic institution into its technological components.

To do so, the competition could build on some recent precedents of a systems approach applied to university design. The Philipps Universität in Marburg (1964) had been the first relevant university project to reason in terms of a coordination of components arranged hierarchically from technical detail to building unit to whole complex. Even more elaborate was the project by ARUP for Loughborough University of Technology (1966), which devised a tartan grid as the regulatory framework for the disposition of building units that were conceived as technologically integrated three-dimensional elements. To be sure, grids were a constant trope of much university architecture of the 1960s. Yet a key difference between ARUP's project and those of other grid-lovers, such as some Team X architects (for example, Candilis, Josic, and Woods's Berlin Free University or Giancarlo De Carlo's competition entry for University College Dublin) was in the former's fixation on approach, organisation, process, and system, which overshadowed altogether any discussion of architectural composition. In this modular complex, reasoning proceeded through a graphic notation where arrows were the literal substitutes for relations usually embedded deep in an architectural plan or section and requiring close reading to be diagnosed. A space stripped down to its bare technological bones, it required the architect to reason with the frame of mind of an engineer. Not coincidentally, an engineer – Mario Ingrami – won the competition at Salerno (Figure 4.7 and Figure 4.8). Also not unexpected was the presence among the winner's drawings of some literal quotations from ARUP's project, specifically a plan diagram indicating the possibilities of growth for the university complex and a perspectival section of the main building unit,[76] in which space was reduced to an amount of air sandwiched between technological horizontal slabs – a perfectly cold-blooded embodiment of Banham's 'well-tempered environment'.[77] Ingrami's scheme was a faultless reformulation of the brief and of the mentality that conceived it. It was a project quasi-automatically coming out of a 'building system' that was thoroughly defined in written form – and much more so than in Calabria, where the brief still left scope for architectural interpretation. Thus, to understand the project it is already sufficient to consider the brief itself.

Its main author was Pierluigi Spadolini,[78] an expert in the industrialisation of the building process whom we have already encountered as a partner with Ludovico Quaroni for the project that received the third prize in the University of Florence competition. As seen, that entry had opted for an ultimate demise of the architectural project. Insisting on process rather than product, their project's flow charts already hinted at the approach that would inform Spadolini's brief for Salerno – tellingly called a 'technical report', as opposed to the 'illustrative' reports of the previous competitions. Spadolini had also taken part in the 1970 ISES conference on university design at which he read a paper on 'Methodology for the industrialisation of university buildings'.[79] There he argued that the growing importance of industrialised construction for an optimal performance of the building process required rethinking the notion of architectural typology, transferring 'the concept of type from the building to its single part'[80] – the basic idea on which the Salerno brief was shaped.

The brief was as much the formulation of an objective as of the method to achieve it. Deploying the obscure jargon of an IT developer, it prescribed that entrants should 'apply the rules of aggregation of the system's components (software) to achieve a spatial model of the entire university organism, which

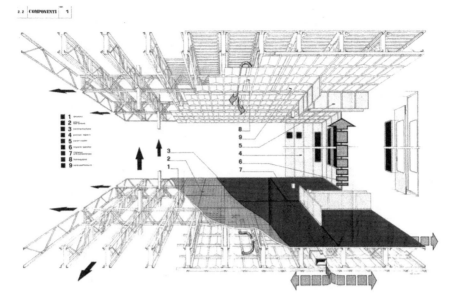

Figure 4.7 Competition entry for the University of Salerno, 1973–75. Architects: Mario
Ingrami *et al.* (first prize). Explanation of a typical technological module.
Source: Archivio Storico dell'Università degli Studi di Salerno, serie *Affari Generali*,
sottoserie, *Edilizia e arredi*, b. 1025, c. 30.

can then be three-dimensionally translated through the system's components
(hardware)'.[81] Put in simpler terms, academic functions were broken down into
a thinner set of human activities that were associated with specific 'spatial
units'. Fifty-four such units were indicated within eight categories of activities:
'teaching and research', 'practical activities and experimentation', 'management', 'complementary activities', 'production of informational materials',
'conferences, congresses, and assembly', 'dining services', and 'healthcare services'. Indications of possible users (individuals, small groups, medium groups,
large groups, very large groups), as well as of the preferable interactions with
other activities, accompanied a list of the technical equipment and the optimal
environmental parameters (lighting and acoustics) for each of the spatial units.

Stretching rhetoric and imagination, Spadolini tried to reclaim the humanistic
roots of this taxonomy, maintaining that it originated from an understanding of
human activities that were only subsequently translated into geometrical
terms – rather than the other way around, as, in his view, was the case in the
precedents of Marburg and Loughborough.[82] He promised the outcome would
be even better than that of those international precedents, since he envisioned
the achievement of an environment responsive to change:

> The building system is, therefore, the most effective device to guarantee the
> construction of spatial organisms whose dimensions can be varied over

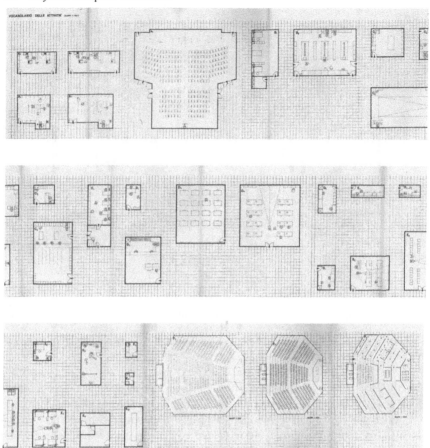

Figure 4.8 Competition entry for the University of Salerno, 1973–75. Architects: Mario Ingrami *et al.* (first prize). Taxonomy of the spatial modules.
Source: Archivio Storico dell'Università degli Studi di Salerno, serie *Affari Generali*, sottoserie, *Edilizia e arredi*, b. 1023, c. 151.

time. These can thus be expanded to adapt to the variation of functions in time and space, responding to the needs of adaptability and flexibility.[83]

In reality, at stake was the ultimate sweeping away of some of the remaining humanism that still permeated even the first quasi-scientific reduction of campus planning proposed by Richard Dober in 1963.[84] While dividing a university into a main building and functional components, Dober still believed in the architect as the interpreter of a brief. Conversely, in Salerno, very little was left to the architect other than a mere mixing of abstract ingredients pre-cooked by engineers.

The outcome could only be, and indeed was, a flat surface on top of which sat a number of architecturally dull, industrially manufactured, repetitive buildings whose only aim was to ensure the university's 'performance'. In fact, performance was the most repeated word in the winning team's report, which urged a reassessment of the possibilities offered by technology and rejected the criticism of technology as a proof of capitalist exploitation and compliance with a productivist paradigm – a criticism that was being popularised across Italian architectural culture, and here the brief clearly hinted at the theories of Manfredo Tafuri.[85] But the attack on architecture by the winning team was aiming at an even bigger target. In complete agreement with the brief's conceptualisation of the project as a sequence of interlinked stages and rational decisions in which a building was the final, logical output, Ingrami and his team condemned any attempt at creativity as a practice based on subjectivity, empathy and impulse.[86] Architecture was reduced to a technical act of coordination that could be realised thanks to the new computer-aided design procedures.

Designed through a primordial use of computer-generated iterations, the winning project 'resulted' in three parallel strips regulated by a tartan grid. Laboratory blocks were linked via bridges to slabs for research activities and connected by a covered walkway to the teaching blocks, in an overall linear configuration that would grow longitudinally over time according to needs. At first glance, similarities with other linear schemes – especially Gregotti's winning scheme in Calabria – would appear to harmoniously place Ingrami's project within an ideological tradition of abstract, even de-humanised, space for a university-machine. However, a big conceptual leap separated the project for Salerno from the type of uncanny abstraction pursued by Gregotti – or, for that matter, in the other Italian university projects such as the Samonàs' and Anversa Ferretti's schemes for Cagliari. The projects of Gregotti, Ferretti and the Samonàs depended on the priority of formal intelligibility over interior performance and were designed, so to speak, from the outside in, with priority given to their overall presence as figures on a landscape. Conversely, Ingrami's process-based project equated abstraction with a total disregard for the outward relations of the built complex; hence, it abandoned the claims (which were also rhetorical) of territorial ordering through architecture made by his architect competitors. Put simply, those claims were not a concern for an engineer who was aiming at optimising the performance of a building system.

Salerno declared the triumph of the productivist mentality that Frampton was still hoping to defeat in his commentary on Gregotti's project for Calabria, written five years after the conclusion of the Salerno competition. Even if, indubitably, the projects of this mostly unnoticed national competition were not among the historian's preoccupations, they signalled a general redirection of architecture and planning procedures in the advanced technological societies of the 1970s that Ferguson – quoted at the beginning of this section – and others endeavoured to explain.

Related to this change of direction was an inevitable clash between increasingly separate specialisms, each of which reclaimed leadership in the design of the built environment. Instances of the clash were evident across the competition entries,[87] which varied in their level of acceptance or rejection of the approach prescribed by the brief, turning the competition into a battleground of positions about the nature of the architectural project.

Resisting the brief's 'statement of distrust in the specific instruments of architecture',[88] one of the competitors, Uberto Siola, reclaimed a role for the architect beyond that of an organiser of objects on a checkerboard. Against this, he opposed a typological argument that tried to defend an autonomous intellectual realm for the architectural project.[89] In a reversal of approach from the winning entry, his proposal started from an *a priori* decision on some basic architectural types extracted from the hyperuranion of architectural ideas and modified by the mind of the architect to intentionally 'shape' the final project (Figure 4.9). However, fatigue was too evident in Siola's project for his defence of formal autonomy to be persuasive. In it was the evidence of a more general stagnation of Italian architectural theory, which continued reiterating ad nauseam the same ideas – namely, the pair typology/morphology – while the world around it was changing undisturbed by those preoccupations. Importantly, it was precisely in 1973, the same year as the Salerno competition, that this mannerist phase of the Italian architectural debate was ratified in *La Tendenza*, the Italian stream of a wider international new rationalism whose wear and tear would soon be attacked as architectural form copied from the past but deprived of utopia.[90]

Defeated by the advance of unbiased technicians, an important strand of Italian architecture faced in Salerno the prospect of its sudden ageing – perhaps most satirically represented in the characterisation of Carlo Aymonino as the 'expert of tech facilities' by the competition jury. To be sure, Salerno was not the end point of the typology/morphology dogma, as more projects along the argumentative lines of Siola's would continue to fill the panels of competitions organised in Italy during the years to come, and Italian architecture continued to be widely associated with a search for formalism, archetype and historical referencing well into the international postmodernist turn of the 1980s.

Conversely, the competition had a deadly impact on the Italian idea of the university. It did not simply provide a partisan victory of engineers over architects, but it also altogether washed away the reasons behind the previous type of discussion that had developed in Florence, Cagliari, and Calabria. In fact, it is totally irrelevant to assess this fourth competition in similar terms as the previous ones. The campus/non-campus debate was overshadowed by a totally different mindset, as architects felt forced to abandon the defence of the university as a piece of city rather than a self-sufficient entity because they had to cope with what appeared a more dangerous attack on their own profession. Now, they had to defend architecture against those who wished to neutralise and completely subsume it to a process-oriented mentality. In other words, they turned to a defence of architecture against the takeover by engineers.

Fate had it that the competition for Salerno was the last with a sufficiently wide scope and ambition to enable large-scale thinking about the future of

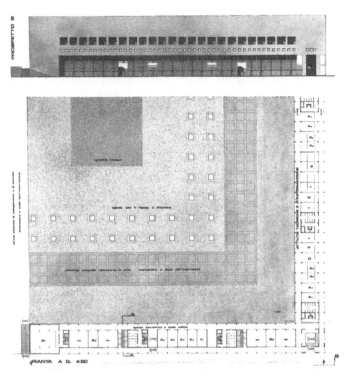

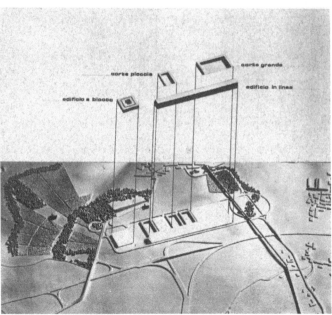

Figure 4.9 Competition entry for the University of Salerno, 1973–75. Architects: Uberto Siola *et al.* (second prize ex-aequo). Bird's-eye view of the complex and project of the large courtyard unit.

Source: Archivio Storico dell'Università degli Studi di Salerno, serie *Affari Generali*, sottoserie *Edilizia e arredi*, b. 1023, c. 151; b. 1022, c. 106.

higher education in Italy. Subsequently, a continuing incapacity to implement even the few results of this short-lived season of university design could only raise doubts as to the possibility of any heroic vision of change.

Notes

1 See Chapter 7.
2 See Law no. 641, 28 July 1967, 'Nuove norme per l'edilizia scolastica ed universitaria e piano finanziario per il quinquennio 1967–71'. See also Chapter 3, note 34.
3 Vittorio Gregotti and Eugenio Battisti, 'Due concorsi', *Edilizia moderna* 82–83 (1964): 109. My translation.
4 Carlo Aymonino *et al.*, 'La nuova Università di Cagliari', *Controspazio* 3 (1973): 30. My translation.
5 'Bando di concorso internazionale per la sistemazione della Università degli Studi di Firenze', *Gazzetta ufficiale della Repubblica Italiana* 110 (4 May 1970): 2747–2749. Eighteen projects were received by the submission deadline (15 June 1971). The results were announced on 22 October 1971.
6 Ibid., Art. 3.
7 See Sandro Rogari, 'Università di Firenze', in *Storia delle università in Italia*, ed. Gian Paolo Brizzi, Piero Del Negro, and Andrea Romano, vol. 3 (Messina: SICANIA by GEM s.r.l., 2007), 183–92.
8 The municipalities involved in the competition were Florence, Sesto Fiorentino, Galenzano, and Prato.
9 'Bando di concorso internazionale per la sistemazione della Università degli Studi di Firenze', Art. 3.
10 The competition was widely covered in the Italian architectural press. See *Casabella* 361(1972): 19–29; *Controspazio* 1–2 (1972): 5–31; *Domus* 509 (1972): 1–12; *Urbanistica* 62 (1974): 45–63.
11 Project *Amalassunta*. The winning team comprised Emilio Battisti, Edoardo Detti, Gian Franco Di Pietro, Giovanni Fanelli, Teresa Cobbò, Vittorio Gregotti, Raimondo Innocenti, Marco Massa, Hiromichi Matsui, Mario Mocchi, Paolo Sica, Bruno Viganò, Marica Zoppi; Collaborators: Francesco Barbagli, Peo Calza, Gian Franco Dallerba, Franco Luis Neves, Franco Purini.
12 The jury was composed of Professor G. Sestini (president and rector of the University of Florence), Professor G. Astengo, Professor J. Barge, Professor L. Benevolo, Professor O. Bohigas, Architect James Gowan, Professor P. Carbonara, Ing. U. Cassi, Professor V. Di Gioia, Professor T. Maldonado, Architect A. Mariotti, Professor G. Michelucci, Architect A. Montemagni, Architect G. Morozzi, Professor L. Piccinato, Ing. E. Salzano. The jury met in September and October 1971.
13 Oriol Bohigas, 'Considerazioni di un membro della giuria', *Casabella* 361 (1972): 21.
14 Massimo Scolari, 'Progetti per due città', *Controspazio* 1–2 (1972): 2–4.
15 James Gowan, 'Firenze università: Appunti di un membro fuggiasco', *Casabella* 364 (1972): 10.
16 'A Florentine Fiasco', *The Architectural Review* 900 (1972): 79.
17 Vittorio Gregotti *et al.*, 'Florentine Fiasco: To the Editors', *The Architectural Review* 905 (1972): 63.
18 Pier Luigi Cervellati and Italo Insolera, 'Aquarius', *Controspazio* 1–2 (1972): 15. My translation.
19 Pier Luigi Cervellati and Italo Insolera, 'Aquarius', *Urbanistica* 62 (1974): 56. My translation.
20 Ibid. My translation.

21 Project *Ariella*. Design team: Carlo Aymonino, Giorgio Ciucci, Costantino Dardi, Vittorio De Feo, Umberto De Martino, Mario Manieri Elia, Giovanni Morabito, and Francesco Pierobon.

22 Project *Continuum*. Design team: Italo Gamberini, Bianca Ballestrero Paoli, Serena De Siervo Cresci, Carlo Cresti, Andrea Del Bono, Loris Macci, Piero Paoli, Rosario Vernuccio. Consultants: Aldo Visalberghi, and Tullio Seppilli.

23 Project *Sistemi Congiunti Tre*. Design team: Università di Roma, Istituto di Progettazione della Facoltà di Architettura (Ludovico Quaroni, Salvatore Diema, M. Vittoria Diema, Antonio Quistelli, Francesco Karrer, Corrado Terzi, Marco Ventura, Egidio De Grossi); Università di Firenze, Istituto di Tecnica delle costruzioni (Pierluigi Spadolini, Mario Zaffagnini, Paolo Felli, Carlo Rocco Ferrari, Antonio Andreucci, Graziano Trippa, Carlo Guerrieri); Università di Bologna, Istituto di Architettura ed Urbanistica della Facoltà di Ingegneria (Fernando Clemente, Leonardo Lugli, Alberto Corlaita, Luisella Gelsomino, Maurizio Mari, Carlo Monti, Giovanni Crocioni, Celestino Porrino, Piero Secondini); Consultants: Alberto Pasquinelli, Piero Barucci.

24 See Romano Chirivi *et al.*, 'Rapporto sui problemi dell'edilizia universitaria nei riguardi delle tipologie e delle tecnologie', in *Atti del convegno di studio sull'edilizia universitaria* (Roma: ISES Istituto per lo Sviluppo dell'Edilizia Sociale, 1970).

25 Scolari, 'Progetti per due città', 4.

26 Ludovico Quaroni *et al.*, 'Sistemi Congiunti 3', *Urbanistica* 62 (1974): 60.

27 See Chapter 2.

28 For a discussion on Archizoom and the related bibliographical references, see Chapter 6.

29 Archizoom, 'Progetto di concorso per l'Università di Firenze', *Domus* 509 (1974): 11.

30 Ibid.

31 See Franco Raggi, 'Firenze università: Concorso per pochi intimi', *Casabella* 361 (1972): 19–27.

32 'Bando di concorso nazionale per il piano urbanistico di sistemazione dell'Università degli Studi di Cagliari', *Gazzetta ufficiale della Repubblica Italiana* 180 (17 July 1971): 4453–4455.

33 Università degli Studi di Cagliari, 'Consiglio di amministrazione integrato del 2 Maggio 1968: Relazione sulla scelta delle ree per l'Università di Cagliari del gruppo di studio incaricato del piano edilizio universitario (22/4/1968)', 22 April 1968, 2.

34 The first, second, third, and fourth prizes were published in a monographic issue of *Controspazio* dedicated to the competition in 1973. The project by Enrico Corti *et al.* was published in a research booklet by the University of Cagliari in 1974 (together with Corti's team project for the University of Salerno). The project by Giancarlo Leoncilli *et al.* was published in *Controspazio* in 1978. See 'Architetture per due concorsi', *Controspazio* 3 (1973): 10–49; Serafino Casu *et al.*, 'Le strutture universitarie: Problemi di metodologia progettuale', in *Atti della facoltà di ingegneria* (Cagliari: Università degli Studi di Cagliari, 1974); and Giancarlo Leoncilli, 'Progetti 1969–77', *Controspazio* 4 (1978): 22–31.

35 Luisa Anversa Ferretti *et al.*, 'Concorso nazionale per il piano urbanistico di sistemazione della sede dell'Università di Cagliari: Relazione tecnica', 1972, 38. (Rome: Studio Anversa Ferretti.)

36 Ibid., 111–112.

37 In the text submitted to the competition, Anversa Ferretti extensively referred to the following university projects of the 1960s: Walter Gropius's University of Baghdad (example of monocentric model), Bakema and Van der Broek's entry in the competition for the University of Bochum (example of polycentric model), the University of California at Santa Cruz (example of disaggregated model), and the universities of Loughborough and Marburg (examples of modular model).

38 See Shadrach Woods, 'The Education Bazaar', *Harvard Educational Review* 4 (1969): 116–125.

39 See Giuseppe Samonà, *L'unità architettura-urbanistica: Scritti e progetti, 1929–1973* (Milan: Franco Angeli, 1975).

40 Giuseppe Samonà *et al.*, 'Concorso nazionale per il piano urbanistico di sistemazione della sede dell'Università di Cagliari: Relazione illustrativa dei concetti informatori della proposta, con le fasi e i metodi di realizzazione e il piano finanziario di massima', 1972, 12. Samonà 1.pro/1/069, Università Iuav – Archivio Progetti, Fondo Giuseppe e Alberto Samonà.

41 Ibid.

42 Alberto Samonà, 'Alla ricerca di un metodo per la nuova dimensione', *Casabella* 277 (1963): 50–54. See Chapter 2.

43 Law no. 442, 12 March 1968, 'Istituzione di una università statale in Calabria', *Gazzetta ufficiale della Repubblica Italiana* 103 (22 April 1968), 2514–2517.

44 'Concorso internazionale per il progetto della sede dell'Università degli Studi di Calabria', *Gazzetta ufficiale della Repubblica Italiana* 188 (20 July 1972), 5229–5231.

45 Decree of the president of the republic, no. 1329, 1 December 1971, 'Approvazione dello statuto dell'Università degli studi della Calabria', *Gazzetta ufficiale della Repubblica Italiana* 53 (26 February 1972): 2–15.

46 See Pietro Di Leo, 'Università della Calabria', in Brizzi *et al.*, *Storia dell'università in Italia*. The founding of the university is here described as a 'real utopia' (p. 487).

47 Ente Studi Economici per la Calabria, *La scelta della sede dell'università della Calabria nelle esigenze regionali e più generali* (Cosenza: Tipografia Chiappetta, 1968), 16. My translation.

48 The three sites measured 320, 200, and 140 hectares respectively. See Università degli Studi di Calabria, 'Concorso internazionale per il progetto della sede dell'Università degli Studi di Calabria: Relazione illustrativa' (first competition call), 26.

49 Ibid., 4. My translation.

50 The twenty-one departments were: philology, history, arts, linguistics, philosophy, education, mathematics, physics, chemistry, cellular biology, ecology, earth sciences, systems, structures, territorial planning, soil preservation, mechanics, electrics, political economy, business, and public administration. See Decree of the President of the Republic, no. 1329, 1 December 1971, Art. 1.

51 The four faculties were: Literature and Philosophy; Mathematical, Physical and Natural Sciences; Engineering; and Economic and Social Sciences. See Law no. 442, 12 March 1968, Art.1.

52 Università degli Studi di Calabria, 'Concorso internazionale' (first competition call), 62.

53 Ibid., 63. My translation.

54 Decree of the President of the Republic, no. 1329, 1 December 1971, Art. 14.

55 See Vittorio Gregotti, *Il territorio dell'architettura* (Milan: Feltrinelli, 1966). See also Chapter 5.

56 The jury consisted of Professor B. Andreatta (university rector, president of the jury), Ing. Ettore De Coro, Professor Ing. Marcello Vittorini, Architect Carlo Cocchia, Professor Ing. Augusto Cavallari Murat, Architect Aleksander Franta, Architect George Candilis, Architect Michael Brawne, Architect Erdem Aksoy, Architect J.F. Zevaco, and Professor and Architect Joseph Rykwert.

57 *Jury Report on the International Competition for the Design of the Seat of the University of Calabria*, Recommendations 7.1.0, 1973.

58 The winning team (competition entry no. 51) comprised Vittorio Gregotti (team leader), Emilio Battisti, G.M. Cassano, Hiromichi Matsui, Pierluigi Nicolin, Franco Purini, C. Rusconi Clerici, and Bruno Viganò.

59 Competition entry no. 27. The team consisted of Costantino Dardi, Carlo Aymonino, Giorgio Ciucci, Bruno Conti, Vittorio De Feo, Mario Manieri Elia, Giovanni
Morabito, Raffaele Panella, and Maria Luisa Tugnoli.

60 The fragments that were assembled in the *Proposta architettonica per Roma Est*
included Aymonino and Dardi's project for the University of Cagliari; Aldo Rossi,
Gianugo Polesello and Luca Meda's *Locomotiva 2* competition project for Turin's
centro direzionale; Le Corbusier's La Tourette monastery; Quaroni's housing scheme
for the Casilino neighbourhood in Rome; Samonà's competition project for the new
deputy chambers in Rome; and Karl Ehn's Karl Marx Hof in Vienna. See Claudia
Conforti, *Carlo Aymonino: L'architettura non è un mito* (Rome: Officina, 1980);
Costantino Dardi, *Semplice, lineare, complesso* (Rome: Magma, 1976); and Carlo
Aymonino and Costantino Dardi, 'Roma Est: Proposta architettonica', *Controspazio*
12 (1973): 45–49.

61 See Carlo Aymonino *et al.*, ed., *La città territorio: Un esperimento didattico sul
centro direzionale di centocelle in Roma* (Bari: Leonardo da Vinci Editrice, 1964). See
also Chapter 2.

62 Competition entry no. 44. The team consisted of Giuseppe Samonà, Cesare Ajroldi,
Cristiana Bedoni, Mariella Di Falco, Gaetana Farfaglio, Rejana Lucci, M. Salvia, M.
Alberto Chiorino, Alberto Samonà, Francesco Tentori, Livia Toccafondi, and G.
Trincanato.

63 Competition entry no. 36. The team consisted of Guido Canella, C. Bono, A. Cris-
tofellis, G. Di Maio, G. Fiorese, V. Parmiani, G.P. Semino, F. De Miranda, F.
Gnecchi Ruscone, M. Ardita, R. Biscardini, G. Goggi, and F. Godowsky. See Guido
Canella *et al.*, 'Progetto per il concorso per l'Università della Calabria', in *Università:
Ragione, contesto, tipo*, ed. Guido Canella and Lucio S. D'Angiolini (Bari: Dedalo
Libri, 1975), 423–442.

64 See Canella and D'Angiolini, *Università*; and Chapter 8.

65 Franco Catalano and Ermanno Rea, 'Le università del sud', quoted in Canella and
D'Angiolini, *Università*, 12.

66 Kenneth Frampton, 'City without Flags', *Domus* 609 (1980): 21.

67 Competition entry no. 25. The team consisted of Ludovico Quaroni, S. Dierna, R.C.
Ferrari, F. Karrer, and P.L. Spadolini.

68 See Reyner Banham, *Megastructure: Urban Futures of the Recent Past* (London:
Thames and Hudson, 1976).

69 Francis Ferguson, *Architecture, Cities and the Systems Approach* (New York: G.
Braziller, 1975), 1.

70 Ibid., 2.

71 Ibid.

72 Ibid., 3.

73 'Concorso nazionale per la progettazione della sede dell'Università degli Studi di
Salerno', *Gazzetta ufficiale della Repubblica Italiana* 157 (20 June 1973): 4358–4360.

74 Established in 1944, the Istituto Universitario di Magistero 'Giovanni Cuomo' was
turned into the Facoltà di Magistero of the Università degli Studi di Salerno in 1968.
See Aurelio Musi, 'Università degli Studi di Salerno', in Brizzi *et al.*, *Storia dell'università in Italia*, 103–110; and Enrico Sicignano, *I campus di Fisciano e Lancusi*
(Rome: Gangemi, 2011).

75 See Corrado Beguinot, 'Il contesto territoriale e le caratteristiche dell'area', in Università egli Studi di Salerno, *Concorso nazionale per la progettazione della nuova
sede dell'Università di Salerno: Relazione tecnica allegata al bando* (1973). Beguinot
also took part in the ISES conference in Rome in October 1970, where he presented
his study of the territory of southern Italy: Corrado Beguinot, 'La rete strutturale del
Mezzogiorno: Estratto dallo studio "Strutture del sapere ed edilizia universitaria in
Italia"', in *Atti del convegno di studio sull'edilizia universitaria*. Beguinot is also
notorious for being the commissioner appointed by the Ministry of Education in

1971 to re-establish order in the School of Architecture of the Politecnico di Milano: see Chapter 8.

76 Besides appearing in many other publications of the time, ARUP's diagram was chosen for the cover page for *L'architecture d'aujourd'hui* 137 (May 1968), an issue dedicated to university design.

77 See Reyner Banham, *The Architecture of the Well-Tempered Environment* (Chicago: The University of Chicago Press, 1969).

78 In addition to Spadolini, the competition brief was produced by a team that included Aldo Bruscoli, Massimo Carli, Sara De Maestri, Gabriela Masi, and Graziano Trippa. See Università degli Studi di Salerno, 'Consiglio di amministrazione: Riunione del 31.10.1972'.

79 Pierluigi Spadolini, 'Metodologia della industrializzazione dell'edilizia universitaria', in *Atti del convegno di studio sull'edilizia universitaria.*

80 Ibid., 2. My translation.

81 Università degli Studi di Salerno, 'Concorso nazionale per la progettazione della sede dell'Università degli Studi di Salerno: Relazione tecnica allegata al bando', 13.

82 Ibid., 10.

83 Ibid., 7. My translation.

84 Richard P. Dober, *Campus Planning* (New York: Reinhold, 1963). See also Chapter 1.

85 The reference was to Manfredo Tafuri's *Progetto e utopia*, which was published in the year of the competition call (1973). Mario Ingrami *et al.*, 'Concorso nazionale per la progettazione della sede della Università degli Studi di Salerno: Relazione', 1974, Chapter 1.3.1, 4. Università degli Studi di Salerno – Archivio di Ateneo.

86 Ibid., Chapter 1.3.1, 14.

87 The competition for the University of Salerno received eleven submissions.

88 Uberto Siola *et al.*, 'Università di Salerno: Concorso nazionale per la progettazione della nuova sede: Relazione illustrativa', 1973, 16–17. Università degli Studi di Salerno – Archivio di Ateneo. My translation.

89 Ibid., 19.

90 See the criticism of the dead end reached by typological reasoning at the end of the 1970s in Rafael Moneo, 'On Typology', *Oppositions* 13 (1978): 23–45.

Epilogue to Part I
End of an illusion

Within the span of two months, between April and June 1974 when the results of the Salerno and Calabria competitions respectively were announced, the Italian season of large-scale university design collapsed – only four years since Florence had launched the heroic prospect of territories restructured around higher education.

In an article entitled 'Gap between Research and Implementation in University Planning' and published in 1976, Paola Coppola Pignatelli commented on the four competitions for new universities of Florence, Cagliari, Calabria, and Salerno:

> A hundred ambitious proposals all grounded on a firm (legitimate?) belief that the university is the beacon – or, to put it in urbanistic terms, the structuring pole – of a territory, the 'unique' opportunity to give an order to the urbanistic and architectural chaos of our cities. However, perhaps, the university is no longer like that at all; perhaps, it is only a poor, modest service that each municipality will offer its inhabitants through the evening use of a computer in the 'common hall' of an elementary school. May the gap between fulfilment and research in university building be nothing but the symptom of the obsolescence of an idea of the university that has been, regardless of anything, overcome?[1]

Concentrating the blame for failure on public authorities, Pignatelli's denunciation was a way for architects and planners to exit the scene by claiming a clean conscience as victims of 'a hundred occasions of frustration and economic pardoning'.[2] Frustration was indeed the only possible sentiment given the fate of the four competitions. Coming out of the realm of fantasy, where everything was possible as long as it remained on paper, and entering the labyrinth of real decision-making, all four ended up in some sort of alteration.[3] Following the loss of the two project leaders in the mid-1980s (Edoardo Detti died; Gregotti left the team), changed feelings about the possibilities of large structures were advanced as a major justification to literally subvert the winning scheme in Florence.[4] With the metropolitan master plan reduced to a drawn memoir to be hung on the walls of the university's planning office, the design of the academic settlement was turned into a conventional set of detached blocks around a lawn. Cagliari went even further, with the university eventually commissioning a new project from a different office[5] that obliterated the bigger picture, leaving only an isolated 'university citadel' for years disconnected from everything else. As anticipated, Calabria was more successful: Gregotti's bridge was eventually built and, at 1.5 kilometres – albeit only half the length of the original design – remains one of the most daring architectural creations on the Italian landscape. Yet, even here frustration was not avoided, as Gregotti attacked the mismanagement that had allowed chaotic private developments in the areas around the university.[6] Confirming the philosophy behind a project first and foremost oriented to exert an outward impact on a vast territory, Gregotti's polemic also confirmed that the Salerno project, by giving up such ambition (or arrogant presumption) from the outset, would be implemented most faithfully to its design – surely not one of the highpoints of Italian twentieth-century architecture, as proved by the *Chiostro della pace*, a collaboration between Ettore Sottsass Jr and Enzo Cucchi in 2006 that manifested a desperate attempt to counter the dullness of the settlement with an injection of irony.

Despite their general failure, all four cases contributed in their own way to the advancement of an architectural discourse around the topic of university design, although it would be hard to place them on a definitive trajectory. The one that I have sketched in my narrative, which presents the idea of *città territorio* gradually losing its centrality from Florence to Salerno and the parallel emergence of a systems approach, is probably sufficiently correct to put this story inside the wider context of an architectural discourse that was generally shifting towards a more techno-scientific approach. Indubitably, Ingrami's victory over Siola's weary attempt at retaining some of the ethos of previous proposals by Gregotti, Aymonino, Anversa Ferretti, and Samonà signalled how the faith in the power of large-scale formal interventions was clearly declining, as was trust in the ability of public authorities to control urban development.

The discussion on university planning re-emerged powerfully around 1976–77, when a novel outburst of social unrest and student protest shed new light on the still very unstable social situation across the country. Over the years 1976 and 1977 architects also resumed their interest in university planning, this time with much more pessimistic tones than only a few years before. New attacks on the government were launched, in particular against a recently passed national law that allowed the creation of new institutions across the country[7] – yet, still with no higher education reform approved. In the pages of *Parametro*, a commentator spoke of 'the end of an illusion', and of the ultimate 'end of university planning': the demonstration of the government's incapacity of going beyond numerical aspects and of really conceiving an idea of the university for the country.[8]

But pessimism was not only directed towards the government. An emergent self-criticism seemed to look back to two decades earlier when Quaroni had attacked the anachronism of the Italian *quartieri* of the 1950s. In 1976, it was again Quaroni who levelled a similar criticism against the design of new universities, expressing it in Marxist tones that posited how only a change of society could lead to making the university a real engine of growth – and not the other way around.[9] In an article asking 'what to do' with the academic institution, he wrote: 'The Utopia of a different world risks remaining utopia forever, at most losing its capital U, and turning into myriad small utopias, some maybe realisable, but overall incapable of providing us with any confidence about the future.'[10]

Considering his anti-architectural proposal for Florence, a critique against determinism was to be more expected than twenty years earlier. But Quaroni's attack was not simply targeted against the advocates of large formal gestures capable of exerting territorial order; more alarmingly, it undermined the very ideology that had moved the discourse on the territoriality of the university, casting doubt on the expectation that higher education could be an engine of territorial restructuring.

Architectural autonomy was wrapped in doubt more than it ever had been. A monographic issue of *Casabella* on higher education in 1977 demonstrated the sense of urgency among the architectural community that discussion needed to be broadened.[11] Adding the voices of politicians and academic officials, a bridge was attempted between two lines of debate that had largely proceeded in parallel over the previous decade. Moreover, broader ideas about academic territories were confronted, pulling together the large-scale visions of the competitions with Giancarlo De Carlo's proposals for universities scattered across the urban fabric. Thus, an important voice that had remained outside of the competitions was included, while at the same time the mounting prospect of distance learning as exemplified by the Open University in the UK started being considered.[12]

A new year zero of debate on the university was promised in 1977. Unfortunately, history shows us that what followed was not better planning and management of Italian higher education. Encouraged by a State more confused than ever as to the meaning of democratic access to knowledge, towns big and small claimed, and often obtained, their own higher education institution. Policies of decentralisation proved the persistence of a quantitative approach that saw universities, often as small as a single faculty or building, proliferate throughout the country.[13] Meanwhile the idea of the university was being reshaped by growing supranational bodies, culminating in the Bologna Process of the early 2000s for a European higher education system that finally established the three-tier degree system proposed and rejected in 1960s' Italy.

Within the general striving for homogenisation of European higher education, the prospect of an 'original' Italian 'take' dissipated together with the steep fall into the abyss of the architect as a figure trusted with vast social responsibility – but perhaps that is, more generally, the story of architecture over the last two decades, a story that would deserve another book to be properly told.

Notes

1 Paola Coppola Pignatelli, 'Gap tra ricerca e attuazione nell'edilizia universitaria: Note su 4 concorsi', *Parametro* 44 (1976): 19. My translation.
2 Ibid. My translation.

3 See Sabrina Puddu, 'Campus o cittadella? Il progetto di un'eredità', in *Territori della conoscenza: Un progetto per Cagliari e la sua università*, ed. Sabrina Puddu, Martino Tattara, and Francesco Zuddas (Macerata: Quodlibet, 2017), 134–151.

4 After the competition, a detailed project was developed by the winning team and presented to the university in 1976. Following the death of Detti and the exit of Gregotti from the team, Francesco Barbagli became the team leader for a new project that was submitted to the university in 1985. See Gruppo Amalassunta, *Nuovo polo scientifico di Sesto Fiorentino*, Project Report, 1985. Università degli Studi di Firenze.

5 In 1982, the university commissioned B&C associati (Tommaso Bevivino and Maurizio Costa) to undertake a new project. Construction of this project began in 1984.

6 See Vittorio Gregotti, 'Università e territorio: Il progetto mancato', *Corriere della Sera*, 17 June 2010, 24–25.

7 Law no. 580, 1 October 1973, 'Misure urgenti per l'università'.

8 See Giampaolo Bonani, 'Fine della pianificazione universitaria', *Parametro* 44 (1976): 4–5.

9 Ludovico Quaroni, 'L'istituzione università: Che farne?', *Spazio e società* 4 (1976): 5–32.

10 Ibid., 17. My translation.

11 See 'Università: Progettare il mutamento', *Casabella* 423 (1977).

12 See Giuseppe Richeri, 'Università, territorio e televisione', *Casabella* 423 (1977): 26–27.

13 A search query using 'university' as keyword on the Italian Ministry of Public Education's website today produces ninety-eight results. See http://ustat.miur.it/dati/dida ttica/italia/atenei#tabistituti (accessed 4 August 2018). In 1967, there were thirty-two Italian universities. See Paola Coppola Pignatelli, *L'università in espansione: Orientamenti dell'edilizia universitaria* (Milan: Etas Kompass, 1969), 196.

Part II

Academic territories

Four takes

Prologue II

The principle of concentration

Ever since Wilhelm von Humboldt reformed it in 1810, 'inventing' the term 'research' as a counterpart to the traditional goal of teaching, the story of the modern university has been ruled by one dominant principle: the principle of concentration. What had existed before von Humboldt was an institution very different from the palaces and settlements of knowledge, modelled on the German example, that popped up around the world afterwards. The earliest European universities were institutions with no ad hoc buildings and which were constantly in search of space to borrow around the city. This nomadic nature held as true at Bologna or Paris in the eleventh and twelfth centuries as it did in the seventeenth-century North American colonial colleges, whose origins have been described as 'ambulatory, like the tabernacle in the wilderness'.[1] Until the nineteenth century, higher education had small spatial and social dimensions overall; in so far as it was thought of on a larger scale, this was generally due to the university's mother institution, invariably the Church. The absence – both institutional and spatial – of an independent entity named 'university' was matched by the parallel rise of learned academies, which developed as a complementary network even less territorialised than its counterpart inside religious colleges and monasteries.[2]

It was only after their re-foundation and redefinition with a new identity as an operative arm of the nineteenth-century national states that universities became large and complex machineries for the production and protection of scientific knowledge. As observed by Jürgen Habermas, by introducing the unity of teaching and research as the central principle of a modern university, Humboldt promoted a conception of 'the scientific process as a narcissistically self-enclosed process'.[3] A paradox was embedded in the way institutional restructuring matched a new canon of open-ended enquiry. This was in contrast to the Aristotelian structure of knowledge in liberal arts and the associated pedagogic canon of repetition of consolidated knowledge – the traditional way of understanding the activity of studying – according to which the unity of teaching and research could never happen within open-ended, spatial dispersion. A concomitant explosion and re-centring of higher education were required, and this happened via the multiplication of the parts of a university – new disciplines, institutes, schools, and departments – and their assemblage inside agglomerations that gradually assumed the scale and scope of industrial complexes – universities, as we know them today.

The university's path to maturity did not unfold only as the desire to gain spatial stability and territorialisation for the institution. Modernity also made the very idea of 'homeless' higher education unthinkable, to the extent that the nomadic past of universities was overshadowed by the affirmation of concentration that was 'essential to their functioning and efficiency',[4] as was proclaimed to the international architectural community in the 1930s. Only the digital turn of the late twentieth century has revamped the idea of a de-centralised university as a possibility, with Massive Open Online Courses (MOOCS) and virtual universities updating the archetype of a 'university of the air' first sketched out by the British Labour Party in 1963.[5] Yet it remains uncertain up to what point information technology has been, or will be, capable of dissolving the stability of power and spaces that made universities among the most immutable and conservative forms of human organisation.[6]

In the second half of the nineteenth century, the United States assigned to the modern research university an unprecedentedly large footprint; in doing so, it was importing the Humboldtian model and turning what had been up to that moment a European story into an American narrative. Johns Hopkins University was the first American university to adopt the German research paradigm, thus initiating a scalar leap from the smaller realities of the colonial colleges at Harvard, Yale and Princeton.[7] But it was at the University of California that, following the transatlantic Berlin–Johns Hopkins reformative trajectory, the jump in scale was matched by architectural grandeur. The 1896–1899 International Competition for the Phoebe A. Hearst Architectural Plan for the University of California at Berkeley marked the first important occasion when a competition was used to compare proposals for a large piece of academic territory – a stretch of landscape 'to be filled with a single beautiful and harmonious picture as a painter fills in his canvas'.[8] To be sure, competitions had previously been launched in Europe for the design of institutes or colleges, such as those organised by the Accademia di San Luca in the eighteenth century.[9] What was new in Berkeley, however, was that the 'ideal home'[10] to be designed for the institution greatly exceeded the limits not only of a single built complex but also of any previous American campus. This scalar jump was sealed with an ambition of immortality, as the competition brief claimed that 'there will be no more necessity of remodeling its broad outlines a thousand years hence, than there would be of remodeling the Parthenon, had it come down to us complete and uninjured'.[11] No longer the cosy, quasi-domestic scale of the old American colonial campuses, Berkeley projected a claim that a big university should be concentrated in space – and it supported this claim by having a footprint as large as the surrounding town.

When, in the 1960s, higher education needed further expansion, spatial concentration had become a widely contested political issue, associated as it was with the growth of top-down control by sovereign national and industrial power. Fate determined that it was on the academic grounds at Berkeley where this association of university and power first came under the fire of student protest, from where it rapidly extended to the old continent.

In Italy, a country emerging from two decades of fascist dictatorship, the critique of top-down authority was charged with added value and was made even more complex by the lack of a tradition of university planning comparable to the Anglo-American one. The series of architectural competitions in the early 1970s clustered discussion around one main question that coupled spatial and political prerogatives: should the university be a concentrated or a dispersed entity? The chapters that follow discuss how five Italian architects and design teams approached the design of universities with this as the underlying question. From different perspectives and achieving strongly contrasting formal results, they all claimed to want to abandon the university as it existed and start afresh with a new university for the mass society. In the wake of 1968, that university could only be a tightrope precariously suspended between authority and discipline, on the one side, and the promise of equality and personalised self-formation, on the other. Reaching either destination implied more than the choice of an idea of the university, as the projects by Vittorio Gregotti, Giuseppe Samonà, Archizoom, Giancarlo De Carlo, and Guido Canella showed by addressing the wider goal of critiquing the discipline of architecture itself.

Notes

1 Carl A. Raschke, *The Digital Revolution and the Coming of the Postmodern University* (New York: RoutledgeFalmer, 2003), ix.
2 See Ian F. McNeely and Lisa Wolverton, *Reinventing Knowledge: From Alexandria to the Internet* (New York: W.W. Norton, 2008).
3 Jürgen Habermas and John R. Blazek, 'The Idea of the University: Learning Processes', *New German Critique* 41 (1987): 10.
4 Ibid.
5 On the Open University, see Joaquim Moreno, *The University Is Now on Air Broadcasting Modern Architecture* (Montreal: Canadian Centre for Architecture, 2018).
6 See John Tiffin and Lalita Rajasingham, *The Global Virtual University* (London: RoutledgeFalmer, 2003); and Raschke, *The Digital Revolution*.
7 See Jonathan R. Cole, *The Great American University: Its Rise to Preeminence, Its Indispensable National Role, Why It Must be Protected* (New York: Public Affairs, 2009).
8 University of California Berkeley Trustees of the Phoebe A. Hearst Architectural Plan, *The International Competition for the Phoebe A. Hearst Architectural Plan for the University of California* (San Francisco: The Trustees, 1900), 8.
9 Paola Marconi, Angela Cipriani, and Enrico Valeriani, eds., *I disegni di architettura dell'archivio storico dell'Accademia di San Luca* (Rome: De Luca, 1974).
10 Berkeley Trustees, *International Competition*, 10.
11 Ibid.

5   Exemplars of order

Vittorio Gregotti, Giuseppe Samonà, and academic gigantism

Ordering eagerness

On 5 June 1974, in Calabria, three years after winning the competition for the University of Florence, Vittorio Gregotti found himself once again in the top rank of an architectural competition for yet another Italian academic settlement. The actual subsequent construction of the winning scheme made his recurring success even more exceptional, given the mostly inconsequential fate of other Italian university projects of similar scale and ambition. And, in terms of ambition, Gregotti's winning design was second to none. Having designed a university as a linear bridge, spanning 3 kilometres of valleys and olive-planted hills, Gregotti had left a tangible mark on the history of Italian large-scale university design (Figure 5.1).[1] This mark had much in common with the project that Giuseppe Samonà had submitted a couple of years earlier to a similar competition for the University of Cagliari – an even more generous celebration of grandiosity at 5 kilometres in length – although the two projects differed in their dialogue with the ground: Gregotti's bridge structure was superimposed on top of the landscape as opposed to Samonà's gigantic inverted bas-relief dug into the ground to make the university disappear from view (Figure 5.2).

Samonà and Gregotti were representatives of two subsequent generations that defended an autonomous role for architectural form. Alongside Ernesto Nathan Rogers (1909–1969) and Ludovico Quaroni (1911–1987), Samonà (1898–1983) was the oldest of a generation that had driven Italian modern architecture across the divide from fascism to postwar democracy.[2] His leadership had particularly been demonstrated during three decades as director of the Istituto Universitario di Architettura di Venezia (IUAV), which he had chaired since 1945. His projects for universities arrived at a late stage in his life and were elaborated with his long-time collaborators, his son Alberto Samonà and Egle Tricanato. These projects inevitably became the summary of a whole career spent writing and designing in defence of the role of architects against the threats of a technocratic approach to planning and urbanism. In 1959, with *L'urbanistica e l'avvenire della città negli stati europei*[3] – the 'first Italian book on urbanism'[4] – he made a fundamental impact on the architectural debate by reflecting on the 'new urban dimension' of postwar society. Written as a

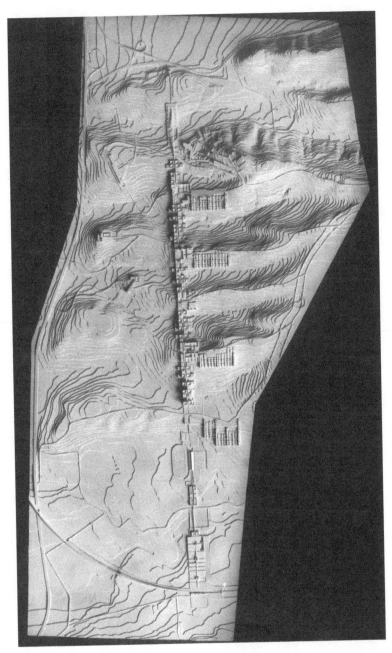

Figure 5.1 Vittorio Gregotti *et al.*, project for the University of Calabria (1972–74). Model.
Source: C.A.S.V.A., Comune di Milano. Archivio Gregotti.

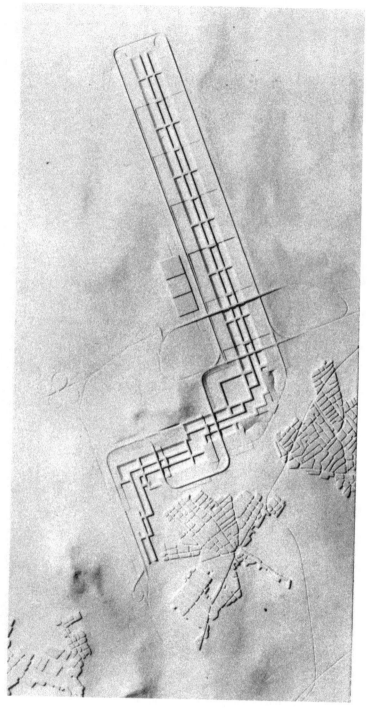

Figure 5.2 Giuseppe Samonà *et al.*, project for the University of Cagliari (1971–73).
Competition model.
Source: Centro Studi e Archivio della Comunicazione, Università degli Studi di Parma.
Fondo Giuseppe Samonà.

critique of the dominant conception of urban planning as a separate practice from architecture – finding the origins of this conception in Ebenezer Howard's Garden City – the book paved the way to the subsequent Italian debate under the rubrics of *città territorio* and *città regione*.

Gregotti never fully demonstrated sympathy for such labels. Formed as an architect and writer of architecture under the influence of Samonà's generation, and in particular of his mentor Ernesto Nathan Rogers, he distanced himself from the 'inventors of easy megastructures' who had come to dominate architectural discourse in the early 1960s.[5] As editor of *Casabella* between 1953 and 1963,[6] when Rogers was the magazine's director, Gregotti was given the opportunity to directly follow the debate on the new urban dimension. In fact, *Casabella* played a major role in disseminating the reflections on vast architect-designed city-territories. In particular, the magazine popularised the ideas of *centri direzionali*: the rational reorganisation and clustering of tertiary services on the outskirts of cities in the form of new architectural typologies.

Both Gregotti and Samonà criticised the handling of a new urban dimension as a mere physical enlargement of architectural structures, a point that Samonà had made clear already in 1961: 'I believe any idea of gigantic spatial parameters to be absolutely out of the question.'[7] Considering their university projects, this opposition to gigantism appears somewhat contradictory if not altogether paradoxical. Yet its rationale dwells inside the very opacity of the brief – university design – and the age – the aftermath of 1968 – to both of which Gregotti and Samonà gave the most heroic architectural responses.

The design of a university settlement offered a way of providing an ordering plan – a large-scale architectural drawing – for a vast stretch of landscape. Samonà's and Gregotti's projects, as perfect manifestations of exemplar and unequivocal pockets of formal order, were paradigmatic in this sense. This fixation on ordering mingled with the need for a new idea of the university that had been violently reclaimed in 1968 and that located these projects in contested territory between the confirmation of top-down control and the acceptance of the students' demands for non-authoritarian forms of higher learning. The architects found a clever way out of this impasse by instrumentally seizing upon the design of new universities to test ideas they had been developing in writing. Ultimately, it was largely an intellectual anxiety about the status of the theory and praxis of architecture that defined the *raison d'être* of their projects.

'New directions in Italian architecture'

As chief editor of *Casabella*, Gregotti did not straightforwardly interiorise the type of discourse promoted by Rogers's magazine. Around 1962, he started to distance himself from the optimism with which the notions of *città territorio*, *città regione*, and *centri direzionali* were being debated by other contributors as an ideal fit between formal expression and social change in an age of growing industrialisation and tertiarisation of the economy.[8] This distancing eventually led to his resignation in 1963, which was rapidly followed by a new editorial position at the magazine *Edilizia moderna*. [9] Emancipated from his intellectual father and various 'step-brothers' at *Casabella*, during the three years before the publication of his major theoretical work, *Il territorio dell'architettura* in 1966, Gregotti developed a personal theoretical investigation on architecture that carved out for him an original position inside Italian architectural circles.

In the 1960s, those circles corresponded to the seven Italian schools of architecture at Turin, Milan, Venice, Florence, Rome, Naples, and Palermo. Notwithstanding some exchange of ideas and migrations of architect–academics from one school to another, these main centres of architectural discussion had over the years developed specific approaches to similar problematics, which Gregotti summarised under three main trends in his 1968 book, *New Directions in Italian Architecture*:

> The first deals with the notion of the city as an artefact and tends to return to architecture its 'monumental' meaning. The second tends to investigate the notion of physical environment and, starting from the idea of formal or functional relationships and materials, attempts to establish a new way of adapting to all dimensional scales. The third, under the influence of American theory, tends to direct its interests toward formalizing the project procedures, replacing the old material technology with project technology. [10]

To illustrate these trends, he selected the work of students, choosing an architectural studio led by Raul Greco and Carlo Aymonino in Rome for the design of a *centro direzionale*, Ludovico Quaroni's studio, also in Rome, on the topic of a University-City, and the work of Ludovico Savioli's students in Florence.

While sharing an interest with aspects of all three lines of reasoning, Gregotti did not explicitly identify the work of his own students at the Politecnico di Milano with any of them. Compared to the other examples, the drawings of his students showed a much larger scale of reasoning, as they dealt with topography and geographical elements. Blurring analysis and intervention, they echoed the investigative line that Gregotti had discussed at length in *Il territorio dell'architettura*, his main theoretical work that, in 1966, formulated the ideas that would later underpin Gregotti's own projects – especially those for universities. Pivoting on the notions of *ambiente totale* (total environment) and of the anthropogeographical project, Gregotti walked alongside other Italian architects on a shared path towards the specification of an original take on the nature of the architectural project and its role within the trajectory of history.

Ambiente totale and the anthropogeographical project

Throughout the 1960s, Gregotti's theoretical investigation ran parallel to the one that prompted Aldo Rossi – another protégé of Rogers – to elaborate a theory of urban artefacts in *L'architettura della città*, also published, like Gregotti's book, in 1966. Gregotti and Rossi shared a sense of urgency about re-establishing a scientific architectural discourse on the built environment after it had been short-circuited by what they perceived as a naïve understanding of functionalism in the nineteenth and twentieth centuries. Re-evaluating the eighteenth-century notion of the revolutionary power of an architecture based on reason, the two became major Italian protagonists of the wider phenomenon of neo-rationalism, although they viewed it from two very different perspectives, as their built work clearly shows.[11] The lyricism and metaphysical poetics of Rossi's work contrasted with Gregotti's more tectonic interpretation of rationalism, and the latter did not allow much space for the amused play with history entertained by Rossi's analogical exercises.

Despite the somewhat colder character of Gregotti's drawn and built work, there were, nevertheless, many commonalities with his colleague that emerged more clearly from their written theoretical investigations. Inevitably, both had to confront the hot topics of the period, especially the expansion of urban territories. But whereas the city was Rossi's favourite subject of discussion, Gregotti showed much less overt enthusiasm in a discourse on a possible new urban theory. This is evident in Gregotti's choice of titles for his book: he purposely avoided the word 'city', opting instead for the wider-ranging term 'territory'. Nevertheless, both his book and that of Rossi built on similar preoccupations derived from their authors' affiliation with Rogers – especially about the dialogue with history – and they shared an interdisciplinary curiosity that drove explorative incursions into anthropology, sociology, semiotics and geography – fields explored with the overarching aim to position architecture alongside them as a specific branch of knowledge.

To accomplish this common mission, they moved from different positions. In his book, Rossi maintained that the city could not be reduced to a single basic idea, composed as it is 'of quarters and districts that are highly diverse and differentiated in their sociological and formal characteristics'.[12] The possibility of finding some unity in a city depended on the existence of dominant formal and spatial characteristics within a single area. As an alternative to this understanding of a city of parts, Gregotti focused on the notions of scale and multiscalarity, an interest best represented by the sequence of topics he chose for *Edilizia moderna* during the years leading to *Il territorio dell'architettura*: product design (issue no. 85), the metropolis and its signification through architecture (issue no. 80, focusing on the skyscraper) and, finally, the project of landscape (issues nos. 87–88).[13]

Orchestrating and commenting on selections of projects and excerpts from already published texts – the format more generally chosen by Gregotti for the magazine – the issue on the skyscraper was particularly instrumental for his entrance into the discussion on tertiary societies. In it, he reflected on the switch from fixed to unstable programmatic requirements for architecture, fifteen years ahead of Rem Koolhaas's ode to congestion and 'Manhattanism'. Among the chosen excerpts was Paolo Ceccarelli's article, 'Affluent urbanism', originally published in *Casabella* as a commentary on a competition for a *centro direzionale* in Turin.[14] Ceccarelli argued that although the insistence on the multiplication and accumulation of functions inside a single architectural envelope could appear to be a reaction to the mono-functionality of modernist zoning, it was ultimately nothing but an arbitrary choice legitimising the architects' design of generic containers for generic bureaucracy. Another excerpt – from Alberto Samonà[15] – elaborated on the exhaustion of the very notion of 'concentration' as a category to understand the urban condition. Instead of thinking of vast landscapes activated by new, punctual and large concentrations of activities – as in *centri direzionali* – Samonà accused the generic building-containers of functions of threatening the figurative intentionality of architecture.[16]

Gregotti praised the skyscraper precisely as architectural machinery capable of combining a generic character, in its interior configuration, with a figurative capacity, in relation to a wider metropolitan condition.[17] Extending such reasoning in *Il territorio dell'architettura*, he claimed that any architectural project should aim at 'the figurative rendition of the whole cultural model that we could define as *ambiente totale* [total environment]'.[18] Taking this point further, he posited:

> Rather than emptying some architectural gestures at certain scales from their significance, [*ambiente totale*] attributes to all gestures a new significance; it is, in other words, a very different approach from the conception of urban design as an enlargement of architectural design.[19]

Gregotti defined the architectural project as the continuous re-signification of existing materials through human action – an 'anthropogeographical project'.[20] Whereas this definition applied to any scale of reasoning – from object to geography – it was best unveiled on a large scale. The name itself was a modified version of geographer Friedrich Ratzel's 1882 book, *Anthropogeographie*, with the rewording instrumental for stressing the projective capacity of architecture in contrast to the descriptive nature of geography.

An anthropogeographical project entailed the difficult synthesis of direct experience and abstract design. Via twofold incursions into phenomenology and structuralism, Gregotti questioned the clash of experiential analysis and top-down planning – the thorny conflict between perspectival and aerial view. Along the lines of modernism and despite famous accusations of retreat from it,[21] Rogers's *Casabella* had mostly promoted the latter viewpoint and had helped to disseminate in Italy the *œuvre* of Louis Kahn and the megastructures of Kenzo Tange. It was only after the change in directorship from Rogers to Antonio Bernasconi in 1965 that other lines of reasoning found wider circulation. Among these was the work of Kevin Lynch at MIT that attributed scientific stature to an experiential analysis of built form and to which Gregotti also directed his attention following his departure from *Casabella*. He thus ended up juxtaposing the analytical readings and graphic methods exposed in Lynch and Lloyd Rodwin's article, 'A theory of urban form' of 1958 and Lynch's book, *The Image of the City* of 1960 with the more canonical form of top-down modernism represented by Le Corbusier's impressions of South American and North African landscapes in the 1920s and 1930s.[22] The issue of *Edilizia moderna* on 'La forma del territorio' (nos. 87–88, 1965) presented this synthesis and marked a critical re-conceptualisation of the very meaning of an architectural intervention as a mere modifying act, viewing it instead as a more complex practice simultaneously combining diagnosis and transformation. Understood in these terms, architecture's role could be conceptualised as an act of unveiling already existing meaning, rather than one of pure creation.

Continuity or amnesia

Claiming that architecture unveils already existing meaning was a way for Gregotti to connect with, and elaborate upon, the central topics on which his master, Rogers, had focused his intellectual endeavours. As noted by Adrian Forty, Rogers's notions of *ambiente* (environment), *preesistenze ambientali* (environmental pre-existences) and, more generally, historical continuity (a real keyword for him, as demonstrated by his changing of the magazine's title to *Casabella-continuità*)[23] owed a debt to T.S. Eliot's 1917 essay, 'Tradition and the Individual Talent'.[24] Eliot had criticised a diffuse emphasis on the artist as a genius gifted with a rare ability of spontaneity. Conversely, he had argued for the impersonality of art, and for the inevitable insertion of any new work of art within a continuum. Such an insertion was, however, never neutral, as it always caused some readjustment of the status quo. Eliot, and Rogers after him, aimed at a different conceptualisation of the relationship between present and past, looking at the former as possessing a consciousness of the latter that the latter could not have of itself.

Gregotti expanded on this idea by stressing the necessary state of amnesia implied by any act of architectural design. For him, it was less important to claim historical continuity; conversely, an architect needed to temporarily exit history in order to enact a transformation of the status quo because 'the pleasure of pure historical contemplation is not sufficient ...; what is necessary is our resolution to revise, suspend, and suspect about a given judgement in order to define a new horizon of historic rationality'.[25]

A perfect embodiment of Gregotti's suspicious view of the specificity of the architectural project between tradition (history) and individual talent was found in an engraving addressing, once again, the geographical scale. This was Fischer von Erlach's *Alexander on Mount Athos*, a print that blurs nature, artifice, and, most importantly, also the demiurge himself and one that Gregotti reproduced in *Il territorio dell'architettura*. Von Erlach's engraving serves as an allegory for Gregotti's understanding of a 'territory of architecture' located at the junction between the mutual interdependency of nature and artifice and the projection of the architect's subjective mind. In other words, architecture was defined as the combination of formal honesty, which renounced a desire for 'the originality of capriccio, formal extravagance, and any rhetorical gesture',[26] with an analytical mind capable of reorganising the existing and providing it with new meaning.

True to his multi-scalar belief, Gregotti stated that such reorganisation would 'be possible through works of high value or, better, capable of over-signification via accumulation on one point, through small functional movements or large structural alterations'.[27] He admitted, however, that the large-scale project was most capable of showing the re-signifying capacity of architecture. What he needed was a project brief offering a large enough object to prove his theory. Coming a few years after Gregotti had fixed the theory on the written page, the design of universities arrived at the right time and place to become the ideal objects awaiting re-signification.

Partisan interests

'Our project seeks above all to direct the construction of the new University of Calabria towards a principle of settlement', wrote Gregotti and his associates about their entry in the University of Calabria competition (Figure 5.3). They claimed interest not so much in the specificities of academic space as in turning 'the university from the representation and functional model of an institution to a model for a new settlement'.[28] Theirs was a settlement that came closer to a piece of infrastructure than to any traditional image of a village – or, for that matter, of a campus. Based on a modular grid of 25.20 x 25.20 metres, within a restricted cross-section of 110 metres, the university ran as a line connecting two major infrastructural nodes: a highway junction and a national railway station. Along the centre of the line was a multi-tiered bridge flanked by buildings designed as cubes and housing the university departments (Figure 5.4). Accessible from the bridge on two levels – a lower pedestrian path and an upper vehicular road – the cubes' roofline was kept at a continuous height, with buildings varying their height according to the rise and fall of the ground. Some extraordinary spaces, such as bigger lecture halls that could not be accommodated within the rigid structure of the cubes, were located as auxiliary bridges suspended between two departments. Residential areas were kept separate from the academic spine and placed on the northern slopes of the hills, whereas the south-facing slopes were preserved for agricultural uses.

Joseph Rykwert, one of the jury members,[29] later commented on the project:

> The University's time and money have been well spent. Probably, I shouldn't be the one to say this, as I was a member of the jury, but I know that the choice was purely based on merit with no influence from partisan interests. After days of hard work during the two selection stages for the competition, and to the best of my knowledge of what is being produced in architecture in Europe and abroad, I think that a better choice could not have been taken.[30]

In line with the architects' framing of the project as a settlement principle of more general applicability, Rykwert's mention of 'partisan interests' implied the existence of a more general, theoretical goal behind the provision of a new idea

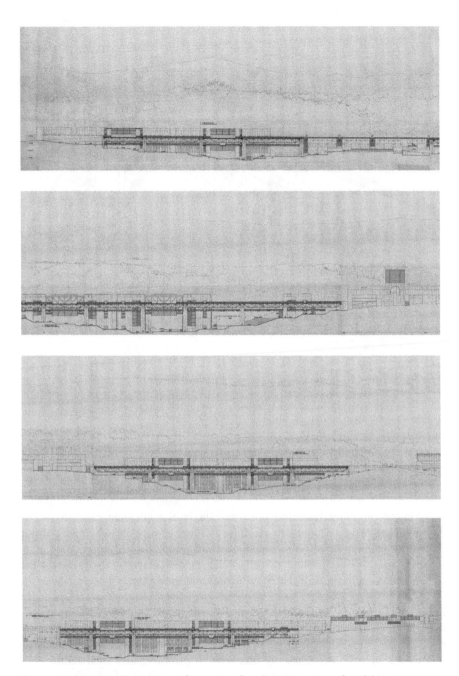

Figure 5.3 Vittorio Gregotti *et al.*, project for the University of Calabria (1972–74).
    Longitudinal section.
Source: C.A.S.V.A., Comune di Milano. Archivio Gregotti.

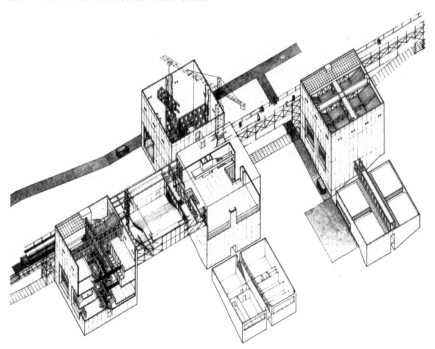

Figure 5.4 Vittorio Gregotti *et al.*, project for the University of Calabria (1972–74). Cutaway axonometric of a typical section of the complex showing the departmental buildings attached to the central three-tier bridge.
Source: C.A.S.V.A., Comune di Milano. Archivio Gregotti.

of university offered by Gregotti and his team. Further confirmation came in a text written by the Italian architect more than ten years later when, reflecting on the Calabria project, he reconnected with Rykwert on a theoretical level:[31]

> The origin of architecture does not lie in the hut, the cave or in the mythical 'Adam's house in paradise'. Before a support was transformed into a column, a roof into a pediment, and stone heaped upon stone, man put stone on the ground in order to recognize place in the midst of the unknown universe and thereby measure and modify it.[32]

Rykwert's *Adam's House in Paradise* was published in 1972, the same year that design work on the Calabria project began. In this study, he famously revealed the ways that architectural discourse had repeatedly explained its origins through the existence of some sort of primitive idea of dwelling. But whereas Rykwert illustrated this idea with the re-use of the frontispiece from Abbé Laugier's *Essai sur l'architecture* (1753), depicting the lineages of architecture as 'a pure distillation of nature through unadulterated reason',[33] Gregotti's preference for Fischer von Erlach's *Alexander on Mount Athos* –

'landscape as a natural or built continuum [as] background on top of which any intervention is necessarily superimposed as a figure'[34] – found in the Calabrese university-bridge its most unequivocal architectural embodiment. Even before receiving a functional label – a 'university' – the project was first and foremost a principle of settlement, 'the synthetic act by which the architect measures the specific place, as geography and as history; like every act of measurement it requires gestures of radical apparent simplicity'.[35]

The simplicity of the project resided in the limited number of clear principles that subsumed it: cubes arranged on a modular grid, a fixed height, and an overall linear settlement that was contradicted only at specific points (the residential areas). It was a clear piece of infrastructure, hence clearly artificial, but it was an artificiality whose *raison d'être* emerged from a conflict with natural topography. If the project for Calabria was an instance of 'man put[ting] stone on the ground in order to recognize place in the midst of the unknown universe', the result was nevertheless not one of total domestication. The only real task for the architect, Gregotti argued, lay in balancing the need to both copy or assimilate this landscape and to internalise it – that is, an architect should be able to simultaneously reflect on reality while maintaining the construction of what he termed its 'double'.[36]

The university-bridge was just such a double that responded to the accommodating image provided by the pedestrian-friendly urban environments of the British plateglass universities – an obligatory reference for anyone called to design a university in the early 1970s – with a strangely unsettling settlement: a megastructure that turned its back on familiar ideas of human scale or of 'townscape' – a central preoccupation of British architectural culture of the 1960s – and sought instead a controlling power over a large territory. It was Gregotti's own Alexander, imposing on the Calabrian hills a marker of pure, rational architectural order.

At the same time, Gregotti managed to integrate – or, at least, to pretend to do so – within this bombasticism an answer to all the elements called for in the brief: a potentially infinite, expandable structure (an absolute must for any new university), flexible interior configurations able to adapt to institutional or pedagogic reorganisation (also essential, given Italy's lack of clarity about the future of the university), and a clear architectural silhouette (acting as a possible future monument to the politicians who enabled it). These successes would also elicit critical praise, with Kenneth Frampton in particular echoing Rykwert's comments in an essay for *Domus* in 1980.[37] Here, Frampton contextualised his endorsement by arguing that the traditional city and its immediate environment had been

> torn to shreds by the imperatives of distribution and speculation ... to the extent that the urbanised area now assumes an apparent size commensurate with the scale of nature herself ... so that the megalopolis invariably asserts itself as the universal reference to which architecture must be addressed.[38]

This condition, Frampton went on to argue, 'bestows a certain typological conviction on the University of Calabria – one which is sufficient to dispel any partisan impulse to dismiss it on the grounds of polemical heresy'.[39]

If Rykwert's own mention of 'partisan interests' had suggested a theoretical prerogative, their return in Frampton's summing-up locates Gregotti's project within the broader imperative to produce a new university for a new society. For Frampton, this overrode any engrained architectural rivalries (or 'polemical heresies') between, for example, rationalism and organicism, or the residual fall-out from the Anglo-Italian spat between Reyner Banham and Ernesto Rogers that contrasted the technological to the historical.

Frampton commented: 'Emerging at a time when the Neo-Rationalist debate on typology, history and the reconstruction of the city appears to have reached its zenith, the University of Calabria initiates a proposition which is both pertinent and undetermined.'[40] In his view, Gregotti had produced a 'city without flags' because it went beyond the limits of the category to which it most evidently belonged – neo-rationalism – as well as beyond the fixation with the traditional city and the related tendency 'to reject outright the possibility of achieving a significant interaction with the reality of modern constructive processes and forms'.[41] At the same time, while more welcoming towards new constructive technologies, Gregotti's endorsement of them did not push him to the extremes of neo-productivism that Frampton identified in the contemporary work of Foster Associates and that, to stay within the realm of university design, found a paradigm in ARUP's project for the Loughborough University of Technology (1964–68). This exemplar of modular design, which was based on the rhetoric of expandability as a response to changing needs, eventually found enthusiastic reception at the competition following that for Calabria, the one for the University of Salerno, launched in 1973. On that occasion, the triumph of technology was celebrated in the winning entry that unashamedly appropriated ARUP's 'spatial unit' as the generator to be assembled on a chequerboard of infinite flexibility. As a side effect of this 'systems approach', architectural reasoning was reduced to the mere coordination of positions on the chequerboard.[42]

Although technology was an integral, even necessary, part of Gregotti's project, it did not take precedence over the role of an architect. The modular design of Calabria was not discussed in terms of endless possible reconfigurations; indeed, the rules given to the architects did not allow many variations in the overall form. Whereas Loughborough (and Salerno after it) *were* system, giving a technological cloak to an all-technological university that could eventually erode its locale by expanding into it, Calabria *used* system as a means to design an orderly piece of landscape. It was *ambiente totale* versus total engineering.

Cities with no outside

The accord Frampton found in Calabria, however, was to a certain extent wishful thinking, because antagonisms were still very much in evidence, not least in the earlier 1970 competition for the University of Florence, which Gregotti had also won, with a bigger team that included Edoardo Detti.[43] More ambitious than the equivalent brief for Calabria, the Florentine competition asked for the production of a regional-scale master plan that not only had to identify a site for a new university between Florence and the town of Sesto Fiorentino (Figure 5.5), but also had to rethink what remained of the existing university in Florence's historic centre. Accordingly, while many participants lamented the requirement to produce a vision of something yet to be defined, others saw this lack of guidance as a free pass to experimentation. The outcome, somewhat predictably, was a diverse set of proposals that fell into two main camps: those which affirmed a faith in architectural form (Gregotti, Aymonino, and Dardi, and Giuseppe Rebecchini) and those which mocked its redundancy (Archizoom, Italo Insolera, and Pierluigi Cervellati, and to a certain extent Ludovico Quaroni).[44]

The resulting tension was not appreciated by the jury, who ridiculed a number of the projects as merely eclectic exercises in drawing. One jury member, James Gowan, even went so far as to resign, criticising the very premises on which the competition was founded – namely, the attempt to detach the university from the city and the promotion of the isolated campus ideal. This polemic would be echoed a couple of years later in an article published in *The Architectural Review* (see Chapter 4). Unambiguously entitled 'A Florentine Fiasco', it declared that

> one of the lessons learnt from this country's postwar university building programme is that a campus of culture, learning and athleticism, sitting in 200 acres of playing fields and parkland two miles from town, is not a final, ideal solution [... but a] romantic dream that research and academic study is best undertaken in rural bliss.[45]

A response by Gregotti and Detti arrived a few months later, published in the letters column of the same magazine:

> Our attempt to pull together a chain of interventions (the university represents one of the central ones), stretching along a service axis which penetrates into Florence's historic centre, was a way of using the competition to regulate the situation as a whole and render it less chaotic ... The whole project provides a clearly complementary and geographically well-defined system. To speak in these circumstances of the university as either in or outside the city is completely meaningless ... The university is separated from the halls of residence and was conceived as a place of work amongst other workers rather than as a privileged ghetto. The intention was to give meaning to the university, to consider it principally as a place of public exchange (a 'social condenser', as the Soviet avant-garde called the factory) that directly affects the region. To do this, it was necessary to break the ideology of the campus.[46]

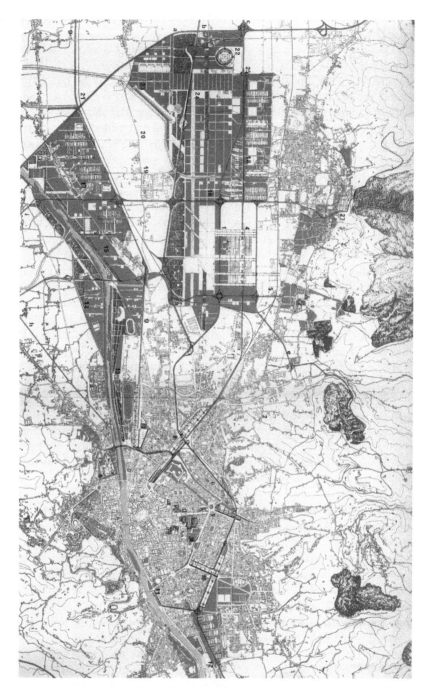

Figure 5.5 Vittorio Gregotti *et al.*, project for the University of Florence (1970–71). General plan of the territory between Florence and Sesto Fiorentino.

Note: From the key to the drawing: 1. New university and service complex; 5. New train station; 7–8/9–10 Parking facility/services/railway terminal; 17–18. New residential settlements; 22. New stadium; 23–24 Park and experimental agriculture; 25. Expo centre; c. service armature (*asse attrezzato*).

Source: C.A.S.V.A., Comune di Milano. Archivio Gregotti.

Gregotti and Detti had entitled their project *Amalassunta* (a name borrowed from the paintings of Osvaldo Licini),[47] and based much of it on Detti's 1962 master plan for Florence, which had refused a clear distinction between city and country – something Gregotti reiterated in *Il territorio dell'architettura*, where he argued that 'the city is no longer something that can be clearly identified in isolation, as in the past'.[48] Their proposal played to this idea with a totalising image that featured a series of large parking garages around Florence's historic core and a capillary infrastructural network delineating a new set of contours for the surrounding landscape – a scheme that clearly displayed the influence of Louis Kahn's Plan for the Center of Philadelphia, which, not coincidentally, was a recurring example in Gregotti's writings in the 1960s. Within this supposedly emphatic representation of territorial coherence, the new university settlement stood as a clearly identifiable figure, a perfect rectangle defined by five linear blocks for the various departments, each almost 1 kilometre long, and held together by a plinth filled not just with lecture halls, auditoria, and libraries, but also with food halls, sports facilities, shops, hotels, and cinemas (Figure 5.6, Figure 5.7). Six years after curating (with Umberto Eco) the introductory section of the 13th Triennale in Milan on the topic of the leisure society,[49] Gregotti's mix of educational, tertiary and time-out activities in *Amalassunta* declared leisure to be compatible with the pure activities of the brain.

Amalassunta was, therefore, hardly a piece of romantic pastoralism, as *The Architectural Review* would make one believe; rather, it was a wholeheartedly urban corridor whose artifice combined both education and leisure. The project asserted that for Italy to learn to be urban at a new scale – as Italian architects had been urging for years – a diversion from the 'peaceful path to real reform' proclaimed by Ebenezer Howard at the dawning of architectural and urban modernism had to be taken. Much more hybridisation was needed than the presumptuous and self-contained rationale promoted by the trajectory of Garden City–new towns–new universities.

The University of Florence was not an entity to be unequivocally associated with a location inside or outside the city because it declared that the very idea of an inside versus an outside was simply anachronistic, and hence to be abandoned. Operating 'within a system that is not anymore the one devised by Poggi [the author of the 1865 Plan of Florence], but coincides with the territory between Florence, Prato, and Pistoia',[50] a peripheral academic settlement like the one proposed by *Amalassunta* only made sense if related to the liberation it would bring to the historic centre. By decongesting the centre of an accumulation of tertiary services and their daily users (800,000 people, according to the architects) and moving them to a new *centro direzionale*/university/leisure park, large areas of Florence, such as San Lorenzo, San Frediano, and Santa Croce, could be returned to their citizens as residential environments. An important part of *Amalassunta* was, in fact, a typological study of how the housing stock of these areas could be reused for student residences, which Gregotti's team saw as a subset of social housing for the working class and which, they insisted, had to be kept separate from the university halls.

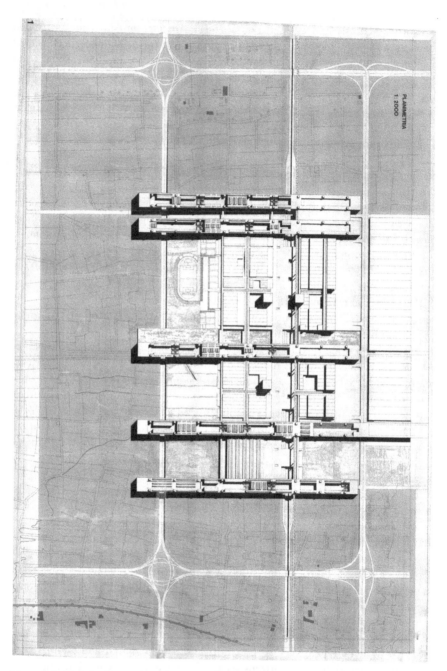

Figure 5.6 Vittorio Gregotti *et al.*, project for the University of Florence (1970–71). The
       university complex with the departmental slabs and the service and leisure
       podium.
Source: C.A.S.V.A., Comune di Milano. Archivio Gregotti.

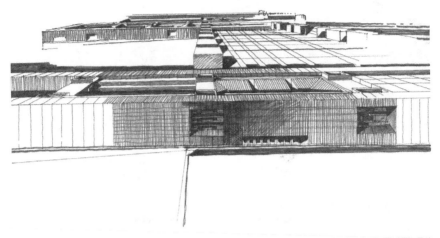

Figure 5.7 Vittorio Gregotti *et al.*, project for the University of Florence (1970–71).
Bird's-eye view of the university complex with one of the departmental slabs
in the foreground.
Source: C.A.S.V.A., Comune di Milano. Archivio Gregotti.

Indeed, the student addressed by *Amalassunta* shared with the working class a similar condition, and in particular the difficulty of accessing affordable housing, with the related problem of the integration of dwelling and workplace.[51] Much beyond reorganising an institution from the inside, reforming the university was an urbanistic, and hence political, problem that had to be solved by confronting the large scale of an urbanised territory. Rather than an abandonment of the city, the university reshaped the city beyond the old walls, inhabiting both the core, in the form of many student residences scattered around the old urban fabric, and its wider territorial dimension, in the form of a service provider among other functions (Figure 5.8). This territorial system surely owed a debt to SOM's University of Illinois at Chicago Circle, which had provided the 1960s prototype of a commuter university with no residences on campus, thus disrupting a staple feature of the American university tradition.[52] *Amalassunta* went beyond its precedent by compromising the purity of an academic environment with other activities and services, and, eventually, making a more general statement that providers of tertiary services – such as regional governmental offices – had to start conceiving themselves as more akin to knowledge-based institutions devoted to ongoing research than to mere administrative institutions.

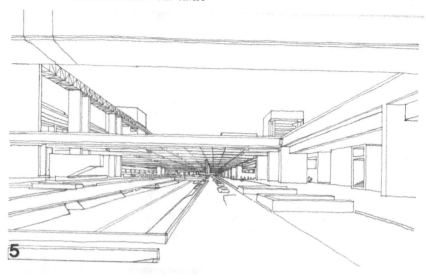

Figure 5.8 Vittorio Gregotti *et al.*, project for the University of Florence (1970–71).
Perspectival view of the freeway crossing the university complex.
Source: C.A.S.V.A., Comune di Milano. Archivio Gregotti.

But the assimilation of universities and tertiary services, together with that of tertiary workers and university students, was a double-edged sword whose effects could not be fully anticipated. Although it could lead to a new conceptualisation of higher education, it would do so by endangering the traditional otherness of the academic realm from the real world, ultimately erasing the former's role as a critical counterpart to the latter. At the same time, it would also endorse an understanding of the university as a professionalising institution – a training ground for a professional career.

It was on this subtle edge, between the professional and the academic world, that a project like *Amalassunta* precariously balanced, perhaps not being entirely conscious of the consequences of amplifying rather than subverting the status quo. Just as Gregotti did not want to think of large-scale space as merely an enlargement of architectural forms, so the same could be said of his argument about rethinking a university for mass culture: echoing the words of his colleague Giancarlo De Carlo, a new (Italian) university could not just be an enlarged version of the old (Italian) university.[53] It had to differ from its national tradition, as well as to diverge from the international idea of a detached, self-sufficient academic compound.

And yet as much as it offered a radical rejoinder to the cosy template of the Anglo-Saxon Garden-City-like campus, Gregotti and Detti's vision also, paradoxically, reinforced Italy's own existing model, merely scaling up the typical university student's daily passage between home (still retained within the city's core) and university (now relocated to an academic shopping mall). At the same time, it paved the way to a narrowing of the university's role as one of preparing for a profession. This role has somehow remained engrained as the dominant way of conceiving a mass university: a paternalistic, top-down institution, channelling individuals on carefully selected paths of promised careers.

The concentration conundrum

Moving from clear architectural objectives, and putting them at the forefront of a response to the problems of higher education, Gregotti's projects unveiled a deep equivocality about how a university could be designed. His own trajectory from Florence (in 1970–71) to Calabria (in 1972–74) found a pivotal point in the second of Italy's big university competitions, for the University of Cagliari (1971–73), ironically one that he did not enter.[54] Giuseppe Samonà's project for Cagliari shared most of the ideas of *Amalassunta* – the university digested inside a service settlement, the student as worker, the separation of residences and academic functions – and anticipated the grand formal response of Calabria. Occupying the entire 400-hectare site on the northern periphery of Cagliari, Samonà had his university sink into the ground (Figure 5.9): 'An emblem (or monument?) turned upside down', was how one collaborator on the project, the anarchist sociologist and planner Carlo Doglio, described it.[55] With a background in law, Carlo Doglio (1914–95) cultivated an interest in urbanism and regional planning that was particularly fostered by his encounter with Giancarlo De Carlo in 1943. In 1952, Doglio published the widely read essay 'L'equivoco della città giardino', in which he criticised the technocratic nature of Ebenezer Howard's idea of the Garden City, a criticism that Samonà would take forward in *L'urbanistica e l'avvenire della città*. The link between Samonà and Doglio was then reinforced through professional collaboration (in 1965–67, they worked on the urban plan for the town of Cefalù in Samonà's native Sicily) and through the appointment, in 1969, of Doglio to teach urbanism at IUAV, where Samonà was the school director. It was during Doglio's time at IUAV (which ended in 1972, when he took on the Chair of Planning at the University of Bologna) that the two collaborated on the competition project for Cagliari, for which Doglio wrote a short 'socio-anthropological' text that was appended to the general description of the project written by Samonà.

Both Samonà and Doglio were highly critical of the English university model and what they saw as its delusion of perpetuating Ebenezer Howard's dream of the friendly synthesis of urbanity and rurality in harmonious, self-contained communities.[56] Their vision, in contrast, depicted a city fuelled by the confrontation of opposing elements, with the strongest of these – that between city and country – reflected in the rigidity of its perimeter (something the architects reinforced in two vast plaster models, whose size and topography alone made them appear as their own chunk of urbanised landscape). It also depended on repetition, for in their university, even more than in Gregotti's Calabria, there was to be no hierarchy (for example, no main library and no student union);

Figure 5.9 Giuseppe Samonà *et al.*, project for the University of Cagliari (1971–73). Competition model of a typical portion of the university settlement.
Source: Centro Studi e Archivio della Comunicazione, Università degli Studi di Parma. Fondo Giuseppe Samonà.

rather, everything was resolved numerically, with the drawings allocating 250 metres to medicine, 100 metres to biology, 150 metres to philosophy, and so on.

For Samonà, the appeal of the generic also lay in its potential to break with the status quo of the paternalistic Italian university. In this he was far more explicit than Gregotti, arguing in his competition text that a 'new' university had to modify the learning process in order to create a similarly 'new' category of worker, whose skills would be less specialised and would encompass more generic tasks, like the organisation of workload. A university student, he continued, was merely a worker in the initial stages of a professional career. This in turn implied a fundamental shift in what a university should be, moving beyond its narrow definition as a special place for teaching and research. Samonà was emphatic on this point, writing that 'it would be impossible but also wrong to conceive the new university of Cagliari as a zoo for teachers and students located within an area of 400 hectares'.[57]

Not a campus, then, but not a dispersed Italian university either. Like Gregotti in Florence, Samonà was presenting the university as a large concentration of activities for an advanced tertiary economy in which offices, laboratories, and classrooms would be mixed together. Inside such a settlement, students would be workers among workers, their constant contact with each other designed to cultivate a more professional mentality that favoured general over specialised knowledge. The social and pedagogic dynamic of the new University of Cagliari would therefore be distinctly bottom-up. Yet the decision to concentrate the whole settlement within a single, geometric structure seemed only to reinforce something fundamentally top-down. This was highlighted by the totally designed natural elements included in the project, such as a series of Italianate gardens that provided an unequivocal response against any claim of informality, organicism or naturalistic mockery appropriate to campus landscaping. As a result, the political associations of Samonà and Doglio's proposal were somewhat vague, which suggests an interesting indictment of 1968: just three years after the global wave of student protests, there remained fundamental doubts as to whether the university of the future should be dispersed or concentrated, urban or rural, and whether its students should be cast as an enlightened elite or, as Samonà would have it, 'an a-political class, limited by false dignity and the preconceptions of a petit bourgeoisie'.[58]

Samonà and Gregotti shared these doubts, to the point of grounding their projects on them. This might explain the double-edged character of their projects, and why the designers' leftist sympathies did not extend to the new left of the students, who had declared war on the old society and its professors – a class that, of course, included people like Samonà and Gregotti. Their universities were thus from the outset riven by paradox: while providing opportunities for more open, mature self-formation, they were at the same time domesticating, even infantilising, large numbers of new students. In this way, the ghosts of centralised authority and paternalism still haunted both Gregotti's and Samonà's ideas of the university, despite their willingness to rethink the scale of these academic settlements and generally to provide greater access to higher education.

Of course, ambiguity might also define the university as a whole, which in all its various incarnations – from the medieval cloister to the bridge and the territorial bas-relief – has always depended on the continual interplay of integration with and detachment from reality. The British plateglass universities, in particular, sought to mask this ambivalence, presenting only a stable typology through a set of fixed images. As a result, the English universities that were built in the 1960s rarely questioned the innermost status quo of the institution, choosing instead to disguise it behind demagogic claims for the university-as-city. In reality, most new campuses played it safe by clearly circumscribing the brief inside a spatially defined compound that in no sense radically challenged the idea of the university.

Italian projects such as Samonà and Gregotti's, in contrast, stood out for their volatility that challenged established models, but also, unwittingly, produced equally unstable solutions. But perhaps more than anything else, this was merely a consequence of their design *after* 1968, unlike their English counterparts, which were all conceived *before* the protests. The fact that this Italian erasure of stability manifested itself through the most heroic architectural gestures imaginable only adds to the difficulty of interpreting this moment.

'We will never revolutionise society through architecture, but we can revolutionise architecture: in any case, this is what we should do':[59] following this claim by Gregotti in *Il territorio dell'architettura*, we are more than tempted to believe that, after all, higher education reform was really just an incident for him – and perhaps for Samonà too. Their real preoccupation was confined within the problems of their disciplines: architecture and urbanism. But if we agree that architecture inevitably encompasses social and political ideas of a broader scope, even when not explicitly uttered, then there is a lot that can be learned from observing the drawings of these grandiose projects for new academic environments. Indeed, in looking back at the images produced by Samonà and Gregotti, we are left with a series of drawings that, with their rejection of the model of buildings clustered around some central urban square within some ersatz campus-city, reveal doubts about the scale at which higher education should be conceived. From this drawn portfolio, the 3-kilometre university-bridge that spans the Calabrian hills stands alone as the only built witness of what was emphatically presented as an alternative narrative to the dominant one of the isolated campus. Contemplating it now, we feel our confusion grow, along with our curiosity as to what this thing we call a university should ultimately be.

Notes

1 See Italo Rota, ed., *Il progetto per l'Universita delle Calabrie e altre architetture di Vittorio Gregotti/The Project for Calabria University and Other Architectural Works by Vittorio Gregotti* (Milan: Electa International, 1979).

2 See Giuseppe Samonà, *Giuseppe Samonà: 1923–1975, Cinquant'anni di architetture* (Rome: Officina, 1975).

3 Giuseppe Samonà, *L'urbanistica e l'avvenire della città negli stati europei* (Bari: Laterza, 1959).

4 Ludovico Quaroni, review of Giuseppe Samonà's *L'urbanistica e l'avvenire della città negli stati europei, Casabella* 236 (1960): 19.

5 Manfredo Tafuri, 'Le avventure dell'oggetto: Architettura e progetti di Vittorio Gregotti', in *Vittorio Gregotti: Progetti e architetture* (Milan: Electa, 1982), x.

6 Gregotti was on the editorial team of *Casabella* between 1953 and 1955 and was subsequently editor-in-chief between 1955 and 1963. He returned to direct the magazine after an almost twenty-year hiatus in 1982 and remained for fourteen years.

7 Giuseppe Samonà, 'Relazione e conclusione al seminario su città-territorio', in *La città territorio: Un esperimento didattico sul centro direzionale di Centocelle in Roma*, ed. Carlo Aymonino et al. (Bari: Leonardo da Vinci editrice, 1964), 91.

8 See Tafuri, 'Le avventure dell'oggetto'.

9 Gregotti edited issues 80–89 of *Edilizia moderna* between 1963 and 1967, choosing a monographic format on selected topics. Of these, issue 87–88 on 'La forma del territorio' (1965) anticipated the arguments presented the following year in *Il territorio dell'architettura*.

10 Vittorio Gregotti, *New Directions in Italian Architecture* (New York: G. Braziller, 1968), 108.

11 See Ezio Bonfanti, ed., *Architettura razionale* (Milan: Franco Angeli, 1973); and Anthony Vidler, Léon Krier, and Massimo Scolari, *Rational Architecture: The Reconstruction of the European City/Architecture rationnelle: La reconstruction de la ville européenne* (Brussels: Éditions des Archives d'architecture moderne, 1985).

12 Aldo Rossi, *L'architettura della città* (Padua: Marsilio, 1966), 64.

13 The full list of topics chosen by Gregotti for *Edilizia moderna* encompasses: 'Il grattacielo' (no. 80, 1963); 'Novecento e architettura' (no. 81, 1963; co-editor: Guido Canella); 'Architettura italiana 1963' (no. 82–83, 1964; collaborator: Emilio Battisti); '3 esposizioni' (no. 84, 1964; collaborator: Emilio Battisti); 'Design' (no. 85, 1965; collaborator: Emilio Battisti); 'Ricerche storiche' (no. 86, 1965); 'La forma del territorio' (no. 87–88, 1966; collaborator: Emilio Battisti); and 'Africa' (no. 89–90, 1967).

14 Paolo Ceccarelli, 'Urbanistica opulenta', *Casabella* 278 (1963).

15 Alberto Samonà, 'Alla ricerca di un metodo per la nuova dimensione', *Casabella* 277 (1963): 50–54.

16 Ibid., 51.

17 Vittorio Gregotti, 'Il grattacielo: Editoriale', *Edilizia moderna* 80 (1963): 92.

18 Vittorio Gregotti, *Il territorio dell'architettura* (Milan: Feltrinelli, 1966), 46.

19 Ibid., 82–83.

20 Ibid., 95.

21 Reyner Banham, 'Neoliberty: The Italian Retreat from Modern Architecture', *The Architectural Review* 125 (1959): 230–235.

22 Kevin Lynch and Lloyd Rodwyn, 'A Theory of Urban Form', *Journal of the American Institute of Planners*, .24, no. 4 (1958): 201–214; Kevin Lynch, *The Image of the City*, (Cambridge, MA: MIT Press, 1960).

23 An early formulation of the idea of continuity was presented by Rogers at the eighth CIAM meeting 'The Heart of the City'. He then elaborated on the idea in his editorials in *Casabella* (in particular 'Le preesistenze ambientali e i temi pratici contemporanei', published in 1954), and in the 1961 essay *Gli elementi del fenomeno architettonico*, which was published posthumously in 1981.

24 See Adrian Forty, *Words and Buildings: A Vocabulary of Modern Architecture* (New York: Thames and Hudson, 2000); T.S. Eliot, 'Tradition and the Individual Talent', in *The Sacred Wood: Essays on Poetry and Criticism* (London: Methuen, 1920).

25 Gregotti, *Il territorio*, 133.

26 Ibid., 177.

27 Ibid., 71.

28 See Vittorio Gregotti *et al.*, 'Università degli Studi della Calabria: Progetto per la costruzione del dipartimento di chimica. Relazione generale', July 1975.

29 Besides Rykwert and the university rector, Beniamino Andreatta, the jury for the Calabria competition included the international members Georges Candilis and Michael Brawne.

30 Joseph Rykwert, 'Vittorio Gregotti e Associati: La nuova università della Calabria, il progetto vincente al concorso internazionale', *Domus* 540 (1974): 15. My translation.

31 An early manifestation of the mutual intellectual respect between Rykwert and Gregotti is found in the publication of an Italian translation of the former's 'The Idea of a Town' (originally published in *Forum* 3, 1963) in *Edilizia moderna* 82–83 (1964): 207–14, an issue edited by Gregotti. Subsequently, Gregotti acknowledged Rykwert's contribution to the conceptualisation of the relation between built form and cosmology in a footnote in *Il territorio* (p. 94). In response, Rykwert published *Gregotti Associati* (Milan: Rizzoli, 1995), a monograph on Gregotti's work, and, most recently, wrote about their intellectual relationship and friendship in his autobiography, *Remembering Places: A Memoir* (New York: Routledge, 2017).

32 Vittorio Gregotti, 'Territory and Architecture', *Architectural Design Profile 59*, nos. 5–6 (1985): 28–34; reprinted in Kate Nesbitt, ed., *Theorizing a New Agenda for Architecture: An Anthology of Architectural Theory 1965–1995* (New York: Princeton Architectural Press, 1996), 342.

33 Joseph Rykwert, *On Adam's House in Paradise: The Idea of the Primitive Hut in Architectural History* (New York: Museum of Modern Art, 1972), 48.

34 Gregotti, *Il territorio*, 86.

35 Gregotti, 'Territory and Architecture'.

36 Gregotti, *Il territorio*, 342.

37 Kenneth Frampton, 'City without Flags', *Domus* 609 (1980): 18–23.

38 Ibid., 19.

39 Ibid.

40 Ibid.

41 Ibid.

42 See Chapter 4.

43 The team comprised seventeen people, divided into two main groups, one based in Florence and headed by Edoardo Detti, the other in Milan and led by Gregotti. Overall, the team consisted of Emilio Battisti, Gian Franco Di Pietro, Giovanni Fanelli, Teresa Cobbò, Raimondo Innocenti, Marco Massa, Hiromichi Matsui, Mario Mocchi, Paolo Sica, Bruno Viganò, and Marica Zoppi; Collaborators: Francesco Barbagli, Peo Calza, Gian Franco Dallerba, Franco Luis Neves, and Franco Purini.

44 The final results of the Florence competition were as follows: Vittorio Gregotti and Edoardo Detti, *Amalassunta*, first prize; Pierluigi Cervellati and Italo Insolera, *Aquarius*, second prize; Ludovico Quaroni, *Sistemi Congiunti Tre*, third prize; Carlo Aymonino and Costantino Dardi, *Ariella*, commendation; Roberto Berardi, *Beltegeuse*, commendation; Italo Gamberini, *Continuum*, commendation; Massimo Pica Ciamarra, *Il Rasoio di Occam*, commendation; Giuseppe Rebecchini, *Stoà*, commendation. Archizoom presented a project entitled *I progetti si firmano* that polemically ignored the request for anonymity, as did their decision to put the office's name on all panels, resulting in their automatic exclusion from the competition. See Chapter 6.

45 'A Florentine Fiasco', *The Architectural Review* 900 (1972): 79.

46 Vittorio Gregotti *et al.*, 'Florentine Fiasco: To the Editors', *The Architectural Review* 905 (1972): 63.

47 From a conversation with Vittorio Gregotti, Milan, March 2018.

48 Vittorio Gregotti, *Il territorio*, 71. My translation.

49 For a discussion of the cultural role played by the Triennale during the 1960s and 1970s, see Gabriella Lo Ricco, 'La Triennale di Milano (1964–1973)', in *Italia 60/70: Una stagione dell'architettura*, ed. Marco Biraghi *et al.* (Padua: Il poligrafo, 2010), 99–113.

50 Vittorio Gregotti *et al.*, 'Concorso internazionale per la sistemazione della Università di Firenze. Motto: Amalassunta', 1970, 32.

51 Ibid., 79–80.

52 See Sharon Haar, *The City as Campus: Urbanism and Higher Education in Chicago* (Minneapolis, MN: University of Minnesota Press, 2011).

53 See Giancarlo De Carlo, *La piramide rovesciata* (Bari: De Donato, 1968).

54 The results of the competition for the University of Cagliari were as follows: Luisa Anversa Ferretti, first prize; Giuseppe Samonà, second prize; Carlo Aymonino and Costantino Dardi, third prize; Uberto Siola, honourable mention.

55 Carlo Doglio, 'L'essenza sarda e l'università come fenomeno', in Giuseppe Samonà *et al.*, 'Concorso nazionale per il piano urbanistico di sistemazione della sede dell'Università di Cagliari: Relazione illustrativa dei concetti informatori della proposta, con le fasi e i metodi di realizzazione e il piano finanziario di massima', 1972. Samonà 1.pro/1/069, Università Iuav – Archivio Progetti, Fondo Giuseppe e Alberto Samonà.

56 For an introduction to Doglio and a collection of some of his main writings, see Chiara Mazzoleni, ed., *Carlo Doglio: Selezione di scritti 1950–1984* (Bologna: Istituto universitario di architettura, Istituto di urbanistica, 1992).

57 Samonà *et al.*, 'Concorso nazionale'.

58 Ibid.

59 Gregotti, *Il territorio*, 25.

6   Information *à la carte*

Archizoom and territorial de-institutionalisation

From knowledge to information

Any architectural competition – or any gathering of discussants for that matter – should include some polemicists. At the competition for the design of the new seat of the University of Florence in 1970, it could be anticipated that the polemical voice would come from the new generation of graduates from that very university – graduates who had already made the headlines in the national architectural press and were on the verge of international stardom. There is no clearer index of a confrontational attitude than the title given by Archizoom to their entry: *I progetti si firmano* (Projects must be signed). Not only was the entry critical of the format of anonymity for a competition, but it was also a more general attack on the brief and, by way of extension, on the entire architectural establishment and its discourse.[1]

The polemical charge was embedded in the panels, with one in particular providing a sense of the opposition to the request to design a new university settlement as part of a solution to the problems of higher education.[2] On a 1:10000 site plan, Archizoom superimposed an abstract 125 x 125 metre Cartesian grid over the whole competition site between Florence and the town of Prato (Figure 6.1). Within the grid, a repeated pattern of numbers was the only signifier of human activities, which were listed in a separate key: housing, kindergarten, playgrounds, petrol station, car parking, warehouses, commercial activities, secondary school, public offices, cultural centre, church, hospital, hotel, cinema and library. Only the library was a reminder of functions traditionally associated with a university. With no classrooms, departments, laboratories, meeting rooms, or any other traditional academic spaces, what the drawing depicted hardly seemed to fit the brief. A continuous horizontal surface of human inhabitation displaced the traditional concentrating apparatus (whether American campus, English college, or European palace) of a university in a move that refused knowledge as something that is created within four walls. Or, in the words of Archizoom, it was the (urbanised) world envisaged as a continuous surface of information.

As a competition entry, Archizoom's would legitimately be called a project – that is, it depicted a scenario of change projected into some future time. Yet,

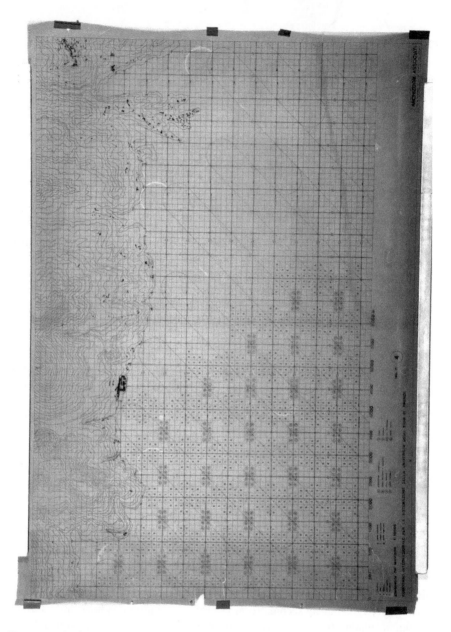

Figure 6.1 Archizoom Associati, project for the University of Florence (1970–71). Competition panel 4.

Note: General plan, scale 1:10000. 1. Library; 2. Kindergarten; 3. Residences; 4. Playgrounds; 5. Parking; 6. Petrol station; 7. Warehouses; 8. Recreational centre; 9. Commercial activities; 10. Secondary school; 11. Public offices; 12. Cultural centre; 13. Church; 14. Hospital; 15. Hotels; 16. Cinema/Theatre.

Source: Centro Studi e Archivio della Comunicazione, Università degli Studi di Parma. Fondo Archizoom Associati.

taken as the first formulation of their more famous proposal, *No-Stop City*, most readings of the Florentine collective's work – starting from Archizoom's own publicised interpretation of it – would rather call it an exaggeration of reality. As such, instead of a projective scenario for a better future society, it could be taken as a comment on society's present condition.

The fact that, alongside the missing word 'university', 'knowledge' is nowhere to be found on Archizoom's panels, and that 'information' is preferred, provides an anticipatory snapshot of the more elaborate and famous analysis of what, eight years after the Florence competition, Jean-François Lyotard named the postmodern condition. Bearing as a subtitle 'a report on the condition of knowledge', Lyotard's book expressed ambivalence between project and commentary similar to that of Archizoom's competition entry. The French philosopher suspended his reflections between diagnosis and prognosis: 'Our hypothesis ... should not be accorded predictive value in relation to reality, but strategic value in relation to the question raised.'[3] Therefore, as much as it was an analysis of the condition of knowledge at the end of the 1970s, the text could also be interpreted as a set of hypotheses that legitimised and implemented the rationale of that very condition.

A central point in Lyotard's argument involved matching the postmodern condition with a conceptual shift from a holistic understanding of knowledge to a piecemeal collaging of information. According to this shift, scientific discourse could be said to have entered a crisis not because science was becoming less important for society – quite the opposite was the case – but rather the legitimation inherent to the very essence of scientific discourse was in crisis. Lyotard discussed how, starting with the seventeenth-century scientific revolution, a premodern unitary conception of knowledge (*savoir*) had been replaced by two opposing categories: on the one side, scientific knowledge (*connaissance*), which would be accorded higher value; on the other, narrative knowledge, which came to be associated with lower, pre-modern and traditional forms of knowledge. For Lyotard, this differentiation was misleading because it falsely oversimplified the concept of knowledge as a mere accumulation of denotative statements that aimed to prove something to be true or false. In his view, it was not only that other dimensions to knowledge exist – such as the prescriptive and the evaluative – but also that knowledge includes as much accumulated and stored matter as it does *know-how* deriving from wider experience of a social nature. It was no coincidence, he argued, that scientific knowledge found it necessary to incorporate aspects of its nemesis to the point that it did not 'know and make known that it is the true knowledge without resorting to the other, narrative, kind of knowledge, which from its point of view is no knowledge at all'.[4]

By the late twentieth century, science was in crisis because it realised the growing impossibility of finding legitimation either within itself or by resorting to a metanarrative such as the will of the nation. The latter had been the operational logic of Wilhelm von Humboldt's invention of a 'modern' institution of knowledge in the early 1800s, but the validity of this logic had been lost after 150 years of geopolitical and social changes. The modern university, as codified in Berlin by von Humboldt, had been a logical response to an age of metanarratives – the culture of a national state being the institution's refer-ent[5] – and *connaissance* – the reproduction of knowledge through its transmis-sion en bloc. The stable limits of a purely scientific discourse nurtured within the fixed boundaries of a university's scientific community descended into crisis as a result of a process of social atomisation that gradually led to the redis-covery of the discursive (or narrative) in the scientific (or non-narrative). Lyo-tard described this rediscovered discourse as 'flexible networks of language games',[6] and he gave as an example the tendency of scientists to look for legit-imisation outside their traditional boundaries in the form of televised interviews or other forms of public appearance.

A consequence of Lyotard's analysis was that the crisis of traditional scien-tific discourse required a deep reconceptualisation of the institution that had been invented to protect and reproduce it. Nowhere was the argument about an urgent rethinking of the university made more explicit than in the dedication of Lyotard's text to his own institution (the Université de Paris VIII Vincennes), which was accompanied by the comment that 'this very postmodern moment ... finds the University nearing what may be its end'.[7] Written ten years after 1968, this statement was proof of the slow, but still unaccomplished, death of the old university. Suspending his discussion in the midpoint between diagnosis and prognosis, Lyotard did not explicitly argue for the ultimate demolition of the old institution, although he admitted that a widened clientele had to be con-sidered for an institution that had shifted from the elites to the masses. His ruminations interpreted the current condition as a field of potentiality, provid-ing a still image of a world at the moment of a difficult choice that stretched before and after 1968. It was the choice between updating or reinventing the university – in other words, it was the old quarrel between reform or revolution.

Once the related processes of the hybridisation of the scientific and the nar-rative, the atomisation of society and a widened clientele for higher learning were recognised, the philosopher's prognosis was very similar to the ambiguous spatial apparatus proposed by architects. Lyotard's words resound with the architectural responses given in Italy by the likes of Vittorio Gregotti and Giu-seppe Samonà that I have discussed in Chapter 5. The philosopher and the architects similarly located themselves in a limbo between the reproduction of the old elites and the creation of a social position for a growing mass of the less privileged who could no longer find a direct route into the job market but had (even when they did not ask for it) to go through the intermediary stage of some form of higher learning. Lyotard depicted a scenario unfolding outside universities, in which the transmission en bloc of knowledge to young people before entering the workforce was replaced with knowledge served 'à la carte' to adults who were either already working or expected to be. The logic of this piecemeal administering of knowledge posited that, by improving generic skills (information, languages, and language games),[8] the occupational horizons of the working class would also grow. In this scenario, however, the old university was not really questioned in its traditional role; rather, it was supposed to be matched with something else that could take the form of a more broadly accessible field of information. For Lyotard, this field of perfect information was still restricted to 'any expert'[9] rather than *anybody*, but in it was embedded the germ of a possible dissolution of the university because, as he admitted, 'the moment knowledge ceases to be an end in itself ... its transmission is no longer the exclusive responsibility of scholars and students'.[10]

By omitting *tout court* to draw and name the word 'university', Archizoom's competition entry for the University of Florence more decidedly took a stance in the direction of the ultimate uselessness of the old institutionalised version of knowledge. But besides being a manifesto of liberation from the university as it had been codified and reproduced over almost two centuries, *I progetti si firmano* was also a critical and polemical response to a similarly institutionalised architectural discourse and its false presumption of designing a better society through architectural form. Archizoom presented their criticism as a series of superimposed surfaces of information: *piano continuo per la ricerca scientifica, piano continuo di parcheggi residenziali, piano continuo per la distribuzione dell'informazione*, and *piano continuo di attrezzature ricreative*. Caught in the urgency of defining new ways of handling ever increasing quantities of data and users, the university was the perfect locus to develop a wider critique of the city as an informational medium.

The Marxist-Operaist helix

Disenchanted with the formal academic exercises they had been asked to produce during their university studies, soon after graduation in 1965–66 Archizoom started developing a critical reading of the modern city and its discourse, with a clear polemical aim towards the propaganda promoted by architectural publications. It was in the pages of *Casabella* that, in the summer 1970, they contributed the more elaborate formulation of their critique to date with the article 'City, assembly line of social issues'.[11] Appearing in the second issue under Alessandro Mendini's directorship of the magazine, the article acted as a sort of programmatic manifesto for the intellectual programme set by Mendini. This programme married most explicitly and helped to promote the polemical and subversive attitude of Archizoom and other Florentine collectives and individuals who, in 1971, would be grouped under the name of 'radical architecture'.[12]

Imbued with political ideology and Marxist vocabulary, Archizoom discussed the architecture/city nexus as the outcome of the continuous cycles of production and consumption that had turned the industrialised world into a gigantic, boundless factory. Their ideas were highly dissonant with the faith in architectural form that the magazine had promoted in the previous decade, especially under the ten-year directorship of Ernesto Nathan Rogers until 1965. In 1970, Rogers's intellectual legacy was still palpable in the words of Mendini's co-director, Giovanni Klaus Koenig, who introduced Archizoom's article with a careful disclaimer. Stating his general disagreement with most of the points presented by Archizoom, Koenig nevertheless justified publishing the article as hopefully to the advantage of 'the young generation of architects, who are more apt than my generation to theoretical ruminations on ideology'.[13]

Archizoom's arguments were indeed saturated with the ideology of young graduates of the mid-1960s who had fought against the established political forces and looked for extra-parliamentary alternatives. By the late 1960s, there were two main alternatives to choose from in Italy. On the one side stood the prospect of Operaism, whose origins dated back to 1961–62 and *Quaderni rossi* and *Classe operaia*, two magazines founded by Raniero Panzieri and Mario Tronti respectively. On the other side was the Student Movement (Movimento Studentesco) with operative groups scattered around Italian universities since 1963. These two groups initially shared a mission to conceptualise the status of the worker and the student as possible emancipatory agents in the struggle to overcome capitalism. They then started parting ways after those two social categories more decisively crossed paths during the protests in the large factories of northern Italy in the so-called 'hot autumn' (*autunno caldo*) of 1969. With the birth of two new magazines within the Operaist strand (*Potere operaio* and *Contropiano*), and one within the Student Movement (*Lotta continua*), the division took the shape of a mutual accusation. The Operaists condemned the students' ultimately bourgeois character, whereas their own 'treatises talking among themselves and citing one another in the best "academic" tradition'[14] were attacked by the students as evidence of hermetic intellectual criticism, for which *Contropiano* provided the main platform.

As narrated by its protagonists and subsequent scholars, the story of Archizoom has been located along the Operaist track and its efforts to define an intellectual theory of the working class opposed to the more activist line promoted by *Lotta continua*.[15] The influence of Tronti's book *Operai e capitale*,[16] as well as of Manfredo Tafuri's 'Per una critica dell'ideologia architettonica', an essay published in 1969 in *Contropiano*,[17] is invariably discussed in the narratives of Archizoom's work. The latter text, in particular, played a decisive role in directing their interpretation of the nexus of capital, architecture, and the city, of which 'City, assembly line of social issues' became a reformulation.

Tafuri had argued that the growth of capitalism had compromised the traditional relationship between architecture and society, which allocated to architecture the role of representing society and providing anticipatory scenarios for its development. Deprived of this role, architecture was left in the status of form without utopia and the city was reduced to a mere accumulation of elements that could, at most, aim to coexist. In this scenario, the architect 'as producer of "objects"' became 'an incongruous figure' whose role was no longer designing but 'organising' the elements of the urban fabric as an extension of the more general cycles of industrial production.[18] Archizoom took this argument to an extreme reformulation, which they developed in words and, especially, in images that represented the urban condition as one continuous interior made of objects floating on an infinite surface. This was a controversial move against Tafuri's opposition to those 'intellectual illusions ... which strive to anticipate, through mere imagery, the conditions of an architecture "for a liberated society"'.[19] Archizoom's response to Tafuri's criticism – which became more explicit in the later expanded version of his essay in which he reproached the Florentine collective for their 'skillful games'[20] – came in the form of a disclaimer about the nature of their drawings. In a letter written in 1969 and quoted by Roberto Gargiani in his study of Archizoom, Andrea Branzi had already specified that their objective was not utopia intended as the prefiguration of a better society; rather, they aimed to unveil 'the real utopian aspects of reality itself'.[21]

Archizoom argued that the eighteenth-century promise of achieving a balance between humans and the natural environment through the medium of the city designed as a formal (architectural) fact had been demystified by the homogenising action of capitalism and its artificial attempt to balance opposites such as private and public, part and whole, individual and group, technology and values, humans and nature. They claimed that this balancing was presented as a '"not" impossible Harmony'[22] through the systematic implementation of the 'plan', the key operative tool of capitalist urbanisation. The megalopolis represented the climax of this process, embodying 'the dimension of the Market itself which goes beyond the distinction between urban and agricultural',[23] and turning the city from a place into a condition. In such a continuous urban field, the metropolis was 'nothing else than the interference of specific interests within the system as a whole [which depend] on the supremacy of "tertiary" activity over all other activities'.[24]

Besides demonstrating Tafuri's influence, these last quotations serve as an oppositional description of the projects discussed in Chapter 5 and which represented the false consciousness against which Archizoom targeted their critique. Both Gregotti's *Amalassunta* and Samonà's University of Cagliari entry evidenced the desperate struggle for retaining a balance of artifice and nature, either by concentrating built settlements within preserved patches of land labelled 'agricultural parks', or by provocatively designing nature as artifice, as shown in the Italian gardens drawn by Samonà as the natural component running alongside his bas-relief university. Moreover, they claimed the sovereignty of tertiary activities to the point of promoting higher education as itself being a service among services, despite both Samonà and Gregotti holding reservations about the positivist and productivist discourse of *nuova dimensione, città territorio*, and *città regione*, in an apparent agreement with Archizoom who also claimed that 'personally, we don't identify ourselves with any of those formulas'.[25]

But it was on another point that, following Archizoom's arguments, the false consciousness of the formal projects of Samonà and Gregotti was most evident. The attempts at achieving harmony that were manifest in the ultimately still modernist way of thinking of the two older architects descended into crisis once they declared their acceptance of the homogenisation of values of late-modern society. In this respect, Gregotti's *Amalassunta* had been more drastic than Samonà's project in taking the university to a level other than just a tertiary service located within other bureaucratic neighbours and turning it into a leisure-work-academic theme park. As evidence of the balancing technique of capitalism, this 'city of spare time' – as Archizoom dubbed it – mixed consumption and production and found its ultimate representation in the supermarket.

By identifying 'the factory model and the consumption model', Archizoom claimed that the supermarket was 'homogeneous utopian structure, private functionality, rational sublimation of consumption. Maximum result with minimum effort [in which] the "landscape" no longer exists as an external phenomenon.'[26] This statement swept away Gregotti's theory of architecture as a mechanism of discontinuity that provides new meanings to the continuity of landscape. Archizoom's counter-argument posited that there is no such thing as discontinuity in capitalism, nor is there any scope for providing meaning through an architectural gesture, no matter how big. Architecture, in fact, had lost any role as a signifier other than that of signifying the logic of capitalist homogeneity.

Identifying the city with a supermarket meant conceptualising the urban as a stratification of homogeneous free plans in which the only possible way to live was, as Branzi later put it, 'weak urbanisation' through elements that renounced their aim to represent something and simply accepted their bare life as undifferentiated co-inhabitants.[27] Reduced to commodities to be produced and consumed in an endless cycle, architectural elements, natural elements and even human beings in the form of the workforce and human capital were no longer figurative; instead, they were merely 'there' – data to be assembled in ever different configurations.

Mixing repetition and anticipation, the continuous surfaces of an informational supermarket drawn over the Florentine plain were the loci where, with anticipatory action, the ideological readings of Operaism and Tafuri met Lyotard's analysis of the postmodern condition of knowledge. The latter's understanding of knowledge as having been reduced to a pick-and-mix process was evidence, as he put it, of an expanding 'mercantilization of knowledge ... in the form of an informational commodity indispensable to productive power'.[28] Put in the unashamed language of Archizoom, the final outcome of this was that 'there is no formal difference between a productive structure, a supermarket, housing, a university, or a sector of industrialised agriculture':[29] all were equal parts of a continuously urbanised territory, as they wrote in the commentary on their competition entry in Florence.

Exaggeration or project

Gregotti and Samonà – and with them various other participants in the competitions for new universities in Italy – had shown that it was possible to design architecturally a university capable of responding to a postmodern condition of knowledge comprising fewer certainties and more hybridisation among disciplines. Its formal configuration, they argued, would be an immense settlement whose overall order could contrast with privately driven urbanisation. Despite their simple, even elementary, formal/geometrical characteristics, these projects retained an understanding of architecture both as a dialectic of figure and ground and as an overall act of signification. Conversely, Archizoom's Tafuri-inspired disillusionment with this traditional notion of architecture drove them to abandon any hope of changing society through architecture. It was only a mere temporal fortuity that *Amalassunta* did not end up caught in Archizoom's critical web. In fact, read under their interpretative lens, Gregotti's project was mocked as nothing more than a 'project of roofs' – as indeed were all the examples that the Florentine group assembled in two introductory competition panels (Figure 6.2).

Collating plans and sections of cities across the nineteenth and twentieth centuries, these panels explicitly referenced the comparative table used by Le Corbusier to contrast his *Ville radieuse* to examples of nineteenth-century city fabric. Archizoom even went beyond the Swiss architect's selection, adding to Le Corbusier's original examples – Paris, New York, and Buenos Aires – the Garden City, Gropius's Siedlung Dammerstock, Le Corbusier's own Unité, Ludovico Quaroni's 'metamorphic pattern', and Archigram's Plug-in City. But beyond the quantitative increase, the real difference from Le Corbusier was that now Archizoom were not aiming to prove a 'better' project. All the chosen examples, they claimed, were nothing but iterations of the same idea, as all fed the unstoppable urbanising machinery of capitalism – often in spite of their blatant progressive theses of social reform. To clarify that they were instances of a single idea, they were summarised at the top of both panels in a plan and a section representing a continuous space of inhabitation cropped at the margins of the page to indicate its endlessness. As Archizoom would later explain in *No-Stop City*, the final version of their drawings, the condition they were faced with could not be opposed with a counter-proposal; rather, the only possibility left to the architect was to represent it, which is what *I progetti si firmano* did for the first time.

Launched in May 1970, the competition for the University of Florence was almost concomitant with the publication of 'City, Assembly Line of Social Issues' in the July issue of *Casabella*. By the submission date in the summer of 1971, Archizoom had further developed their critique of the city with a contribution to the *Design Quarterly* issue on 'Conceptual Architecture' curated by Peter Eisenman and, more importantly, with the article that gave the critique its final name, 'No-Stop City: Residential Parkings, Climatic Universal System'.[30] This sequence of steps shows the central position occupied by the Florence competition in the formulation of a theory of the architecture/city nexus.[31] It was a theory that, rather than openly opposing the status quo, proposed the maximisation of the current logics in order to work as a Trojan horse to demolish the system from within. Yet, when applied to a reading of the condition of the university at that specific moment in time, the thesis of a maximisation or exaggeration of reality as opposed to a projective scenario loses much of its conviction.

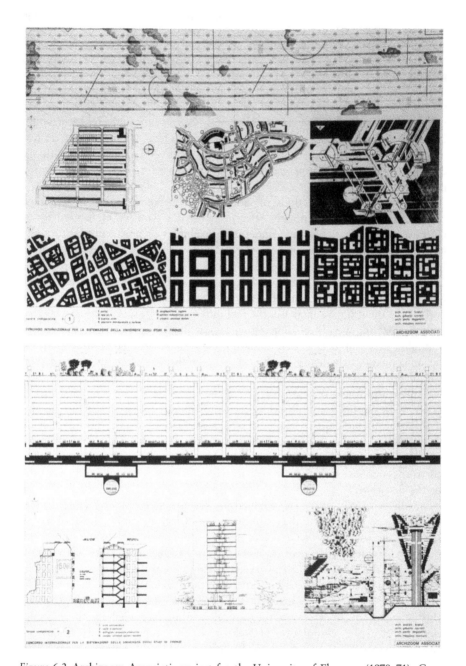

Figure 6.2 Archizoom Associati, project for the University of Florence (1970–71). Competition panels 1 and 2: Comparison of urban plans and sections.

Source: Centro Studi e Archivio della Comunicazione, Università degli Studi di Parma. Fondo Archizoom Associati.

The Italian university of the early 1970s was the opposite of the continuous surface of information for free individual use depicted by Archizoom. If it can be said to have been everywhere, this was only because it was an extremely fragmented reality – a fragmentation that mirrored the interior battles for power within faculties and between chairs and professors. Rather than ubiquitous open source information, it was still an elitist system controlled from the top and strongly discriminatory both geographically and socially. In the face of this situation, the 'surface of continuous research' or the 'surface of continuous learning' drawn by Archizoom assumed the role of a proposal and of an alternative scenario. In a word, they were a project.

The drawings for the University of Florence were not an exaggeration of an existing condition but a prefiguration of a possible scenario of ubiquitous access to information that only the digital turn and the Internet could enable many years later. On a pedagogic level, this scenario implied an understanding of knowledge as something that could be achieved not exclusively through the traditional equation of education and instruction, as argued by other radical thinkers of the time. As well as being shaken by the student protests for more equitable forms of learning, the 1960s was a period of fertile thinking about alternative forms of education, and *I progetti si firmano* ended up adding a drawn representation to a wider range of radical ideas of pedagogy that were being discussed internationally. While a Marxist-Operaist-Tafurian helix constituted its DNA, this was interwoven with a second helix of a more specific pedagogic nature. This second helix would be unveiled only later, when Archizoom, and the radicals in general, were approaching the end of their lives. Significantly, the sunset of the radicals was marked by the implementation of a proper pedagogical project called Global Tools, a diffuse system of laboratories across Italian cities aimed at 'stimulating the free development of individual creativity' by rescuing a 'de-intellectualized man provided with archaic wisdom, allowing all possible consequences including the recovery of nomadism and the destruction of the city'.[32] Global Tools was started in 1973,[33] the same year when the pedagogic preoccupations behind Archizoom's ideological proclaims about the condition of the city in late capitalism were unveiled. Such unveiling happened most explicitly in January of that year, when Andrea Branzi threw a bridge across the Atlantic to connect Florence and Cuernavaca, where Ivan Illich had been operating an alternative school for more than a decade.

The deschooling helix

In the January 1973 issue of *Casabella*, Andrea Branzi reviewed Ivan Illich's book *Deschooling Society* [34] as part of his 'Radical Notes', a column he had been curating since October 1972 and for which he published 27 short texts by 1976.[35] The fourth in the series, his piece about Illich was the first and only to adopt the format of a review, a literary genre that Branzi approached in an autobiographical way. In fact, by talking about Illich, Branzi was actually aiming to talk about Archizoom.

By the early 1970s, Illich had become a prominent critic of modernity, attacking it as a project of institutionalisation and commodification of all human values that hindered individual freedom through the imposition of a code of standardised rules.[36] Having been forced by the Vatican to resign from his post as vice rector at the Catholic University of Puerto Rico, he had set up his own educational institution at Cuernavaca in Mexico in 1961, CIDOC, the Centro Cultural de Documentación that became a stronghold of alternative thinking and education capable of attracting worldwide attention. It was here that Illich delivered a series of seminars that ended up in *Deschooling Society*.

Published in 1970, the book was the first consistent formulation of Illich's critique of the modern industrial and technological society.[37] Beginning his attack with a discussion of the school was a clear statement about this institution's paradigmatic status in relation to a wider phenomenon of top-down social engineering in which 'medical treatment is mistaken for health care, social work for the improvement of community life, police protection for safety, military poise for national security'.[38] What Illich called a schooled society referred, in fact, to a condition that was wider than the specific case of schools. For him, it was intended as the social addiction to an imposed view of the world that obliterated the freer formation of individuals. This was most evident in the institution of the school, which he attacked for its false promise of equality that masked the reality of its promotion of social disparity. Schooling, he argued, misguidedly equated learning with obligatory instruction and set up a client–provider relationship between individual and institution.[39] Based on a process of continuous escalation to build a person's curriculum – a mechanism by which new steps can be made only if previous steps have been legitimised by the granting of a certificate – schooling hampered the possibility of independent accomplishment.

Illich's book posited that the prospect of a deschooled society could be achieved only through the deployment of alternative routes that value learning as necessarily a personal activity controlled by the learner. Alternatives needed to be designed, and they could be built on the acknowledgement of the double-sided nature of knowledge. On the one side, knowledge derives from a set of data that each individual absorbs, as if into a personal archive, and learns how to handle. This kind of knowledge could more appropriately be called information – or explicit knowledge – which can be transmitted through a teacher–student relation or conventional media such as books, instructions, and so on. On the other side, there is knowledge that, differently from information's dependence on a quantifiable set of data, is based on the existence of an immaterial culture shared among members of a community. This dimension is what, in 1958, Michael Polanyi named 'tacit knowledge', defining it as something that cannot easily be stored in a database.[40] In fact, tacit knowledge depends not only on particular skills but also on the existence of an environment for sharing that adds a level of informality to the formal mechanisms of learning. Deschooling means defining the possibility for such an environment to exist.

Illich distinguished between 'convivial' and 'manipulative treatment-institutions', which he located at the left and right ends respectively of an ideal institutional spectrum.[41] The former offer themselves to the free use of individuals, and include telephone link-ups, subway lines, mail routes, public markets, parks, sidewalks, and so on. Conversely, manipulative institutions shape their users by turning services into commodities. For Illich, schools were the paradigmatic case of the latter category because they 'create a demand for the entire set of modern institutions which crowd the right end of the spectrum'.[42]

In opposition to manipulative institutions, learning as a convivial activity depends on the unpredictable ways in which individuals interact with one another, and where the role of the teacher is that of a facilitator 'concerned with helping matching partners to meet so that learning can take place'.[43] To paraphrase this definition: learning is not a product but a condition that is never confined within a univocal boundary. This conception stands in contrast to learning as it has traditionally been understood, an understanding that equates it with obligatory schooling and, spatially, with school buildings.[44] The story of education has for the most part been one of spatial compounds that made the school partake in the more general logics of a growing industrial economy based on concentrations of capital in space. It is here, within a polemic ultimately targeted against the modern industrial city and its social and economic logics, that Illich and Archizoom crossed paths.

From the outset of his review, Branzi revealed an instrumental use of Illich, as he moved the deschooling theses onto a critique that was personal to him:

> Illich's criticism deals with a strictly disciplinary field such as the school, but as he himself declares, the choice of such a field is only an instrumental matter ... for the fact that this sort of analysis could be applied indifferently to other branches and to other forms with identical results: the army, the family, work, etc. And, we wish to add, the town.[45]

The fact that Illich's written and Archizoom's drawn critiques were elaborated simultaneously forestalls any attempt to look for an originator among the two. Rather, they strengthened one another, and Branzi's later review simply served to make the alliance official. In particular, Archizoom's drawings added a further level of complexity to Illich's argument about deschooling, demonstrating how it should not be confused as a simplistic eradication *tout court* of formality and order from the learning process. A closer analysis of some of the drawings of *I progetti si firmano* unveils a more complex picture that depicts informality not as mere spatial anarchy in the name of individual freedom but as the careful orchestration of elements that enable the interplay of freedom and control, openness and closure. So, the continuous surface of the 'distribution of information' proposed a scene of personalised and localised spatial appropriations that only apparently followed a totally free logic. In fact, the drawing strongly relied on zoning and allocated different uses to specific areas while also signalling the reappearance of a traditional double-loaded corridor that could contradict a prospect of complete learning freedom (Figure 6.3). Through the

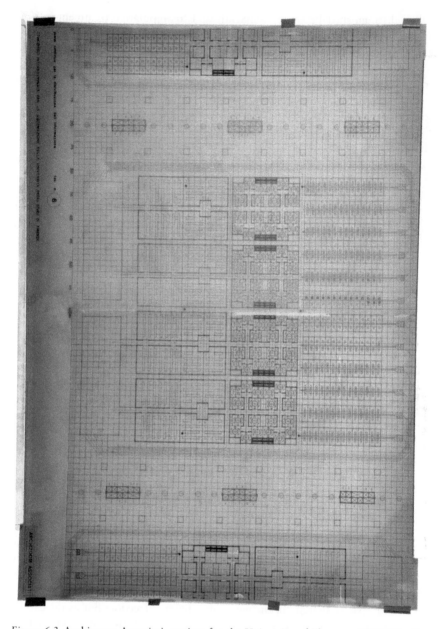

Figure 6.3 Archizoom Associati, project for the University of Florence (1970–71). Competition panel 6: Surface for the distribution of information.
Source: Centro Studi e Archivio della Comunicazione, Università degli Studi di Parma. Fondo Archizoom Associati.

juxtaposition of formal lecture-hall arrangements, convivial layouts based on a central table with chairs surrounding it in a seminar fashion, and single cells for individual retreat, this drawing declared the equivalence of different moments of learning that should be conceived as simultaneous rather than hierarchical.

The simultaneity represented in Archizoom's drawings postulated a degrading of architecture from a hierarchical apparatus impacting on people's behaviour to an allegedly neutral substratum. Here stands the critical distance between their entry in the Florence competition and the other projects of the 1960s that apparently shared a similar ethos of a freer concept of learning – in particular, the famous project for the Berlin Free University by Candilis, Josic and Woods, which controversially turned freedom of learning into the carefully designed architectural machinery of the mat-building.[46] Conversely, the Florence project did not devise any such architectural machinery because, as Archizoom put it in more general terms, 'We are seeking to propose not a new "form" of the city, but rather a different way of "using" it.'[47]

Territory of learning webs

If, as it has usually been presented, *No-Stop City* was an exaggeration of reality – the depiction of a city-as-factory based on Operaist theses – its first formulation as a university more ambiguously placed it between the commentary and the projective scenario for a different future. This hesitancy could be related to the deep crisis of learning and education that the Florence competition entry was responding to, and which required the architect to retain some of his or her traditional role as designer of different scenarios. This is what Branzi retroactively unveiled by deciding at the outset of his 'Radical Notes' to review the ideas of Ivan Illich, which ultimately further confused the already unstable characterisation of Archizoom's view of the city as an exaggeration of reality rather than a project anticipating a different scenario.

Mario Tronti argued that capitalism had turned the factory into a state of mind and an organisational logic that extended well beyond the walls of the production building to permeate the whole city.[48] Archizoom presented *No-Stop City* as the drawn version of this condition taken to its extreme figuration. Illich argued that a schooling mentality had appropriated the city by cancelling the possibilities for personal learning and turning education into a service perfectly fit for the producer-consumer logics of capitalism. Related to this scenario, *No-Stop City* – as anticipated in the drawings for the Florence competition – did not represent the existing situation; rather, it envisaged the alternative scenario that Illich was also seeking.

Illich and Archizoom agreed that an alternative to the school as a manipulative institution could not be a physically bounded institution, however better designed such a building might be. For Illich: 'The alternative to dependence on schools is not the use of public resources for some new device which "makes" people learn; rather it is the creation of a new style of educational relationship between man and his environment.'[49]

These words were echoed in Branzi's review, in which Illich's ideas were translated to an urbanistic domain:

> The battle to improve towns as they are at present is limited by having to operate on a body that is full of structural rather than social contradictions which no new equilibrium will ever manage to regenerate, a body that is too old to absorb a newly-conceived vision of existing and living.[50]

Rather than improving the existing scenario, a totally different scenario had to be designed that understood learning as a network comprising as many and varied institutions and spaces as possible. Illich wrote of 'learning webs', which extended to places such as restaurants, commuter trains, and department stores.[51] These webs were intended to enable a learning environment made of four main sets of resources: things (physical objects), models (masters of a specific skill who could demonstrate how to practise it), peers (people with similar interests), and elders (experienced people providing criticism). All of them were to coexist, floating simultaneously in an expanded environment. In this alternative scenario, Illich described the library as an open source service for individual exploration, and the last remaining fragment of an educational institution that had dissolved into a less physically recognisable arrangement. Not coincidentally, the library was also the only detectable element extracted from a traditional university that remained in the continuous informational surfaces projected by Archizoom on the plain outside Florence.

Notes

1 The motto 'I progetti si firmano' (Projects must be signed) was a complaint against the common practice of anonymity in design competitions. According to Archizoom, such practice produced the opposite of what was intended, since it generated a tendency to make projects as recognisable as possible to the jury. Consistent with their position, the group printed the label 'Archizoom Associati' on all the panels, which led to their exclusion from the competition.

2 The panels submitted by Archizoom were: Panel 1. 'Comparative panel 1' (urban plans); Panel 2. 'Comparative panel 2' (urban sections); Panel 3. 'Elements of the Universal Climatic System'; Panel 4. 'Territorial plan 1:10000'; Panel 5. 'Plan 1:2000'; Panel 6. 'Surface for the distribution of information'; Panel 7. 'Surface for scientific research'; Panel 8. 'Surface for residential parkings'; Panel 9. 'Surface for recreational activities'. They are kept at the Centro Studi e Archivio della Comunicazione, Parma.

3 Jean-François Lyotard, *The Postmodern Condition: A Report on Knowledge* (Minneapolis, MN: University of Minnesota Press, 1979), 7.

4 Ibid., 29.

5 See Bill Readings, *The University in Ruins* (Cambridge, MA: Harvard University Press, 1996). Readings suggested that the modern research university created in Germany in the first decade of the nineteenth century marked a fundamental switch from previous understandings of the institution. He explained this switch in terms of a

change in the 'idea' that acted as a referent for the university, suggesting that three ideas succeeded one another in the evolution of the modern university: 'reason' in the university of the Enlightenment; 'culture' in the university of the nation states; and 'excellence' in the postmodern, corporate university of the late twentieth century. According to Readings, it was Humboldt's reform that, by electing culture – that is, national culture – as the central idea of the university, made the academic institution a mediator between the subject and the State. In his view, this is what made the university 'modern' and fundamentally different from the somewhat autonomous early universities of the Middle Ages.

6 Lyotard, *The Postmodern Condition*, 17.

7 Ibid., xxv.

8 Ibid., 49.

9 According to Lyotard:
    It is possible to conceive the world of postmodern knowledge as governed by a game of perfect information, in the sense that the data is in principle accessible to any expert: there is no scientific secret. Given equal competence ... what extra performativity depends on in the final analysis is 'imagination', which allows one either to make a new move or change the rules of the game (ibid., 52).

10 Ibid., 50.

11 Archizoom Associati, 'Città, catena di montaggio del sociale: Ideologia e teoria della metropoli. City, assembly line of social issues', *Casabella* 350–351 (1970): 43–52.

12 The label 'radicals' was first used by Germano Celant in 1971: Germano Celant, untitled article, *IN: Argomenti e immagini di design* 2–3 (1971): 76–81.

13 Giovanni Klaus Koenig, untitled article, *Casabella* 370–371 (1970): 43. My translation.

14 Guido Viale, *Il sessantotto: Tra rivoluzione e restaurazione* (Milan: Gabriele Mazzotta Editore, 1978), 187.

15 For an interpretation of Archizoom and its relations with Operaism, see in particular Pier Vittorio Aureli, *The Project of Autonomy: Politics and Architecture within and against Capitalism* (New York: Princeton Architectural Press, 2008); and Andrea Branzi, *Una generazione esagerata: Dai radical italiani alla crisi della globalizzazione* (Milan: Baldini & Castoldi, 2014). Aureli underlines the impact on Archizoom of the theses proposed by Mario Tronti that
    were not about the destruction of capitalist culture and bourgeois history per se but, on the contrary, their deep analysis and instrumental use [proposing] an audacious effort to appropriate the political realm in order to construct an alternative to capitalist domination.
                                                    (Aureli, *The Project of Autonomy*, 14)

    In his autobiographical recollections, Branzi clarifies that Archizoom followed the Operaist path rather than aligning with the Student Movement: 'Our sophisticated political ethos kept us outside the whirl of student assemblies and the ritual occupations of institutional places' (Andrea Branzi, *Una generazione esagerata*, 70; my translation).

16 Mario Tronti, *Operai e capitale* (Turin: Einaudi, 1966).

17 Manfredo Tafuri, 'Per una critica dell'ideologia architettonica', *Contropiano* 1 (1969): 31–79; republished in English as 'Toward a Critique of Architectural Ideology', in *Architecture Theory Since 1968*, ed. K. Michael Hays (Cambridge, MA: MIT Press, 1998), 6–35. After publication in 1969, Tafuri expanded the essay and published it as *Progetto e utopia: Architettura e sviluppo capitalistico* (Rome: Laterza, 1973), an English edition of which was published as *Architecture and Utopia: Design and Capitalist Development* (Cambridge, MA: MIT Press, 1976).

18 Tafuri, 'Per una critica dell'ideologia architettonica', 22.

19 Ibid., 32.

20 Tafuri, *Progetto e utopia*, 130.

21 Andrea Branzi, letter to Beate Sydhoff, 23 January 1969, quoted in Roberto Gargiani, *Archizoom Associati, 1966–1974: Dall'onda pop alla superficie neutra* (Milan: Electa, 2007). My translation.
22 Archizoom Associati, 'Città, catena di montaggio del sociale', 165.
23 Ibid., 167.
24 Ibid., 169.
25 Archizoom Associati, manuscript note from 1967, quoted in Gargiani, *Archizoom Associati*, 40.
26 Archizoom Associati, 'Città, catena di montaggio del sociale', 51. My translation.
27 See Andrea Branzi, *Weak and Diffuse Modernity: The World of Projects at the Beginning of the 21st Century* (Milan: Skira, 2006).
28 Lyotard, *The Postmodern Condition*, 7.
29 Archizoom, 'Progetto di concorso per l'Università di Firenze', *Domus* 509 (1974): 12.
30 Archizoom, 'No-Stop City: Residential Parkings, Climatic Universal System', *Domus* 496 (1971): 49–54.
31 Roberto Gargiani explains how the theoretical project *No-Stop City* was developed as a phased process that, following a Marxist line of reasoning, aimed at the ultimate liberation of humans from the tyranny of work. In sequential order, the stages were defined as follows: the 'destruction of architecture' intended in its traditional figurative role; the 'destruction of the object'; the 'elimination of the city'; and, finally, the 'dissolution of work': see Gargiani, *Archizoom Associati*.

  A chronology between 1969 and 1971 helps to clarify the role of testing ground played by the Florence competition within the development of Archizoom's critique of the city/architecture/capitalism nexus, which culminated in No-Stop City.

  September 1969. Archizoom, 'Congrès de Turin 26, 26, 27 Avril 1969', *L'architecture d'aujourd'hui*, 40, no. 145 (1969): lxiv–lxviii.

  December 1969. Archizoom, 'Discorsi per immagini', Domus 481 (1969): 44–45.

  May 1970. Announcement of the competition for the design of the University of Florence.

  July 1970. Archizoom Associati, 'Città, catena di montaggio del sociale: Ideologia e teoria della metropoli', Casabella 350–351 (1970): 43–52.

  December 1970. Original deadline for the University of Florence competition (postponed).

  January 1971. 'No-Stop City Residential Park Climatic Universal System', Design Quarterly 78–79 (1971): 17–21 (issue dedicated to 'Conceptual architecture' and edited by Peter Eisenman).

  February 1971. Archizoom, 'Utopia della qualità, utopia della quantità', Argomenti e Immagini di Design 1 (1971): 30–35.

  March 1971. Archizoom, 'No-Stop City: Residential Parkings, Climatic Universal System', Domus 496 (1971): 49–54.

  March 1971. Deadline for the University of Florence competition (postponed again).

  June 1971. Archizoom, 'La distruzione degli oggetti', Argomenti e Immagini di Design 2–3 (1971): 4–13.

  June 1971. Final deadline for the University of Florence competition.
32 'Bollettino Global Tools,' cited in 'Appunti su Global Tools', Gizmoweb, 2011. Available at: www.gizmoweb.org/2012/06/appunti-su-global-tools/ (accessed June 17, 2018).
33 Global Tools was founded by Archizoom, Riccardo Dalisi, Superstudio, Ufo, Zziggurat, Ugo La Pietra, and 9999.
34 Andrea Branzi, 'The Abolition of School – Radical Note no. 4', *Casabella* 373 (1973): 10.
35 The first 'Radical Note' was published in *Casabella* 370 (October 1972) and the last in *Casabella* 412 (April 1976). The latter was also the last issue to be edited by Alessandro Mendini, who directed the magazine from June 1970 to April 1976.

36 See Todd Hartch, *The Prophet of Cuernavaca: Ivan Illich and the Crisis of the West* (New York: Oxford University Press, 2015).

37 Ivan Illich, *Deschooling Society* (New York: Marion Boyars, 1970). The other main books in which Illich developed his critique of institutions are *Tools for Conviviality* (New York: Harper & Row, 1973), *Medical Nemesis* (New York: Pantheon Books, 1976), and *Toward a History of Needs* (New York: Pantheon Books, 1978).

38 Illich, *Deschooling Society*, 1.

39 Ibid., 11.

40 See Michael Polanyi, *Personal Knowledge: Towards a Post-Critical Philosophy* (Chicago: University of Chicago Press, 1958); and Michael Polanyi, *The Tacit Dimension* (Garden City, NY: Doubleday, 1966). Summarised in the claim that we know more than we can tell, Polanyi described a dimension of knowing that is inherently personal and cannot be transmitted – as information can be – via any media. Tacit knowledge became an operative concept for thinkers like Illich, for it sustained the argument against the total institutionalisation of education and the imposition of top-down instruction. Tacit knowledge challenges the teacher–student dyad in so far as it is something that cannot be taught but only learned.

41 Illich, *Deschooling Society*, 53.

42 Ibid., 60.

43 Ibid., 17.

44 This argument was most clearly formulated by Giancarlo De Carlo who questioned the absoluteness of the school building as the dominant way to approach the spatiality of education. See Giancarlo De Carlo, 'Why/How to Build School Buildings', *Harvard Educational Review* 4 (1969): 12–35. See also Chapter 7.

45 Branzi, 'The Abolition of School', 10.

46 See Chapter 7.

47 Andrea Branzi, letter to Charles Jencks, 16 May 1972, quoted in Gargiani, *Archizoom Associati*, 276.

48 Tronti, *Operai e capitale*.

49 Illich, *Deschooling Society*, 72. Illich returned to discuss the need of finding alternatives to the school in the follow-up text to *Deschooling Society*: Ivan Illich, *After Deschooling, What?* (London: Writers and Readers Publishing Cooperative, 1976; first published in 1973).

50 Branzi, 'The Abolition of School', 10.

51 See Illich, *Deschooling Society*, Chapter 6, 72–104.

7   Reversing the pyramid

Giancarlo De Carlo and the dilution of the university

The founding of *Universicittà*

> After the floods and earthquakes a new cataclysm upsets our country: the revolt of the University.[1]

While the Italian experience of university design in the 1960s and the 1970s has generally been neglected by architectural historians, there is one architect who has been widely celebrated for his substantial work in that field. This exception is Giancarlo De Carlo.

A key contributor to the debate on the new urban dimension – in 1962, he organised the important seminar on 'La città regione' in Stresa[2] – De Carlo, unlike his colleagues, did not consider the university as simply a new brief for the postwar debate. Rather, he was the architect who most explicitly accepted and rephrased Joseph Rykwert's 1968 statement of the paradigmatic status of the university:[3]

> There was a moment when the university, which was undergoing striking expansion and was variously imbricated with society, appeared to my eyes as a possible founding element of a new city, together with housing and other significant collective services that have multiplied and diffused in later years.[4]

For De Carlo, more than any other architect, the university offered the key to understanding how the consolidation of a consumerist mass society required a complete change in the ways that knowledge was produced and diffused. The question for him was not so much how to reform higher education as how to subvert it by turning the existing pyramidal structure of the academic world upside down. In 1968, he wrote: 'The only feasible hypothesis seems to be the creation of a state of permanent fluidity in which the diffusion of information and experience is continuous, ubiquitous, and widespread.'[5]

Although this argument echoed Archizoom's polemic at the University of Florence competition, De Carlo differed from his radical colleagues in not giving up a belief in architectural form. Yet he also distanced himself from the proposers of large architectural gestures that populated many of the panels submitted in Florence and at the other competitions of the early 1970s, none of which he entered. In fact, he occupied a third position deriving from a starting point that differed from those of his colleagues. Whereas Archizoom's critique originated from Operaist theses, and Gregotti's and Samonà's from their own intellectual preoccupations with the discipline of architecture, De Carlo's point of departure was more decisively the student unrest of the 1960s. Observing the violent spilling out of the students from the academic halls onto the city streets (Figure 7.1), but also listening to and criticising their calls for a different higher education, he elaborated the hypothesis of a diluted university that was perfected through a triad of projects, each associated with a specific city and its academic institution: Urbino, Dublin and Pavia.

Embedded between two direct commissions – the projects produced for Urbino since the late 1950s and the master plan for Pavia initiated in 1971 – the one for University College Dublin (1963–64) was De Carlo's only participation in an international competition on the topic. Responding to a canonical brief typical of the time – a new university campus on an out-of-town site – he began elaborating an idea of a dispersed university that would abandon stable hierarchies and promise ever changing levels of association, thereby connecting with the idea and ethos of Team X of which he was a component.[6] In Dublin, De Carlo's link with the follow-up to CIAM became all the more explicit, to the point of leading him to develop his own counter-proposal to the canonical

Figure 7.1 Student protest in Milan, 4 October 1968.
Source: © Cesare Colombo.

university design generally associated with Team X – the Berlin Free University by Candilis, Josic, and Woods.[7] The idea of the university as a diffused, open-source service first outlined in Dublin then found its ultimate formulation in Pavia, which De Carlo himself considered his most complete achievement in university design.[8]

The prospect of a dissolution of the university derived from a conceptual switch that placed De Carlo – who notoriously had anarchist sympathies – within that line of thinking about the de-institutionalisation of values that, at various levels of theorisation within the social sciences and branching into architectural and urban studies, included Ivan Illich, Cedric Price, John Turner, Colin Ward and, in Italy, Carlo Doglio.[9] Like them, De Carlo questioned the traditional equation between school and building and argued for a much wider understanding of learning beyond the four walls of an ad hoc architectural container. The project for Pavia, where De Carlo conceived multiple academic poles scattered throughout the city and reaching out to the regional territory through mobile research satellites, provided a possible physical representation of a reflection on the status of education and its necessary de-institutionalisation. In doing so, it offered an alternative formulation for the large-scale conceptualisation of higher education proposed by Price's Potteries Thinkbelt.[10] In a substantial departure from Price, De Carlo's similar argument of alternative and multiple paths to learning did not lose sight of the traditional city as its main focal point, and it ultimately proclaimed a belief in the quality of a mid-sized Italian town which, in line with the ideas of a city-territory debated in Italy since the early 1960s, he reconnected to its wider territory by means of an expanded higher education institution.

Through the projects for Urbino, Dublin, and Pavia, but also through his parallel written elaborations on the condition of higher education, De Carlo anticipated some of the trends of what was later called the 'knowledge economy', such as the blurring of boundaries between different spheres of human existence and a conception of learning as a ubiquitous condition that is not confined within a unity of time and space. Informality, serendipity, flexibility, open source, and other notions that have become common labels within twenty-first-century talks on education were all integral to De Carlo's identification of the university with the city – his notion of a *Universicittà*. [11]

Urbino (or the cell and the collective)

De Carlo's commitment to university design is commonly associated with his projects for the University of Urbino.[12] Before receiving from Carlo Bo, the rector, the commissions for which he is most known – such as the Faculty of Education (Magistero) and the complex of the university colleges – De Carlo had produced, between 1958 and 1964, an urban study and a master plan for the city, which he published in 1966.[13] The plan was based on a detailed survey of all the city's buildings, and this provided him with the necessary background knowledge for the subsequent series of architectural interventions inside the historic city.[14]

It was from outside the historic core, however, that De Carlo started his urban remodelling through academic buildings. His first relevant commission was the Collegio del Colle, designed and built between 1962 and 1966 as the initial nucleus of an academic residential compound that De Carlo implemented over the following years on a hill overlooking Urbino. Splitting the residential component off from other academic functions was a way of formulating an interpretation of that new urban dimension that was being debated in Italy at the time. In 1962, the year work on the Collegio del Colle project started, De Carlo organised a congress in Stresa at which he articulated a definition of what he called *città regione*, [15] a 'dynamic set of relations that contrasts with the static condition of the traditional city'.[16] Elaborating on this generic definition, in his urban study of Urbino, he highlighted how the city was trapped between two problems: on the one side, there was the decaying historic centre, with numerous buildings in a severe status of degradation; on the other side was the amorphous periphery that was continuing to grow uncontrollably outside the ancient city walls – that same periphery which had been depicted by many Italian neo-realist films of the 1950s. Arguing for the simultaneous consideration of both parts of the city, De Carlo proposed that the university could play an exemplary role by infiltrating the old urban fabric as much as it did the amorphous periphery. A modern city-region, he suggested, necessarily required the coexistence between the two parts.

The project of the colleges had already expressed De Carlo's main arguments about higher education, which revolved around a conceptualisation of a main actor: the (individual) student. Addressing the relationship between the individual and collective dimensions of education, Collegio del Colle deployed a spatial diagram combining enclosure and openness and playing with the clear differentiation between private domestic (quasi-monastic) cells and shared spaces. Where the presence of a central focus (the service core for collective facilities) defined a centripetal, inward-oriented complex, the dormitories for 150 students stretched to create an inverse crescent in which each cell faced the landscape (Figure 7.2). In the part-to-whole relationship of this complex was a representation of the condition of the student inhabitant, which produced a spatial organisation that only superficially bore some similarities to a project of comparable topographic ambitions, namely, Denys Lasdun's University of East Anglia. In the latter, as in most other British new universities of the 1960s, a basic module for the academic community stood at the core of the spatial organisation of the university and, in particular, its residential areas. This module was defined in relation to a group of ten to twelve students and derived from a tradition dating back to the collegiate models of Oxford and Cambridge. The 'staircase principle' was the way in which this sub-community, organised around a staircase distributing rooms and shared spaces on each floor, found its architectural representation.[17] Conversely, no basic sub-community was considered by De Carlo to be the ideal module of the university population; rather, the basic module was the individual student. Each student was given their own monastic cell overlooking the landscape, and the grouping

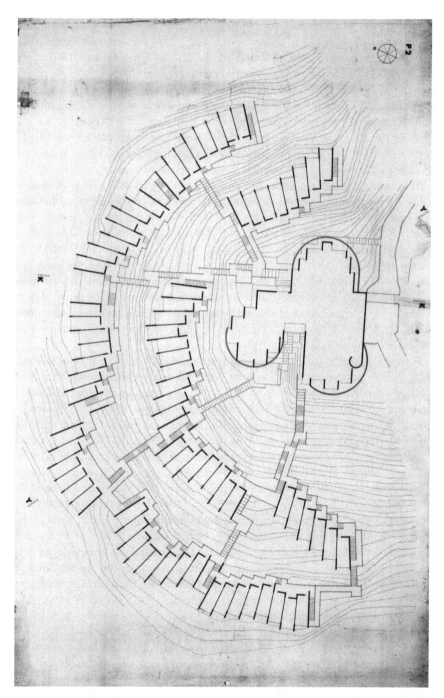

Figure 7.2 Giancarlo De Carlo, project for Collegio del Colle, Urbino (1962–66). General plan showing the structural elements.
Source: Università Iuav di Venezia, Archivio Progetti. Fondo Giancarlo De Carlo.

of six to eight cells did not aim to create domestic sub-communities. Instead, the project juxtaposed the wholly individualistic (the cell) and the forced collective (the communal service core).

In line with De Carlo's argument that 'students should not be treated as dispersed quantities out of a mass; rather, they are to be enabled to find the ways of developing their own individuality',[18] the individual and collective poles of the project were mediated by a system of pathways positing a dynamic dimension to education. These paths added an element of chance and of the unprogrammed to the clearly designed private/collective dichotomy, and they elaborated on an interest in the spaces of movement as fundamental structuring devices typical of Team X's ethos. In the Urbino colleges, De Carlo combined the movement lines that could be observed in the Smithsons' proposals for Golden Lane or the University of Sheffield,[19] as well as in Candilis, Josic, and Woods's 'stems',[20] with an interest in modularity and singularity that was expressed through the repetition of the cells. Instead of a clear hierarchy between the two, the result merged them into a single formal structure, as the circulation paths 'read' the topography rather than just contrasting it in a tendency to dissolve in an extension of the cells themselves. The dissolution of movement and its concomitant declaration as a moment of continuity with the overall experience of the student are what the dormitories of Urbino anticipated about De Carlo's idea of the university, ultimately becoming the overarching principle of the proposal for Pavia. In the spatial diagram of a residential complex there was already embedded a wider idea of the university and, in turn, a wider idea of the city.

Dublin (or disciplinary reshuffling)

While De Carlo was working on the Urbino colleges, in May 1962, University College Dublin announced the 'International Architectural Competition for the site layout of the new buildings for the College and for a block for the Faculty of Arts (with associated faculties), administrative offices and examination hall'. The competition brief required the extension of a cluster of buildings located outside Dublin into a proper campus on a 'large, flat and well treed site'.[21] As De Carlo commented in a booklet he published in Venice in 1965 to present his entry, 'the object was explicitly that of obtaining a dispersed disposition of elements, continuing the rural type plan already established by the arrangement of the existing buildings on the site'.[22] The results, announced in July 1964, were unsatisfactory for both De Carlo and his Team X colleague Shadrach Woods, who also took part in the competition with a scheme clearly modelled on his previous winning entry for the Berlin Free University and which shared with De Carlo's project a refusal of the pavilions-in-the-park solution – the solution that the jury ultimately preferred.[23]

Anticipating his own criticism of the Italian university as an incoherent system made of detached faculty buildings, De Carlo opposed the very idea of a campus made of discrete built elements:

The relation of the University to its immediate surroundings has been a central concern that has shaped our proposal. Rather than limiting the aim to the organisation of a University in a park, the proposal considered the University as a cultural centre. As such, the University and the park – understood as a leisure destination – could become focal points for the surroundings and for the city at large.[24]

As in Urbino, the attempt at opening up the university and turning it into an episode of 'transition between the urban centre and the countryside' was a statement about a new territorial dimension of a city. Eight years before Vittorio Gregotti and Edoardo Detti would propose a new outlying academic-service-leisure complex for the University of Florence, and a couple of years before Gregotti would curate the introductory section of the Thirteenth Milan Triennale (1964) on the topic of *tempo libero*, [25] De Carlo interpreted a campus as a leisure destination for a vast urban population.

The goal of responding to the demands of a *città regione* by blurring both the specialised and the leisure dimensions of a campus was coupled with the internal reorganisation of the university as the machinery for teaching and research. In contrast to an array of clearly defined faculties, De Carlo proposed a system with a lower degree of rigidity that refused a conceptualisation of the university as a juxtaposition of disciplines. Instead, he argued for a constant process of regrouping disciplines into what he called an 'organisational systematisation', which related to the perceived impossibility of translating the university into a fixed figurative form. In De Carlo's understanding, the university was indeed far from being a stable system. Rather, it was the most unstable and incoherent of institutions, its keywords being flexibility, adaptability, expansion and phasing. The only way architectural design could claim a controlling role over the physical layout of this entity was by deploying a set of rules that, however, could never be sufficient to provide a definite final image for the institution.

Three levels of systematisation overlapped in the Dublin project. The first broke down the university not into disciplines but according to a privacy/collectiveness spectrum ranging between the communal, general, particular and specialised.[26] Conceiving all parts of the university as services,[27] this taxonomy suppressed the modernist servant/served dichotomy. A second systematisation related to circulation, which was divided into primary and secondary routes. The former was a central linear spine organised on two levels and running across the whole university complex, whereas the latter superimposed a layer of parallel and perpendicular paths that reiterated the idea of serendipity and chance already encountered in the Urbino colleges.[28] Finally, the third level of systematisation related to the actual organisation of built form by means of a planning grid whereby De Carlo reconnected with modernism – unashamedly, as he based the grid on the golden section (Figure 7.3). The grid regulated the position of all the built masses in such a way as to avoid the segregation of residences into a specific cluster, a segregation found in most projects of the time, such as the British universities of Lancaster and Essex. Unlike in those

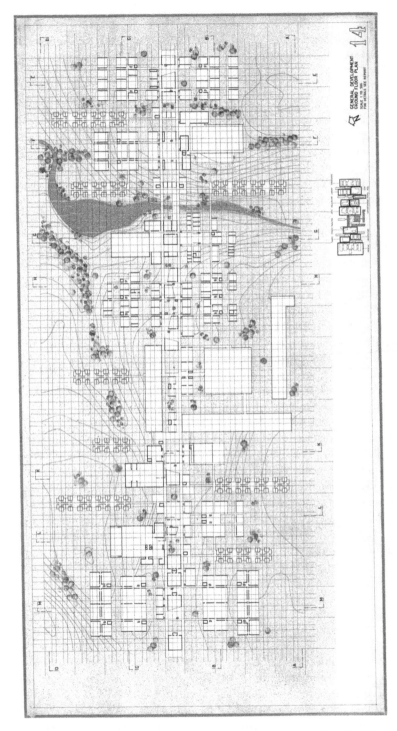

Figure 7.3 Giancarlo De Carlo, competition entry for University College Dublin (1962–64). General plan, scale 1:500.
Source: Università IUAV di Venezia, Archivio Progetti. Fondo Giancarlo De Carlo.

university projects, De Carlo's student residences mingled with other academic activities and concurred to activate the central spine throughout the whole day.[29]

Commenting on his plan, De Carlo wrote:

> The drawings show a determined final configuration: that was the only way to make explicit the system we are proposing. However, the solution we are showing is just one among the possible many. Moreover, it is very unlikely that this solution will actually correspond to reality once construction is over ... The plan is capable of total rearrangement, while still maintaining the order of the system.[30]

Modularity was thus not handled in terms of indefinite repetition of the same module – as was the case, for instance, at the Loughborough University of Technology designed by ARUP. At the same time, the grid remained as an underlying rationale that did not explicitly manifest itself in space. This was a major difference between De Carlo's project and Shadrach Woods's proposal for the Dublin competition that, as anticipated, reiterated the previous year's proposal for the Berlin Free University. As with his Berlin project, Woods materialised the underlying grid in the form of a horizontal landscape of rooms and courtyards that provided the canonical image for what was then labelled a mat-building.[31] It was precisely this materialisation that De Carlo explicitly criticised a few years later. In 1973, at a Team X meeting held in the newly built Free University, De Carlo commented on the project:

> Can a university become an opportunity for broad cultural interaction, which implies creative disorder, if its pattern is entirely and perpetually conditioned by the strait-jacket of a materialized grid? ... Shouldn't a grid be just an intellectual discipline that ought to fade out, and allow a counter-move of contradiction, as the generation of space and forms takes place? ... We are all indebted to Shad for the rediscovery of the grid as a powerful tool for reunifying varied architectural events. The grid cannot, however, be more than a frame. As soon as it becomes a closed system that compels activities and forms to adhere to its over-simplified geometry, the designing process freezes and authoritarianism manifests itself again.[32]

Woods's reply came in the form of a short poem entitled 'Remember the Spring of the Old Days?' in which he ironically claimed that 'the intellectual grid is all in your head'.[33]

It is indubitable that De Carlo and Woods shared an ethos about architecture's social significance. Indeed, these words by Woods could just as easily have been written by his Italian colleague: 'Education loses its relevance by being locked up in ivory towers. The theatre of our time is in the streets. Education, then, is urbanism. And urbanism is everybody's business, as is education'.[34]

Elaborating on the notion of an 'educational bazaar', these words come from a 1969 article, published alongside De Carlo's own essay 'Why/How to Build School Buildings', in a special issue of the *Harvard Educational Review* on 'Architecture and Education'.[35] While Woods's essay was a retroactive manifesto distilling lessons from projects already executed, De Carlo's text had the taste of a declaration of intentions that still had not reached their final coagulation in space. Contrasting Woods's choice to illustrate his essay with his own drawings and diagrams for Berlin and Dublin – which in turn presented the two projects as variations on the same idea – De Carlo did not relate to any of his own projects. Rather, he selected photographs of students protesting on the streets of Milan as illustrations of a potentially different idea of the university – one that was not contained within any four walls.[36]

Despite making similar claims for the city-as-university, Woods still hoped to solve the contradictions of higher education from within the architectural machinery. With their insistence on the need to break down barriers among the 'rings of isolation' inside a university, the diagrams for the Free University confirmed this interiorised approach.[37] And, while sharing an intention to reshuffle disciplines, the formal results achieved by the two architects were ultimately opposites, as demonstrated by their Dublin entries: a clearly controlled and controllable rectangular figure for Woods in contrast to the much less rigidly bounded settlement for De Carlo.

Differences extended to the proposed urbanistic action of a university. Woods understood it as a salvific presence within an already compromised condition. His university aimed to operate in a manner not too dissimilar from the regional shopping mall that had been pioneered by Victor Gruen in the United States to remediate the suburbanisation that was already in place.[38] With his invention, Gruen did not aim to subvert reality; rather, he accepted it, and tried to approach it from within by injecting a new social condenser wholly devoted to consumer culture. In a similar fashion, Woods conceived of the university as an opportunity for a new centrality within the European suburb. As suggested by Alexander Tzonis and Liane Lefaivre,[39] his aim was to attract the residents of Dahlem – 'one of the wealthiest suburbs in pre-war Europe'[40] – and 'make them rethink their views, shed their suburban identity, and ultimately be converted to a more humanistic way of life'.[41] The dense built mass of the university, placed in stark contrast to the sparse suburban area, was clearly oriented to this goal of social concentration.

The paradox of Woods's project – and probably the reason why it is still studied and considered a milestone of postwar architecture and urbanism – is that it concomitantly pursued and rejected formal configuration. Although it was promoted via the rhetoric of extensibility and open form, it was intrinsically finite, complete and stable. The overall form was defined *a priori* as the final result to be achieved. Inevitably, it could only end up as an inward-looking device that hoped to draw diversity from the outside due to the allegedly mighty mixing capabilities of its interior complexity.

Woods thus created a universal system – a prototype that could be endlessly reiterated.[42] Conversely, while sharing the same belief in a socially engaged architecture for the 'man in the street' – as a posthumously published book by Woods was titled[43] – De Carlo did not define a prototype. There was not, for De Carlo, the equivalent of a Berlin diagram that could be applied to subsequent projects. For him, the project for Dublin was a stepping stone towards the formulation of an alternative model of the university that he would later name 'university centre' (*centro universitario*) to oppose it to the traditional labels – the 'campus', the 'university complex' (*complesso universitario*). and the 'disarticulated university' (*università disaggregata per facoltà*).[44] None of the latter, he suggested, was capable of achieving the renovation of the academic institution that was being advocated in the 1960s.

Pavia (or diluting the university)

Whereas Shadrach Woods had found in the building the ultimate scale of application for a reshuffled university – although a new building (the mat-building) aimed to drastically rethink usual school typologies – De Carlo's willingness to disrupt the university could not stop at the scale of the building. His referent was the whole *città regione*, a scale that he reached with the plan for the University of Pavia, which responded to this definition given in 1968:

> In order to keep its consistency and integrity the University Centre does not need any unity of place: it can as well be articulated and intermingle within the urban fabric as long as the exchange among its parts continues unperturbed. In other words, it can be dispersed across the city and also use some of its parts without falling into pure disaggregation.[45]

De Carlo received the commission for a master plan from the University of Pavia's rector, Mario Rolla, in October 1970.[46] The commission included the overall reorganisation of the university inside the historic centre and a study for a new academic pole in a peripheral area.[47] and was split into three separate commissions: (1) an urban study and plan for the historic centre; (2) an urban study and plan for the peripheral area of Cravino; and (3) an architectural project for the Department of Engineering on the latter area. This allowed the budget for each commission to be contained below the limit indicated by the law (500 million liras, Law no. 641, 1967 – see Chapter 3) and beyond which the university would have had to launch a public competition.[48]

In fact, the university envisaged its reorganisation into two separate clusters corresponding to a conventional disciplinary division between the humanities and the sciences, with the former inhabiting the old fabric and the latter relocating to a brand new peripheral complex. This proposed division was clear evidence of that split between the 'two cultures' famously diagnosed by C.P. Snow in the 1950s and which, perhaps, appeared to the academic officials as an insurmountable obstacle. To De Carlo, on the other hand, the implementation of the twofold scheme envisaged by the university would be nothing but the confirmation of the status quo of a fragmented institution appropriate to most Italian universities.[49] As such, it had to be avoided, and he set out to show how this could be done by working from the outset on the idea of a multi-polar academic system.

The initial steps in setting up the plan were a questionnaire sent to all faculty members and a series of meetings with the academic community and local residents to discuss practical issues.[50] This methodology built upon the participatory planning that De Carlo was developing at the time for housing projects and which found in Villaggio Matteotti at Terni (1969–74) the first tangible response to De Carlo's polemical announcement intended to redirect architectural thinking away from orthodox modernist dictatorship: 'architecture is too important to be left to architects.'[51] Following this diktat, which was part of his 1970 essay 'Architecture's Public', still considered today seminal for the development of participatory planning and design,[52] between 1971 and 1973, the urban plan for Pavia was developed through twelve stages[53] according to a process of continuous consultation with various urban actors, including faculty members, local residents, landowners, city councillors, students, and possible benefactors (see Appendix 4).[54] De Carlo built his plan on top of what he considered the two complementary roles of a university: the 'continuous observation of reality' and the act of 'generalisation and theorisation'.[55] The university thus operated to balance, on the one hand, permeability towards the outer world, which implied the 'precise knowledge of the class conflicts of society',[56] and, on the other hand, 'technical autonomy', which required a certain degree of operative closure. The latter, as he had already argued in the Dublin competition, relied on the abolition of the barriers between disciplines that characterised the Italian university and obstructed circulation of information across the academic spectrum.

Neither a concentrated campus of Anglo-American derivation, with its striving for autonomy and self-enclosure, nor, despite its apparent mingling with the urban fabric, a dispersed university of European origins could achieve the two roles simultaneously. Even less could the accomplishment come from a typical Italian university, which De Carlo criticised as a deteriorated manifestation of the dispersed model. This 'disarticulated university' was merely the mirror of interior power conflicts that produced separate feuds corresponding to single faculties or even single chairs and professors. As such, this model was doubly unsuccessful, since it both failed to enable interdisciplinary investigation and it hid an even stronger willingness for isolation behind its apparently ubiquitous presence.

De Carlo's multi-polar alternative suggested that the very nature of the city, with its multiple and contradictory dimensions, could avoid the reiteration of closed loops of knowledge formation and instead nurture open-ended processes that would prevent the consolidation of power in fixed arrangements controlled from the top down. Like a city, knowledge was based on a continuous process of constant iteration, and it had to be continuously open to scrutiny and questioning.

For instability to be achieved, a dilution of power concentrations was needed. The plan for Pavia translated this into a literal dislocation of the academic presence onto a vast urban field and according to a taxonomy that envisaged three categories of university poles: central, intermediate and peripheral.[57] The central poles pursued the role of theorisation and were thus relatively more introverted. Nevertheless, being among the most complete parts of the university in terms of the facilities they needed for their everyday functioning, they constituted a major interface with the urban population through their museums, theatres, libraries, restaurants, sports facilities, and outdoor areas. The central pole in the area of Cravino – the one to be built from scratch as opposed to the other one housed inside the old seat of the university in the historic centre – added to its public service provision an experimental school to serve the local social housing neighbourhood and a centre providing information on the programme for further education for the workers recently launched by the Italian government.[58] Besides the central poles, the intermediate and peripheral poles were aimed at the direct observation of real-life phenomena and were located in closer contact with urban areas that lacked access to a sufficient array of services or that offered the subject matter for scientific inquiry (Figure 7.4).

Similar to what De Carlo had been doing in Urbino since the late 1950s, the theoretical multi-polar model was adapted to the physical fabric of Pavia via a mixture of new constructions and re-use of historic buildings. So, beyond the historical seat of the university one of the central poles encompassed two repurposed buildings – a former military barracks and an orphanage – chosen because their courtyard typology could lend the open spaces to general public use. This pole would be complemented by another, a new one on the site indicated by the university in its original two-area scheme. Faithful to De Carlo's wish to disrupt this scheme, the intermediate and peripheral poles were broken down into three categories – permanent, temporary and mobile poles – and dislocated across peripheral sites. The mobile poles, in particular, added to the idea of the university as a permanent territorial observatory in the form of literally nomadic structures travelling across the surrounding region because, as De Carlo put it, 'it is not difficult to imagine that, besides allowing the movement of people across a territory, a means of transport could fulfil educational functions, even if only at the level of observation or information'[59] – words that clearly recalled Cedric Price's university-on-a-railway, which was in fact an example selected by De Carlo in his research and book on the state of the art of university design and planning published in 1968.[60]

Taken together, the multiple components of the restructured university created a picture that was different both from the status quo and from the simplistic ideas to reform higher education proposed at a political level. Subverting the dictatorial regime of the mono-disciplinary faculties had been a central topic of debate for over a decade and the creation of multidisciplinary departments was widely considered the answer to the lack of communication across the academic system. Disillusioned with solutions that the system would very easily

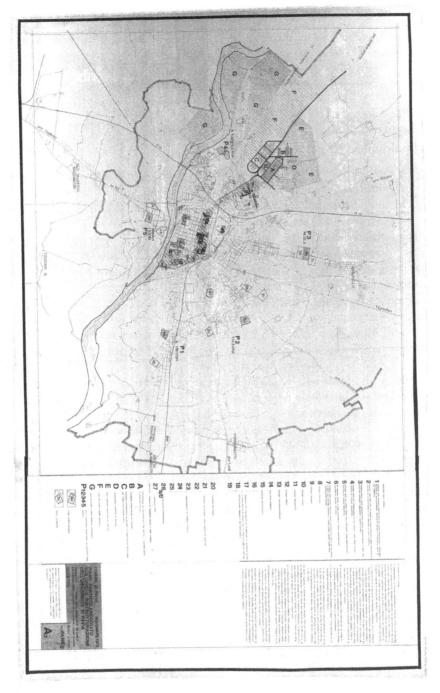

Figure 7.4 Giancarlo De Carlo, urban plan for the University of Pavia (1971–76). General plan, scale 1:10000.
Source: Università IUAV di Venezia, Archivio Progetti. Fondo Giancarlo De Carlo.

turn upside down to its own benefit by replicating the existing feudal organisation only through differently named institutes, De Carlo went beyond the
mere passage from a 'university of faculties' to a 'university of studies'. The
answer had to be more radical: the disruption of the equation:

education = educational building.

School buildings: why/how?

In the essays he wrote in parallel to his design work on universities, De Carlo
set out an overall reading and critique of the current state of higher education
in Italy and abroad, mixing a review of the student unrest and of the situation
of the schools of architecture in Italy in *La piramide rovesciata* (1968), a discussion of international case studies in *Pianificazione e disegno delle università*
(1968), an attack on the equation education = school building in 'Why/How to
Build School Buildings' (1969) and reflections on mass education in 'Il territorio
senza università' (1973).[61]

Using the metaphor of the pyramid to describe the academic power structure,
the first essay elaborated on how the Italian university was a strange kind of
pyramid. Although it retained a strong hierarchical structure, De Carlo noticed
how its vertex was not clearly identifiable; rather, it tended to blur within the
maze of national politics, eventually defining an institution deprived of any real
autonomy and made overly convoluted as a gigantic bureaucratic apparatus. *La
piramide rovesciata* stemmed from his observation of the student protests as they
developed throughout the 1960s in the Italian architecture schools in opposition
to the false consciousness of the government's reform proposals.[62]

De Carlo agreed with the students that the reform merely confirmed the old
logics that had historically governed the Italian university as an authoritarian
system. Taking a long historical excursus, he pointed out how a principle of
authority had ruled Italian higher education since the first post-medieval
expansion in the sixteenth century under the control of the Jesuits. Authority
was then reinforced immediately after the unification of Italy in 1861.[63] At a
time when the country needed a national modern university, De Carlo argued,
the government moulded one onto the worst features of the French and German
models: from the latter it took a certain detachment of research from reality,
while from the former it inherited an academic system kept firmly in the hands
of the State – a militarised university, as Martin Pawley unashamedly put it
around the same time.[64] Unsurprisingly, the fall into dictatorship during the
fascist period reinforced authoritarianism, also giving higher education the
structure it would take well into the postwar democratic turn. By the late
1960s, the principle of authority had not dissolved after twenty years of
democracy; rather, it had disintegrated into myriad small microcosms – the
disaggregated model. But more than the status quo, what De Carlo (and the
students) found alarming was the cure proposed by the State that proclaimed
the possible adjustment of the system through ad hoc operations. The result

was a mere enlargement of the old system to respond to expanding student numbers, rather than a proper rethinking of its very nature.

Quantity, for De Carlo, was just the visible tip of an iceberg of social change that was infecting all institutions and, in particular, education. 'Il territorio senza università', a conference paper presented in 1973, elaborated on the multiple challenges related to mass education by putting its author's reflections within the wider umbrella of the 'problem of the greater number', the phrase used by De Carlo and other Team X members to address the relationship between individuality and the collective in an age of homogenisation and commodification of values. As discussed by Tom Avermaete in relation to the work of Candilis, Josic, and Woods, De Carlo and his colleagues agreed that the greater number required 'a radical shift of attitudes within the realm of modern architecture, in which quantity was too often regarded negatively'.[65] It was the search for a positive reconsideration of the quantitative aspects of architecture and urbanism beyond the 'less is more' approach that characterised the modernist canon. Furthermore, it implied accepting that society had become all about greater numbers, as seemed evident from the notions of mass housing, mass education and mass leisure. Along these notions, postwar societies were being reshaped as traditional family-based relations gave way to a much more atomised, even anonymous, way of life.

De Carlo rejected as nonsense the very idea of a mass culture,[66] as well as the related one of a mass university, in particular if the latter was intended as the old elite university, the 'old Napoleonic and Humboldtian models' simply made bigger: 'the old models cannot be adapted to present needs because ... it is impossible to find the necessary financial resources'.[67] So, a larger university made of larger classrooms and laboratories for larger student numbers was not a smart solution enabling more democratic and open access to knowledge. Instead, the only way a larger university for a larger audience could make sense was if it catered to the empowerment of the individual. 'How can a university without individuals generate culture?' he later asked.[68] Choosing the theme of the greater number for the Fourteenth Milan Triennale that he directed in 1968 – and which never took place, due to student protests on the opening day[69] – he set out to raise public consciousness on the limitations on individual freedom imposed by welfare state policies in democratic disguise. One key institution used to such ends was the university, which De Carlo presented as the paradigm of the socio-cultural crisis of the times. In this analysis, the university could be rethought only by redefining a place for the individual who would be made responsible for his or her own self-formation. This was the role of a new model of the university, which De Carlo defined in *Pianificazione e disegno delle università*:[70]

> From a structural perspective the University Centre is an open organisational system. It is coherent with the principles pursued by the renewal of higher education, namely: the recovery of a unity of culture through the continuous exchange among different specialisations; the setup of a free

curriculum of studies; the unification of teaching; the expansion and inter-disciplinary convergence of research; the highest degree of mobility for group work; and the fluid and incessant interpenetration between university activities and the social and cultural activities of the city and its territory. From a morphological perspective the university centre is a flexible system of forms capable of adapting to a constantly changing organisation without ever losing its identity during its mutation.[71]

Echoing his equally slippery definition of *città regione* as a dynamic condition that replaces the fixity of the traditional city, these words hinted at the core of De Carlo's argument: a questioning of the school building as the dominant way of conceiving educational space. It was in the article published in the *Harvard Educational Review* in 1969 ('Why/How to Build School Buildings') that this argument was more explicitly elaborated and in which its author's anarchic mentality more powerfully emerged. Here he suggested that the main force hindering any possibility of consistently subverting the existing system was the persistent and anachronistic conceptualisation of institutional education in terms of unity of time and unity of place. Late twentieth-century advances in communication technologies allowed information to be transmitted at different times, with the time of the sender not necessarily having to coincide with the time of the receiver. As a consequence, the transfer of information no longer needed to happen in a specific place, or, at least, not solely in a specific place as the architecture of education still obtusely proposed.

The 1969 article was arranged in the form of a questionnaire, with the first question being crucial to De Carlo's argument. Asking 'Is it really necessary for contemporary society that educational activity be organized in a stable and codified institution?', the reply connected with the ideas of Ivan Illich, as it claimed that educational institutions hinder learning via the selection of a pur-posely limited set of tasks preventing the individual subject from engaging in a 'total experience' of learning. In De Carlo's words, the school was thus 'a physical structure exclusively dedicated to teaching, teachers, and students just as the prison is a physical structure exclusively dedicated to detention, wardens and inmates; its function is to accommodate a specific activity and isolate it from other activities'.[72] He went on to remind how the bulk of education – 'the richest and most active part' – happens outside school hours and outside a school building, 'or perhaps it has not yet found the appropriate spaces in which it could take place as a whole, becoming a part of a sphere of total experiences'.[73] Only during revolutions, when institutions get 'interrupted', De Carlo concluded, is total learning achieved – a statement that explains his interest in the student protests around the world as a powerful short-circuiting of the status quo.

In more general terms, De Carlo's reflections on education were equally as valid if considered as ruminations on architecture and its conventional logics that accorded a dominant role to enclosure. Questioning enclosure as archi-tecture's goal put the architect in a situation of identity crisis – a situation in which De Carlo gladly accepted to immerse himself. Inevitably, any response would remain trapped in the contradiction of giving formal value to the most a-formal of institutions. He tried to circumnavigate the problem by exploding the university, as he most clearly demonstrated in Pavia where he kept only the innermost, necessary academic core while removing the external envelope that had historically shielded it from outside interferences.

Time, however, proved the operation a failure. Reviewing the project for Pavia almost thirty years later and, more generally, reflecting on the aftermath of that brief period between the 1960s and 1970s of heroic belief in the possibility of subverting the traditional university and, by doing so, reinventing the city, De Carlo concluded:

> Like at the end of the 1940s, at the end of the sixties it looked like all common places on which the old world had been grounded were on the verge of collapsing. It was as if we had arrived at the threshold of a new world ... At the turn of the sixties and seventies there was a strong civic sense and the university had been put into deep crisis by the student revolts. Then, the institution recovered its old position, reaffirmed its traditional arrogance, and broke its pact with society ... The university has not only gone back to what it was before 1968; it has even worsened because its expansion turned it into a gigantic and detached body that suffocates the city. Students are considered but a mere accident; they could be totally discarded if it wasn't for the fact that they are essential for the reproduction of the system.[74]

Putting the accent again on the students is a way of rephrasing De Carlo's concern towards architecture's public instead of architecture per se. Yet this is only partly a similar position to the fierce accusation levelled against architecture by Archizoom that I discussed in Chapter 6. As I have already pointed out, where the Florentine group rejected any possible 'project of roofs' – that is, any formal configuration of walls and other architectural elements – as capable of representing society at a given moment in history, and found refuge in furniture and object design, De Carlo remained faithful to the profession of architecture, his *œuvre* ultimately being of skilful mastery of space through the articulation of architecture's traditional vocabulary. On another point, however, De Carlo agreed with the radicals, and this is the idea that the built world is the register of human activity happening at the divide between collectiveness and individuality. Perhaps less emphatically anti-architectural than Archizoom's chairs and tables scattered on a continuous grid, the plans drawn for Urbino, Dublin and Pavia, with their scaling-up of ambition, argued that a similarly vast territorial extension could be reached only by considering the academic institution as the sum total of inevitably different individuals. Perhaps, De Carlo even went a step further, surpassing Archizoom's carefully drawn repetitiveness and, ultimately, accepting the possibility of disorder.

Notes

1 Giancarlo De Carlo, *La piramide rovesciata* (Bari: De Donato, 1968), 5.

2 Giancarlo De Carlo et al., *La nuova dimensione della città: La città-regione* (Milan: ILSES, 1962).

3 Joseph Rykwert, 'Universities as Institutional Archetypes of Our Age', *Zodiac* 18 (1968): 61–63.

4 Franco Buncuga, *Conversazioni con Giancarlo De Carlo: Architettura e libertà* (Milan: Elèuthera, 2000), 151.

5 Giancarlo De Carlo, ed., *Pianificazione e disegno delle università* (Rome: Edizioni universitarie italiane, 1968), 14.

6 The 'hierarchy of human associations' was first discussed by Alison and Peter Smithson at the eleventh meeting of CIAM in Otterlo in 1959, which famously marked the end of CIAM and the birth of a new chapter in the history of modernism under the auspices of Team X. The Smithsons developed an argument about 'the problem of re-identifying man with his environment' that proposed to change the categories on which urbanism and architecture had operated during the first half of the twentieth century by constructing 'a hierarchy of human associations which should replace the functional hierarchy of the Charte d'Athènes'. Instead of categories such as 'house-groupings, streets, squares, greens, etc.', they proposed to consider the human environment as based on four levels of human association: 'the house,' the street, the district, the city'. See Oscar Newman, *CIAM '59 in Otterlo* (Stuttgart: K. Krämer, 1961), 68.

7 The project for Berlin was amply covered by the international magazines on architecture. See, in particular, *Architectural Design* 8 (1964), issue on Team X; *Architectural Design* 1 (1974); and Shadrach Woods, *Free University Berlin*, ed. John Donat (New York: The Viking Press, 1965), 116–17. See also Gabriel Feld et al., eds., *Free University, Berlin: Candilis, Josic, Woods, Schiedhelm* (London: Architectural Association, 1999). For a general discussion of the work of Candilis, Josic, and Woods, see Tom Avermaete, *Another Modern: The Post-War Architecture and Urbanism of Candilis-Josic-Woods* (Rotterdam: NAi, 2005).

8 See Buncuga, *Conversazioni con Giancarlo De Carlo*.

9 An occasion at which all these figures gathered to discuss common ideas about de-institutionalisation and the empowerment of the self was a congress on 'Auto-costruzione e tecnologie conviviali' ('Self-Build and Convivial Technologies') held in Rimini on 1–2 March 1980 by the collective Collettivo per un abitare autogestito. Some of the papers presented at the congress were published in Renzo Agostini et al., eds., *Il potere di abitare* (Florence: Libreria Editrice Fiorentina, 1982).

10 See Chapter 1 and the related notes.

11 The term *Universicittà* was used by De Carlo in an article published in 1976 where he presented his proposal for the University of Pavia: Giancarlo De Carlo, 'Un caso di studio: L'universicittà di Pavia', *Parametro* 44 (1976): 20–22.

12 For an overall account of De Carlo's work in Urbino, see Giancarlo De Carlo and Pierluigi Nicolin, 'Conversation on Urbino', *Lotus International* 18 (1978): 6–22.

13 Giancarlo De Carlo, *Urbino: La storia di una città e il piano della sua evoluzione urbanistica* (Padua: Marsilio, 1966).

14 De Carlo's main interventions inside the historic core of Urbino were the Faculty of Law (1966–68, in a former convent), the Faculty of Letters (1968–76, in a former orphanage), and the area of Mercatale where he designed a theatre and a garden.

15 De Carlo contributed to the debate on *città regione* in various ways and on different occasions. In 1959, he took part in the roundtable on the topic at the Ninth Congress of the Italian Urbanists Association (INU) held in Lecce (see Chapter 2). In 1962, as part of the research programme on metropolitan areas, of which he was the director, he organised on behalf of ILSES (Istituto Lombardo per gli Studi Economici e Sociali)

the international seminar 'La nuova dimensione della città – la città regione'. The seminar promoted an interdisciplinary approach to urban studies that would eventually become institutionalised by the promoters of integrated planning, as exemplified by the work of Centro Piani and their *Progetto '80*. See De Carlo *et al.*, *La nuova dimensione della città* (see also Chapter 2). Also in 1962, he participated in a roundtable discussion organised by Saul Greco and Carlo Aymonino on 'La città territorio'. See Carlo Aymonino *et al.*, ed., *La città territorio: Un esperimento didattico sul centro direzionaled di centocelle in Roma* (Bari: Leonardo da Vinci Editrice, 1964).

16 Giancarlo De Carlo, 'Relazione conclusiva al seminario dell'ILSES sulla nuova dimensione e la città-regione', in *La nuova dimensione della città*.

17 Discussing the project for the University of East Anglia at a symposium held at the University of Sussex in July 1964 and organised by the Architectural Association and the Royal Institute of British Architects, the university's vice chancellor, Frank Thistlethwaite, said:

There was clearly a need to provide some architectural means for fostering the undergraduate's natural inclination to live cosily, bearing in mind that students like to live, as well as be taught, in small groups. To solve the problem we turned back for inspiration, not to the college, but to what some would regard as its secret strength: the staircase.

See Frank Thistlethwaite, 'University of East Anglia', in Michael Brawne, ed., *University Planning and Design: A Symposium* (London: Lund Humphries for the Architectural Association, 1967), 39.

18 Buncuga, *Conversazioni con Giancarlo De Carlo*, 156.

19 See Alison and Peter Smithson, *The Charged Void: Architecture* (New York: Monacelli Press, 2000); and Alison and Peter Smithson, *The Charged Void: Urbanism* (New York: Monacelli Press, 2005).

20 See Avermaete, *Another Modern*.

21 Giancarlo De Carlo, *Proposta per una struttura universitaria* (Venice: Cluva, 1965), 2.

22 Ibid.

23 Out of 105 entries received from twenty-four countries, the first prize went to Andrzej Wejchert from Poland who proposed a scheme of detached pavilions kept together by walkways. The second prize was awarded to Brian Crumlish and Don Sporleder from the United States, and the third prize to a team headed by Vladimir Machonin from Czechoslovakia. See 'Assessor's Report and Award of the "International Architectural Competition for the Site Layout of the New Buildings for the College and for a Block for the Faculty of Arts (with Associated Faculties), Administrative Offices and Examination Halls"', July 1964. Avery Drawings & Archives, Shadrach Woods Archive, Papers collection, Avery Box 12.

24 De Carlo, *Proposta per una struttura universitaria*, 3.

25 See *Casabella-Continuità* 290 (1964), a monographic issue on the Thirteenth Triennale.

26 De Carlo, *Pianificazione e disegno delle università*, 31–32.

27 Ibid., 31: 'All parts of a university are services in so far as each pursues its role in a relation of dependency to all others'. My translation.

28 'To pass from one element to another there is a wide choice of routes, the principal, the secondary or the exterior tertiary, or one can pass over the main route and take another line on the other side': De Carlo, *Proposta per una struttura universitaria*, 6.

29 De Carlo deployed a double-ladder diagram of circulation in the Dublin project with vehicular traffic serving the buildings from the outside and pedestrians accessing the buildings from the central spine. The project aligned with much of the contemporary university design production, as evidenced by various projects he compiled in *Pianificazione e disegno delle università*. Similar decisions were identifiable in the projects for the University of Middle East in Ankara (by Cinici and Cinici), the University of

Zambia (by Julian Elliott) and the University of Bath (by Matthew & Johnson-Marshall).

30 De Carlo, *Proposta per una struttura universitaria*, 8.

31 See Alison Smithson, 'How to Recognise and Read Mat Building', *Architectural Design* 9 (1974): 573–590. Smithson took the completion of a first part of the Free University to dig back in time and 'recognise those thing that led up to it' (p. 574). For a wider discussion on mat-building, see Hashim Sarkis, ed., *Le Corbusier's Venice Hospital and the Mat Building Revival* (Munich: Prestel Verlag, 2001). For a comparative discussion of the De Carlo's and Woods's approaches to higher education reform and university design, see Francesco Zuddas, 'Pretentious Equivalence: De Carlo, Woods and Mat-Building', *FA Magazine* 34 (2015): 45–65.

32 Giancarlo De Carlo, 'Comment on the Free University', *Architecture Plus* 2, 1 (1974): 51. These words come from the publication of the comments made by the other Team X members at the meeting in 1973 on the construction site of the Berlin Free University, which Shadrach Woods could not attend. Woods asked Manfred Schiedhelm, a collaborator on the competition project in 1963 and subsequently the director of Candilis, Josic and Woods's office in Berlin during construction of the university, to present the project at the meeting. The discussion was taped and sent to Woods who later replied in poem form (see note 33). The tape is held in Avery Drawings & Archives, Shadrach Woods Archive, Columbia University, New York.

33 Shadrach Woods, 'Remember the Spring of the Old Days?', *Architecture Plus* 2, 1 (1974): 51.

34 Ibid.

35 Giancarlo De Carlo, 'Why/How to Build School Buildings', *Harvard Educational Review* 4, no. 4 (1969): 12–35; Shadrach Woods, 'The Education Bazaar', *Harvard Educational Review* 4, no. 4 (1969): 116–125. Besides the texts by De Carlo and Woods, the special issue of the *Harvard Educational Review* included contributions by James Ackerman, Saul Steinberg, Herman Hertzberger, and Aldo Van Eyck. A preliminary handwritten draft of Woods's article entitled 'The Education Super Mart' is held at Avery Drawings & Archives, Shadrach Woods Archive, Papers collection, Feld Box 08.

36 De Carlo in 'Why/How to Build School Buildings', 16, stated:
    With the student revolt, education has returned to the city and to the streets and has, thus, found a field of rich and diversified experience which is much more formative than that offered by the old school system. Perhaps we are headed toward an era in which education and total experience will again coincide …

37 Some conceptual diagrams for the Berlin Free University were published in the *The Architectural Review* 806 (1964). The complete series, which Woods later reproduced in 'The Education Bazaar', appeared in Woods, *Free University Berlin*, 116–117.

38 See Alex Wall, *Victor Gruen: From Urban Shop to New City* (Barcelona: Actar, 2005).

39 Alexander Tzonis and Liane Lefaivre, 'Beyond Monuments, Beyond Zip-a-Tone, into Space/Time', in *Free University Berlin: Candilis, Josic, Woods, Schiedhelm* (London: AA Publications, 1999), 138.

40 Ibid.

41 Ibid.

42 Three iterations of the mat-building as applied to university design are found within the portfolio of Candilis, Josic and Woods, namely, the projects for Berlin and Dublin and the academic complex proposed to fill the space between the residential 'stems' at Toulouse-Le Mirail.

43 Shadrach Woods, *The Man in the Street: A Polemic on Urbanism* (Baltimore, MD: Penguin Books, 1975).

44 De Carlo first formulated this classification of university planning models in the introductory text to *Pianificazione e disegno delle università* in 1968 (pp. 9–34). He

returned to it in subsequent texts: Giancarlo De Carlo, 'Il territorio senza università', *Parametro* 21–22 (1973): 38–39; and 'Un ruolo diverso dell'università: Il modello multipolare per l'Università di Pavia', in Giuseppe Rebecchini, *Progettare l'università* (Rome: Edizioni Kappa, 1981), 144–151.

45 De Carlo, *Pianificazione e disegno delle università*, 31.

46 Collaborators on the project were Fausto Colombo, Antonio di Mambro, Gianni Ottolini, Antonio Vecchi, Carla Zamboni, Bruno Dell'Era, Akinori Kato, and Vittorio Korach as consultant structural engineer.

47 See Giancarlo De Carlo, 'Pavia Piano Universitario: Relazione generale', 18 February 1974. Università Iuav, Archivio Progetti, Fondo De Carlo, pro/057.1/18/22, 040550.

48 The University of Pavia opted to use national funds only for the architectural project of the Department of Engineering, whereas the two urban studies would be financed by autonomous funds. The plans were submitted for approval by the university in 1974 after having been approved by the municipality of Pavia.

49 According to De Carlo:
    With few exceptions, the universities inside Italian cities are fragmented and dispersed in the urban fabric, suffering from strong isolation that is disadvantageous as much to social development as to the development of the neighbourhoods within which the university fragments are randomly located. ('Un caso di studio', 20. My translation)

50 A preliminary discussion on the development opportunities for the University of Pavia took place at a conference on 22 May 1971 among representatives of the academic community and the municipality (Incontro di studio sullo sviluppo dell'Università di Pavia). See De Carlo, 'Pavia Piano Universitario'.

51 Giancarlo De Carlo, 'Il pubblico dell'architettura', *Parametro* 1, no. 5 (1970): 4–12.

52 The essay was chosen as the opener to a collection of recent essays on participation and was republished as Giancarlo De Carlo, 'Architecture's Public', in *Architecture and Participation*, ed. Peter Blundell Jones, Doina Petrescu, and Jeremy Till (London: Spon Press, 2005), 3–18.

53 The twelve stages were: 1 (30/03/72) – study of the situation of the university and the student population, possible scenarios of growth, first localisation hypotheses in the historic centre, and accessibility studies for the area of Cravino. 2 (30/05/72) – re-use of former barracks inside the historic centre (Caserma Calchi) for the Department of Political Sciences. 3 (21/07/72) – re-zoning proposal for the Cravino area from agricultural to university use. 4-5 (7/11/72) – modification request of the city plan regarding the area around the former Caserma Calchi and preliminary project for the engineering pole in the Cravino area. 6 (23/11/72) – preliminary project for sport facilities in the Cravino area. 7-8-9 (10/05/73) – preliminary projects for the Department of Economics, the Department of Biological Studies, and the Department of Pharmacy. 10 (15/06/73) – preliminary project for the Department of Mathematics. 11 (3/12/73) – development plan submitted to the municipality of Pavia ('Piano per la ristrutturazione urbanistica dell'Università di Pavia'). 12 (4/12/73) – report produced by Gianni Ottolini and Remo Dorigati on the decentralisation of the university.

54 In December 1970, an unidentified woman (referred to as 'signora benefattrice' in the 1974 report produced by De Carlo) stated her willingness to donate two billion liras for an extension of the Collegio Ghislieri, one of several colleges in Pavia. The extension was to be located in the area of Cravino and a project was proposed by De Carlo's team. However, the benefactress's idea of an introverted college modelled on traditional ones was opposite to De Carlo's idea of opening up the academic community. The project was thus abandoned and the benefactress funded the college independently of De Carlo's plan. See De Carlo, 'Pavia piano universitario'.

55 Ibid., 38.

56 Ibid.

57 Ibid., 40.

58 The workers statute (Statuto dei Lavoratori) was passed in 1970 with Law no. 300, 'Norme sulla tutela della libertà e dignità dei lavoratori, della libertà sindacale e dell'attività sindacale nei luoghi di lavoro e norme sul collocamento'. It introduced the notion of the student-worker and established an allowance of 150 hours for further education to be included in contracts.

59 De Carlo, 'Pavia piano universitario', 43.

60 De Carlo, *Pianificazione e disegno delle università*.

61 *La piramide rovesciata* (Bari: De Donato, 1968) derived from a conference paper read by De Carlo on 2 February 1968 in Turin and subsequently presented in Genoa, Milan and Rome in the following months; 'Why/How to Build School Buildings' was republished in *Casabella* 368–369 (1972): 65–71 with the title 'Ordine, istituzione, educazione, disordine'. *Pianificazione e disegno delle università* was the outcome of a two-year research project funded by the Italian Ministry of Public Education and developed by De Carlo in conjunction with his courses on urban planning at IUAV in Venice. In addition to these texts, while a visiting professor at the Massachusetts Institute of Technology in 1967, De Carlo led a design studio for a university-led redevelopment of the South End area of Boston.

62 The pamphlet – as the publisher, De Donato, called *La piramide rovesciata* on the back cover – was composed of two parts: De Carlo's own text, which was a reworked version of the paper presented in Turin, and a collection of documents produced by the student assemblies at the schools of architecture across Italy. For a reconstruction of the context from which *La piramide rovesciata* stemmed, see the introduction by Filippo De Pieri to the new edition of the book: Filippo De Pieri, 'Il breve e il lungo '68 di Giancarlo De Carlo', in *La piramide rovesciata: Architettura oltre il '68*, ed. Filippo De Pieri (Macerata: Quodlibet, 2018), 7–36.

63 De Carlo, *La piramide rovesciata*.

64 See Martin Pawley, 'The Demilitarisation of the University', *Architectural Design* 4 (1972): 216–219.

65 Avermaete, *Another Modern*.

66 'Mass culture does not exist; the mass cannot have culture': Bunčuga, *Conversazioni con Giancarlo De Carlo*, 163.

67 De Carlo, 'Il territorio senza università', 38.

68 Bunčuga, *Conversazioni con Giancarlo De Carlo*, 163.

69 On the Fourteenth Triennale of 1968, see Carlo Guenzi, 'La triennale del re', *Casabella* 333 (1969); 'Dibattito sulla triennale', *Casabella* 333 (1969); 'Milano XIV Triennale', *Domus* 466 (1968). For a recent reading, see Paola Nicolin, *Castelli di Carte: La XIV Triennale di Milano* (Macerata: Quodlibet, 2011).

70 *Pianificazione e disegno delle università* presented a selection of recent international projects for universities alongside essays by foreign contributors discussing the state of the art of university planning in Britain, the United States, France, Germany, Switzerland, Japan, and the USSR. In his Introduction, De Carlo discussed the Italian university and anticipated some of the topics that would be central in his project for Pavia, such as the notion of permeability of academic buildings, the principles of spatial and temporal diffusion of higher education, and the university's direct relationship with its immediate context. The book is one among many collections of international projects for new universities that were published in the 1960s and the 1970s.

71 De Carlo, *Pianificazione e disegno delle università*, 30.

72 De Carlo, 'Why/How to Build School Buildings', 17.

73 Ibid., 19.

74 Bunčuga, *Conversazioni con Giancarlo De Carlo*, 121–126.

8   The anti-city

Guido Canella and the nomadic university

A system of learning

On 23 November 1971, the Italian Ministry of Education suspended eight members of the architecture faculty at the Politecnico di Milano, indicting them for collusion with students who were sheltering in a group of shanties inside the university halls. The academics included the dean of school, Paolo Portoghesi, and professors Franco Albini, Lodovico Barbiano di Belgioioso, Piero Bottoni, Guido Canella, Carlo De Carli, Aldo Rossi, and Vittoriano Viganò. (Figure 8.1). Spanning two generations – the oldest was Bottoni (1903–1973) and the youngest were Portoghesi, Canella and Rossi (all born in 1931) – they represented the most progressive part of a faculty that had, since 1967, supported students' requests for a radical restructuring of the architectural curriculum. Hosting a group of shantytown dwellers was only the most ostentatious in a series of ideas to renovate the outdated methodologies and preoccupations of the school and, more generally, the role of a university.

Between 1963 – when students first occupied the school of architecture – and 1974 – the year of the readmission of the suspended eight – the Politecnico di Milano experienced its own cultural revolution[1] to 'transform architectural education from discipline-based to problem-and-research-based', as Portoghesi commented on it.[2] 'Research' was the single word most uttered at the time to express the desire of disrupting a learning process still grounded on one-way instruction from professor to students and the repetition of the same old curriculum and design exercises of alleged professionalising value. In the 1960s, architectural education was largely intended as a training ground for practice and little space was left for free investigations into the wider domains implied in an architect's work. It was precisely to expand the gaze towards a wider scope that the Milanese revolution aimed, driven by unbiased ideological inclinations.

A glance at the titles of some of the research projects that were proposed to be developed collectively across full faculty members, teaching assistants and students, provides clear evidence of the politicisation permeating that moment: 'The condition of housing for the working class' (Maurice Cerasi), 'Tools of Marxist culture for architectural and urban criticism' (Paolo Portoghesi), 'History of modern architecture as bourgeois architecture in power' (Portoghesi and

Figure 8.1 Photo taken outside of the Politecnico di Milano during the student occupa-
tion in May 1971. In front of the military, from left: Fredi Drugman, Guido
Canella, Paolo Portoghesi (with megaphone), Federico Oliva, Pierluigi
Nicolin.
Source: Courtesy Studio Portoghesi, Rome.

Vercelloni), 'The struggles of the building worker' (Bianca Bottero), 'Social
struggles in the creation and use of the Milanese urban environment' (Giuseppe
Campos Venuti) and 'The factory city' (Alberto Magnaghi). Even more
unequivocally imbued in ideological referencing was the 'Document of the
October Revolution', a manifesto signed by some of the younger academics,
which endorsed the teaching experimentation and refused a professionalising
role for the university:

> We don't want to normalise the university so that it can be aligned with
> the system – wrote the authors of the document. Rather, we want to set up
> a condition that can expand the university's role in attacking the system at
> its weakest part, namely education for the few and culture subsumed to
> Capital.[3]

Among the signatories were Guido Canella and Aldo Rossi who, besides their
year of birth, shared a common status as Ernesto Nathan Rogers's protégés.
Like Rossi, Canella was a member of the editorial team at *Casabella*[4] and his
affiliation with Rogers extended to the teaching realm through his role as
teaching assistant on Rogers's third-year course on 'Elementi di composizione'.

The collaboration with Rogers left a fundamental mark on Canella's own approach to pedagogy, making him one of the most radical teaching innovators in the faculty.[5]

Between 1963 and 1971 – the year of his academic suspension – Canella wrote briefs for design studios that interpreted the student requests for closer ties between university education and real-life problems. In as much as they aimed to contribute to architectural theorisation – especially elaborating on the then popular notions of typology and morphology – the studios were experiments with mass education, which required rethinking teaching methodologies to adapt to ever increasing student cohorts. To understand this twofold objective, there is no better index than the sequence of themes explored in the studios: the school (1962–63 and 1963–64, with Rogers), the theatre (1964–65 and 1965–66, when Canella and Rogers ran parallel modules), the prison (1966–67), the university (1967–68 and 1968–69), and the expo centre (1969–70 and 1970–71). Taken together, these constituted what Canella called a 'system of learning', the title he gave to a research report produced in 1971 at the end of this first phase of his teaching activity.[6]

Politecnico di Milano 1963–74: experiment with a mass university

Commenting on the period of teaching experimentation in Milan, Portoghesi framed it as an active response to the political impasse in which reform of higher education in Italy had been trapped for years. While the idea of reorganising universities around interdisciplinary departments had not yet achieved consensus, the Milanese school of architecture had independently set up its own 'open department'. This, however, had not happened smoothly: the experimentation in Milan had been shaped by continuous conflicts among those involved, both within and outside the school of architecture.

Written in 1973, when still expiating the sentence inflicted on him by the Ministry of Education, Portoghesi's comments introduced an issue of *Controspazio* wholly devoted to discussing the school of architecture in Milan.[7] The editor of *Controspazio* since its foundation in 1969 as a magazine born with the twofold (and subtly contradictory) objective of reconnecting architecture with politics while also sustaining the autonomous discourse of architecture against the growing interdisciplinary fascinations of the 1960s as well as against *Casabella*'s incursions into product design under the directorship of Alessandro Mendini between 1970 and 1976, Portoghesi had also been the dean of the Milanese architecture school since 1968, when he was elected to replace Carlo De Carli after the latter had been deposed by the Ministry of Education for his excessive anti-conformism.[8] De Carli was the first victim of repeated acts of repression by the State against the experimental spirit promoted by the architecture students and vitally supported by a group of progressive professors. In fact, as much as the Student Movement claimed a hegemonic role in reorienting the methods of work within the school away from its old-fashioned academic structure and towards an alignment with real-world problems, the cultural revolution that was put in place in Milan could not have been achieved without a unique dialogue established between students and teachers. This was not, however, a peaceful path, but one marked by the jealousies and concealed attempts at accumulating power that undermined any project of direct democracy.

The Milanese students had, in 1963, started asking to update curricula and for more direct involvement with the daily management of the university. Since then, they had been advocating a switch from sterile and technical academic exercises supervised by the professors to research activities conducted collaboratively with them. Following an initially negative response by the faculty and the subsequent occupation of the school by the students (the first such in Italy, and one that opened the way to 1968), a mixed committee of faculty and students began discussions on the possible modifications to curricula and programmes, as a result of which they reached some agreements that helped ease tension for a few years. Peace did not last long and, triggered by the events happening at Berkeley and other universities worldwide in 1967, a growing political consciousness in the students led to their consolidation into a student movement that aimed at direct government of the university. Taking advantage of a newsletter by Luigi Gui, the Minister of Education, that allowed the schools of architecture to undertake 'prudent experimentation for the renovation of curricula',[9] the attack on the academic power structures found its first mature elaboration in a declaration of opposition to 'a service of the bourgeois society that guarantees the reproduction of qualified technicians while simultaneously generating consensus towards the System through the transmission of ideological culture'.[10] More generally, the critique was targeted at the higher education reform proposal that Gui had presented in 1965 and that after two years was still being debated in parliament. Among the main points of the proposal were the establishment of a three-tier degree system and of the departments, the latter conceived as a solution to the isolation between single-discipline faculties. In the eyes of the students, the proposals merely shuffled the existing situation without, however, impacting on the very balance of power, so that the university that would come out of the reform would be basically the same institution as before, perhaps just with more students.[11]

Taking the Politecnico as a laboratory to test alternatives to the reform, the architecture students made three radical proposals. The first was the abolition of all exams and of the existing system of prerequisites that set a rigid sequence in the curriculum, and their replacement with discussion seminars happening at various moments through the academic year. A second point posited the centrality of research as a learning methodology. The three-tier system of university degrees – *diploma*, *laurea*, and *dottorato* – proposed in the 1965 higher education reform allegedly aimed at opening up university pathways to a wider section of society. According to the students, however, it would only augment the traditional discriminatory nature of institutional education, further differentiating opportunities according to socio-economic conditions, and promoting research as an activity open only to the few. Research, they claimed, had to be extended to all as the very founding logic of higher learning. Finally, a third point took aim at the professionalisation role of universities and argued for a school of architecture as a place in which theoretical and ideological positions were critically considered.[12]

The Student Movement's requests found the support of the recently elected dean, Carlo De Carli, who committed to the idea of using the architecture school as a laboratory of teaching experimentation. This resulted in the establishment of 'horizontal' research groups comprising professors, assistants and students (and allowing the latter to mix regardless of their year of enrolment). Even more radical were the decision-making mechanisms about programmes and themes, which would be proposed by the professors and agreed in consultation with the students.

An obvious threat to central authority, the experimentation unsurprisingly walked into a minefield from day one. In February 1968, as the formal activities of the school were temporarily suspended to allow for a collegiate seminar discussing the contents for the new academic year, the Minister of Education sent a letter to the Politecnico's rector intimating that the academic year might have been invalidated had normal teaching activities not already begun. In turn, the rector addressed a letter to De Carli with the provocative title 'Nil sub sole novi' ('nothing new under the sun'), in which, citing the repressed attempt by students in Turin in 1799 to overturn power, unmistakably highlighted the risky position of the dean. A risk soon turned into reality, as De Carli was dethroned by ministerial decision.

De Carli's progressive views, expressed in his idea of education as a 'gathering: speaking of human affairs, and not having exams because we have already discussed at length',[13] were confirmed by his follower, Paolo Portoghesi, who declared his willingness to continue supporting the Student Movement. Yet the programme he proposed at the beginning of the 1968–69 academic year was as much opposed by the students as by De Carli himself, with the latter accusing his successor of re-centralising decision-making. Portoghesi attempted to restore order to the experimental environment of the school by defining clearer rules, such as a prescribed number (twelve) of research projects that each student should complete in order to graduate, and a sequence of three consecutive stages within the five-year curriculum. With the events of May 1968 still fresh in the memory, the mantra had now become the total opposition to the status quo and any attempt to restore power would inevitably be rejected by the students – as they did with Portoghesi's plan.

But opposition was not limited to the students, since it also met with the support of a group of professors. The 'Document of the October Revolution' targeted Portoghesi's plan and confirmed the urgency of continuing a radical teaching experimentation – a position firmly promoted by Guido Canella.

The complication of school

Alongside Vittorio Gregotti, in 1962–63, Canella was an assistant to Ernesto Nathan Rogers. From Rogers, he received a strong pedagogic imprint and to him he also owed his earlier opportunities to position himself as an essayist on architecture. After two articles co-authored with Rossi, one on industrial design and the other on the work of Mario Ridolfi, Canella's career was facilitated through Rogers's *Casabella*, starting with an essay written in 1957 on the school of Amsterdam of the 1910s–1930s.[14] As noted by Paolo Portoghesi, this article provided evidence of Canella's controversial biography. He was born to a middle-class family that already nurtured architecture, as his older brother, Luciano, was a respected Milanese architect. Whereas his brother did not disdain working to the architectural briefs of Milanese bourgeois society, such as the design of typical middle-class dwellings,[15] Canella always showed an oppositional attitude that eventually led him to decide to fully devote his career to public and civic commissions. Yet, his was not mere outright refusal of bourgeois values as, in the words of Portoghesi, 'He did not ignore the guilt and ambiguity of a social class whose distress and decadence he understood but that he also appreciated for its extraordinary self-criticism and to which he was not ashamed to belong.'[16] The specific bourgeois class that attracted Canella, Portoghesi observed, was exactly the one represented by the architects he discussed in his first *Casabella* essay, in which he considered the work of Berlage, Behrens and de Klerk as evidence of architecture's civic engagement.

But more than his essays,[17] or even his practice work, it was his teaching that characterised Canella as an innovator – although with the contradictions to be expected of his Janus-faced persona trapped between bourgeois values and progressive views. The 1962–63 design studio with Rogers, which focused on the design of primary schools, provided him with the entry point into the problems of mass education, as well as of architecture for the mass society more generally.[18] Convinced that 'the School is a laboratory of culture and not a gigantic bureaucratic technical office',[19] Rogers opposed traditional teaching based on the cyclical repetition of pedantic exercises and briefs, and he set up a working methodology that assimilated the design studio to a research group aimed at the cultivation of an architect's civic responsibilities. In the book *L'utopia della realtà*, published in 1965 and presenting the projects and ideas discussed during the two-year design course on the primary school, Rogers wrote:

> The more you communicate to them [the students] that the past continues through them, the more will they take pride and responsibility in creating a future in which the current day might be seen as a past worthy of belonging to collective memory.[20]

Between the lines of this statement was a reiteration of Rogers's belief in the continuity of history and, by extension, of architecture as practice and theory.[21] Reclaiming continuity also implied, as a postulate, a careful balancing between an enabling attitude towards the cultivation of the students' socio-political conscience and the conservation of discipline and control. In other words, Rogers's sentiments appear to rule out revolution and opt for more cautious reformism.

Yet his innovatory charge within the traditional academicism of the early 1960s is indisputable, as Canella himself recognised by calling it a response to the pedagogic alternative, requested by the students, that aimed to instil self-reflection on the condition of the learner.[22] In his text published in *L'utopia della realtà* he noted that more than for 'sociologic or demagogic motivations' the topic of the school was chosen because it enabled university students to reflect on themselves by looking at their previous experiences as learners.[23] This idea embedded awareness of the impossibility of solving the crisis of higher education by considering it in isolation from the rest of the learning system. Moreover, it highlighted the urgency of expanding the definition of what constituted this system – a definition that had to go beyond a traditional understanding of school.[24]

An expanded notion of school was the first occasion for Canella to reflect on what he regarded as a complication of the architectural concept of typology. In his early writings he often returned to a description of the postwar urban condition as one that had left behind the rigidity of functional typologies codified in the nineteenth century.[25] At the basis of his critique of typology was a political position that opposed the degeneration arising from bourgeois culture, as he expressed more clearly at a seminar on architectural design theory (*teoria della progettazione architettonica*) organised by Giuseppe Samonà at the Istituto Universitario di Venezia (IUAV) in the academic year 1965–66.[26] The concept of building type, he suggested, had been neutralised by the bourgeois construction of the city according to private prerogatives. Reducing urban space to classifiable types was an objectification of architecture subsumed to the needs of the accumulation inherent in capitalism, which enabled a 'process of stratification that is presented as irreversible'.[27] A way out of such simplification was offered by the complexity of the functions of a modern city, where any definite taxonomy no longer held true so that, by the late twentieth century, it had become impossible to categorise a building type with the same degree of certainty as in the past. Favourite pieces of evidence that Canella frequently mentioned in his lectures and writings were the American shopping centres or the Italian *centri direzionali*, both of which aimed at functional congestion across the domains of work, commerce and leisure.[28]

From the outset of his teaching activity, Canella posed to the students the problem of functional complexity, and on the course with Rogers he proposed that a school should be understood as an 'uninterrupted activity for human development [that] is not limited to a few years of obligatory study but unfolds – as much in work as in leisure time, in individual as in communal life – like an expression of free personal will'.[29] That a school could be more than just a set of classrooms for instruction was proved by the selection of exemplars, which included the project of a model school for 1,000 students in Leningrad, designed by Atelier A. Nikolskij in 1927 as a blurred school-factory (and which linked to Canella's wider interest in Soviet socio-architectural experiments);[30] Geoffrey Copcutt's Urban Centre for the new town of Cumbernauld, an example of the integration of multiple services with residential and educational uses; and the five 'super-schools' proposed by Copcutt with David Lewis and James N. Portman for the city of Pittsburgh in Pennsylvania.[31]

Proposing an idea of school as territory, these exemplars were echoed in the projects of Canella's students. These projects extrapolated elements from inside a school building – such as lecture theatres, libraries, dining and sports facilities – to project them onto a wider urban field, at times dispersing and at times repackaging them in dense multi-functional complexes. Ultimately, the aim was to instil some civic spirit and sociality in the amorphous urban periphery of Milan – the territory that Canella's own practice work sought to redeem from dull, privately driven urbanisation.[32]

On a pedagogic level, the complexity of the school and its opening-up to wider urban communities tied into John Dewey's differentiation between progressive and traditional education.[33] The freer possibilities of expression that were to be allowed to the pupil by the former, Dewey had argued, were to be matched with an overall rehabilitation of the teacher's maieutic function, as a facilitator of learning in multiple ways beyond the mere transmission of established knowledge. Whereas the drawings of Canella's students that were published in *L'utopia della realtà* never depicted the interior organisation of a single room by showing furniture, the intention to break with the traditional hierarchical settings of pupils facing a teacher's desk was openly expressed in the texts of the book in which the projects were published. A recurring term in the book was 'research', which appeared in the diagrammatic representations of the stages of a learning process oriented to a disruption of old deductive methodologies solely based on the a-critical transmission of pre-packaged concepts. As the second cycle following a first cycle of 'information and elaboration', research was proposed as an inductive process based on critical analysis and ultimately intended to answer the question 'who are we?'[34]

Understanding the primary school as already a research environment was a way of projecting onto the earliest stages of education a vision of learning that was diametrically opposed to the daily academic experience of the university students who were drawing these progressive ideas. It was, in other words, a way to exorcise the continuation of the status quo for future generations. Changing the school was the first and necessary step to change the university.

Theatrical pedagogy

In the late 1950s and early 1960s, when the baby boomer generation resulted in a massive expansion of the number of pupils to be schooled, designing and rethinking schools unsurprisingly became a main concern for architects. By the late 1960s, following the coming of age of those same pupils, the attention switched to the design of universities. Canella's own teaching trajectory followed this sequence, which proceeded through an intermediary stage between school and university, as Rogers and he decided to devote two years (1965–67) of work to the architecture of theatres.[35]

The reasons for moving from the school to the theatre were explained by the two architects in terms of the opportunities that the latter offered for devising reasoning on the city for a mass society. Acknowledging a crisis for the theatre of similar gravity as that for the school, Canella nevertheless recognised the apparently minor urgency of the former. The intention, however, was precisely to distract from a consideration of an obvious theme of social urgency – the school – in order to redeem proper architectural reasoning on how to achieve a direct relationship between individuals and the city by means of a system of spaces for social aggregation. The results were the *Prototipi didattici per il sistema teatrale a Milano* ('educational prototypes for the theatre system in Milan'),[36] the elements of an urban archipelago of multi-use buildings located throughout the Milanese hinterland and revising the school complexes designed in the previous years by Canella and Rogers's students as architectural condensers of functions for collective use. More explicitly than before, with these prototypes Canella was playing with the metaphor of urban life as a staged theatrical performance.

The work on the theatre built on an initial hypothesis explained by Canella in the book *Il sistema teatrale a Milano* (1966), which derived from the design studios and constituted the follow-up to *L'utopia della realtà* (1965). The hypothesis posited the different viewpoints of directors, actors and set designers on the one side, and architects and urbanists on the other. Whereas for the former a theatre was always contingently linked to the specificities of a performance, Canella suggested that the latter could only understand an ideal theatre as 'the system of physical places that unveil the city as theatrical multiplicity'.[37] During the twentieth century, he went on to argue, the theatre had entered a crisis because of growing competition from cinema and television, both of which had been able to better interpret and accommodate the switch from an elite to a mass audience, whereas the theatre had proved incapable of being distributed across urban societies.[38] Taking Milan as a case study, Canella's studio developed a reading of the history of theatres in the city as a dispersed system in the urban fabric that mirrored changes in the taste and technological advances of bourgeois culture. The avant-gardes of the second half of the twentieth century, with their claims to abolish the 'fourth wall' and break from a conception of theatre as an enclosed space, opened an additional opportunity to rethink the architectural typology (Figure 8.2). Once the direct link between stage and performance was challenged, the theatre exited its typological classification and instead colonised an outer environment and hybridised with other urban functions. The resulting multiplication of the theatrical encompassed a whole series of what Canella named 'crypto-theatres ..., latent forms of theatre induced by other functions' that included 'pedagogic theatres' (those inside schools and universities), 'debate-theatres' (those that were part of the spaces of leisure, culture, and politics), 'study-theatres', and so on.[39]

Besides the urbanistic reasoning behind the metaphor of the city as theatrical multiplicity, it was Canella's pedagogy that was itself theatrical. The clearest manifestation of this came in his two *Montaggi didattici* (teaching montages),

Figure 8.2 Guido Canella, Project for a theatrical system in Milan, produced in the
architectural design studio led by Canella at the Politecnico di Milano (1965).
Source: Courtesy Studio Canella, Milan.

which he conceived in 1965–66.[40] Switching attention from the topic of the
school to the theatre (and later to the prison), Canella considered it necessary to
find ways of replicating the direct sense of involvement that the first topic had
managed to stimulate in the students. He thus elaborated a *mise-en-scène* of
architecture in which four 'actors' chosen among Canella's own collaborators
gave their voices to the protagonists of City, Architecture, Literature, and
Teaching, with the first three being the domains from which text excerpts and
images were derived and the fourth playing the role of offstage voice keeping
the narrative together and providing commentary.

The *Montaggi* drew inspiration from the crossing of paths of theatre and
architecture that materialised in 1966 when the Living Theatre – the American
avant-garde company that in the mid-1960s was touring Europe – performed at
the School of Architecture in Milan at Rogers's invitation. Canella translated

the Living Theatre into a teaching methodology and a *tour de force* throughout the history of Western thought. From Aeschylus to Engels, from Vitruvius to Kafka, from Palladio to Sartre, the breadth of sources he picked from was not merely a showcase of his own cultural breadth. Instead, ranging across authors, ideas, and times was necessary to waken the critical consciousness of a student cohort that was coming out of a still-traditional type of schooling in which disciplines were taught in isolation from one another. Against this tradition, Canella presented his eulogy to multilateral knowledge, which went hand in hand with his architectural theories of typological complexity and added to the idea of a vast learning territory.[41]

The *Montaggi* involved young academics from the Politecnico (such as Gae Aulenti, Ezio Bonfanti and Maurizio Calzavara, the latter co-author with Canella of the scripts) as well as some professional actors, including Alberto Sironi of Piccolo Teatro in Milan and later, among other things, a director of popular television shows in Italy. Canella acted as the general director and the mind behind the conception of the *Montaggi*, of which he staged two in 1966 and 1967, respectively on 'Architecture, City and the Theatre' and 'Architecture, City and the Penal System'. Taking place in one of the university's lecture theatres, the performances were choral works both in terms of the people involved and the intellectual sources they assembled. Their format mixed the projection of slides, as in a normal lecture but with multiple projectors showing plans and photographs of works of architecture, and a series of readings by teaching assistants and students. Each of them was called to give voice to one of the knowledge domains assembled in the script, for texts were extracted from literature on architecture, the city, theatrical theory and penal theory, and were combined with wider literary sources. The latter were interpreted by the professional actors while an omniscient offstage voice – the voice of teaching, played by Calzavara and Aulenti – acted as a narrator holding the script together and providing commentary that could help the students navigate across the intellectual archipelago assembled by Canella across the whole spectrum of Western culture and history.

It was not long after this that Canella would commence work on the most elaborate version of this territory. In 1967, he embarked on his most ambitious teaching project to date, and one that moved the focus up the scale to the logical ultimate level: the university.

The university is everywhere

At the dawn of 1968, focusing an architecture studio on the topic of university design would appear to have been an obvious choice. Yet specific national reasoning was also attached to Canella's decision to consider this topic. The brief he set for his students – a cohort that by then numbered more than one hundred – proposed to reflect on the creation of a new university in the southern region of Calabria, a socially and economically depressed region that reflected the severe developmental gap of southern Italy. More than previous studios, the topic was contingent with real Italian politics, as the creation of the University of Calabria had for years been central to parliamentary debate on higher education reform.

Led with interdisciplinary teamwork from urbanist Lucio Stellaro D'Angiolini, a long-time collaborator with Canella,[42] the studio marked the apex of his (and, before him, Rogers's) objective of raising the students' socio-political consciousness. The students, who were from all years of study, were taken – some even physically, on aeroplanes offered by the military[43] – on a cultural shock trip from the privileged bubble of the industrialised North, which had been blessed by the postwar 'economic miracle', to one of the most depressed regions in Europe. It was here, in Calabria, where Canella believed the implementation of a radically different idea of higher education was possible.

His key reference for an educational alternative was the alphabetisation campaign of rural Cuba, which he frequently mentioned in his lectures as an instance of education understood as activist practice, and which he illustrated with a photograph in *Università: Ragione, contesto, tipo* (1975), the third book in the series extracted from his design courses that was published only after Canella's readmission at the Politecnico following the ministerial suspension.[44] The system of learning that his studio elaborated for Calabria opposed the traditional boundaries between primary, secondary and tertiary education. It proposed that university students would act as teachers in primary and secondary schools and live a life constantly on the move, as their education would not be limited to activities inside the university halls but would be complemented by additional learning inside industry, thus merging the spheres of education and work. Canella and D'Angiolini contended that a new university for the Italian South could make sense if, and only if, it was related to wider interventions across the productive and educational fabric. With unrestricted ambition, they opposed the government-backed creation of petro-chemical plants in Calabria, claiming that it was instead possible to turn the region into a science and technology hub centred on a new university and an understanding of science-based industry – an equivalent, they believed, to the Massachusetts Institute of Technology for the Italian South. The overarching idea that grounded the projects developed by the students in the design studio led by Canella and D'Angiolini was that the establishment of a new university in Italy required changing the national industrial policies to overcome the traditional divide between technology and research. Moreover, they argued that only by thinking of the university as industry itself could the opportunity of a new academic institution in the south of Italy work positively towards the wider goal of narrowing the development gap between the north and the south of the country. D'Angiolini proposed that a more precise definition of strategic industrial sectors (he mentioned electronics, the iron industry, agriculture, and thermo-electronics) could help set the conditions for most technological innovation to happen in the South, which in turn would break the usual pattern of northern industrialists establishing in the South large industrial enterprises that have no relationship with the surrounding territory.[45]

Behind the unbiased ambition was the will to ignite a proper revolution for Italy. Canella and his collaborators were proposing to redeem scientific and technological thinking from the neglected position to which they had been relegated by the dominant role traditionally accorded to a humanist type of education in Italy. In their view, this historical situation had led to an approach to industrial development that totally discounted the need for an educated workforce, excluded technical education from the tasks of the public university and left professional courses to the private sector.[46] Making the university the core of a system combining all levels of learning and production thus entailed three concomitant goals: (1) coordinating scientific research in all branches of knowledge; (2) offering academic-level knowledge to the needs of secondary schooling; and (3) directing the strategies of industrial development at a national level.[47] To accomplish this threefold mission in the hostile context of Calabria, much more than higher education reform was needed.[48] Calabria lacked sufficient established institutions, businesses and levels of education to sustain industrial development. Moreover, there was no widespread perception of the possibilities offered by technical culture, let alone shared feelings of what an industrial society might be.[49]

For Canella and D'Angiolini, the task ahead equalled nothing less than the founding of a 'new city'.[50] They did not mean by this the creation of a physically concentrated urban agglomeration, but quite the opposite. Myth helped sustain a different vision of a vast urban territory that could reinstate the ancient Greek city of Sybaris, an urban system allegedly founded in the eighth century BC but which archaeologists have struggled to locate definitively. Like Sybaris, Canella's learning territory longed to be 'everywhere':

> On the one side, we can say that the university settlement is 'everywhere'; this corresponds to a nomadic attitude as continuous movement that rejects any physical limitation. On the other side, the university settlement is a 'laboratory' conducting experiments on itself and its surroundings; this must necessarily be matched with a finite typology, although still with some degrees of indeterminacy.[51]

As these words expressed, the path towards ubiquity entailed two consecutive stages, the first of which was necessarily spatially bounded. To initiate the city, a pioneering act of colonisation was required to implant a 'base-camp'. Intended as a territorial observatory, Canella defined the main objective of the camp to be the building of a body of knowledge about the socio-cultural condition of the territory it aimed to reshape (Figure 8.3). A germ of a new university, it would grow while becoming aware of its surrounding condition. This process could be accomplished only through a level of operative closure; more generally, Canella maintained that an image of total continuity between universities and their environments was mere fantasy that was used demagogically by politicians to promote the alleged integration of knowledge in the fabric of society. He elaborated on this argument in the article, 'Passé et avenir de l'anti-ville

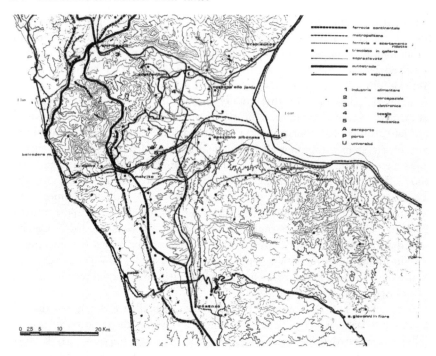

Figure 8.3 Guido Canella, Lucio Stellaro D'Angiolini *et al.*, territorial plan for a new
          university in Calabria, produced in the architectural design studio led by
          Canella and D'Angiolini at the Politecnico di Milano (1967–69).
Source: Courtesy Studio Canella, Milan.

universitaire', published in the May 1968 issue of *L'architecture d'aujourd'hui*,
[52] and in which he defended detachment, singularity and enclosure as the
necessary 'invariants' of academic space throughout its history.

Invariantly, Canella suggested, the university's history had been marked by
segregation. This was most evident in older epochs, from the proverbial town-
and-gown divisions in Oxford and Cambridge to the cloisters that gave European universities a monastic detachment. Nineteenth-century bourgeois ideology pretended to disguise academic segregation, giving rise to palaces of
knowledge inserted with apparent continuity inside the urban fabric. This
'forced and artificial integration of the university within the city'[53] concealed
the goal of reducing the university's confrontational role in relation to reality,
instead turning it into one more institution within the amalgam of the bourgeois State. Canella interpreted the campus revolts of the 1960s not as aiming at
the abolition of the university's conflict with the city but as a claim for restor-
ing the critical role of the university as an 'anti-city, the dialectical contrast of a
world against another, of an environment against another, without believing
that this would negatively impact on the necessary permeability of the university towards citizens'.[54]

A new university for the mass society that built on the invariant of critical detachment was, by necessity, a big anti-city. To resist the commercialisation of values resulting from the growth of capitalist systems, the university had by necessity to operate from within those systems. As with schools and theatres, universities also partook in the general hybridisation of functions of contemporary societies with the aim of engraining critical thought within their consumerist and leisure-based tissue. Adding to the portfolio of crypto-theatres, a new university would be a 'great architecture [that defines] indoor and outdoor spaces, squares and rooms, porticos and steps for free use'.[55]

If the unity of place and the enclosed and finite nature of the base camp were an obvious statement of detachment, a new city created around it should maintain tension throughout its whole life in the form of constant critical assessment and confrontation. Canella envisaged the second stage of the Calabrese project – when the university would finally be 'everywhere' – as an infiltration of a learning component inside 'all those institutions and activities that need undergoing thorough transformation (industries, primary and secondary education, public administration, etc.)'.[56] The infiltration would proceed in parallel to an interior reorganisation of the academic structure through 'mass departments', institutions within the institution catering to the education of large numbers of professional workers from across the territory and digesting and making sense of the apparently unstoppable growth of student numbers across Italian universities.

Canella did not limit these ideas only to the Italian South. In fact, the Calabria project was an alter ego of the idea of the university that he had desired for Milan. This seems to have been why he chose to end one of his key lectures delivered during the two years of work in southern Italy with a quotation from Frantz Fanon's *The Wretched of the Earth*: 'Therefore, comrades, let's not pay homage to Europe by creating States, institutions and societies that take inspiration from it. Humanity is expecting from us something else than grotesque, obscene imitation.'[57] These words show how the 'other' civility found in Calabria was to be approached neither tragically nor through the logics of conventional north-to-south colonisation. Rather, it offered an opportunity to start over and create a totally different university that would be harder to achieve in the culturally and economically developed context of northern Italy. In fact, it would be impossible to achieve, as Canella would experiment on his own persona through the repression of his progressive ideas that came with his academic suspension in 1971 – the starting phase of a restoration of order by the State.

Rappel à l'ordre

In 1968, while Canella's team was working on the project for an activist idea of the university, the Italian parliament passed a law creating the new University of Calabria.[58] Four years later, there was an international competition for the design of the seat of the institution, which was eventually won by Vittorio Gregotti.[59]

In 1975, in a narration of the two years of nomadism between the university classrooms in Milan and the Calabrese territory, Canella expressed his disillusionment about how the State had handled the creation of the new university. The choice of a single large site of 660 hectares on the outskirts of the city of Cosenza contrasted with the diffused strategy devised by his team and was too rigid to allow for any future adjustment. In this choice was the confirmation of the accumulative logics of capitalist urbanisation, which would see the existing city expand but without altering the existing imbalanced territorial condition. 'Impatience ultimately won', Canella commented, 'as the Rector, Nino Andreatta, opted to give immediate birth to an offcut of future, a bit of university at any cost.'[60] Despite some notable innovations inscribed in the constitution of the new university – such as the departmental structure and the adoption of an Anglo-Saxon collegiate model for the first 'residential university' in Italy[61] – the Calabrese story ended with the ultimate confirmation of the status quo, as the central government backed the institution's founding fathers in making the more innocuous choice of a single large campus.

This unhappy institutional ending combined with Canella's own personal misfortune as an academic when, on 23 November 1971, he was one of the faculty members to be escorted out of the university halls in Milan, suspended for almost three years for an attitude to teaching that was considered a threat to the well-being of a university. In January 1972, the suspension was followed by an attempt to restore former methods and logics in the Politecnico by putting it under the external administration of a technical committee (Figure 8.4). Orchestrated from above by the Ministry of Education, the restorative action included the non-renewal of teaching contracts, the annulment of twenty-one courses and their related exams, and a review of all resolutions passed during the years of the teaching experimentation under the deanship of Portoghesi.[62] Finally, in November 1972, the rector established a fixed number of new enrolments for the 1973–74 academic year, just a few years after the Italian parliament had passed a law opening up access to universities to all secondary school students regardless of their previous secondary studies.[63] It was as a response to this law, which marked the official adoption by Italian universities of mass higher education, that Canella had devised the idea of 'mass departments', central to his and his students' proposals for Calabria and constituting, on the one hand, a statement of acceptance of a mass system, and, on the other, a radical alternative to just such a quantitative growth of the existing system. Canella and his team refused a widespread and simplistic interpretation of the department that interpreted it as a mere reshuffling of the existing components of a university or as a facility shared among different sections of the academic community. What they intended by mass departments were completely new institutions that experimented with forms of hybridisation and collaboration between higher and lower levels of education, and were open to large numbers of professional workers. Based on a classification of three main professional figures to be trained by the new academic institution, a tripartite organisation for the University of Calabria was proposed that encompassed: a Department

Figure 8.4 Graffiti against the technical committee appointed by the government to restore order at the school of architecture of the Politecnico di Milano (197?). Source: Politecnico di Milano, Archivio Storico di Ateneo, Titolo X Cattedre e istituti scientifici, fascicolo Facoltà di Architettura.

of Administration (*Dipartimento amministrativo*) aimed at educating a new generation of public bureaucrats with a scientific-technical mentality; a Department of Education (*Dipartimento dell'istruzione*) targeted at a wide restructuring of the teaching staff and directly linked with the lower levels of education (in particular, the secondary school), with university students acting as teachers; and a Department of Technology (*Dipartimento tecnologico*) educating researchers whose work would benefit the restructuring of the industrial sector in southern Italy.[64]

Not only did Canella's proposals for Calabria not materialise, but also the situation at his home institution in Milan remained untouched by the more generally valid changes to the protocols and habits of higher education that those proposals entailed. Within the span of two years, between 1971 and 1973, the combined suspension of Canella and his colleagues and the decision to fix the number of students showed how the government – and in turn the state university – had descended into a condition of incurable sclerosis.

Canella and the other seven faculty members were eventually rehabilitated to their academic posts in May 1974 after two and a half years of forced academic exile. During that time, he had not remained inactive but, together with some students who had taken part in his previous teaching experiences (including in

Calabria), he had moved the parallel studio created inside the academic halls back into his own professional studio in Milan.[65] Here, in a final polemical act, he revisited the ideas he had elaborated with the students for a different university by submitting an entry to the 1972 competition in Calabria.[66]

In an attempt to adapt the idea of a nomadic university infiltrated within the vital organs of a region to the requirements of the brief, Canella's team proposed to divide the university between two main locations. This decision aimed to reach out to nearby industrial areas in line with the overall philosophy of devising a knowledge-based industrial territory. The university itself was designed as an industrial complex, with shed structures that housed scientific laboratories, a museum, a dining facility for 500 people, and smaller teaching classrooms, libraries and study rooms. The other half of the university was located on a hill facing the laboratories, around an old villa that was repurposed for the central academic administration and where Canella organised the teaching and research spaces, an arts and performance centre, the central library, a residential village, and an agency for territorial consultancy. The latter, symbolically designed in the form of a bridge that would return in Canella's competition entry for the new regional offices in Trieste in 1974,[67] aimed to rescue the activist role of the base camp as an observatory focused on its surrounding territory. Giorgio Fiorese, a student and then collaborator with Canella in the late 1960s and 1970s, has suggested that the competition project for the regional offices in Trieste should be read as the logical consequence and development of the ideas discussed for Calabria. Clearly out of tune with the requests set in the brief of merely creating the new headquarters of the regional administration (and in this way very similar to the approach taken on the occasion of the competition for the University of Calabria), Fiorese puts the proposal in strict dependency on the context of Trieste and, in particular, the pioneering work done at the local asylum by Franco Basaglia. In line with Basaglia's theses against total institutions, Canella's project for Trieste went far beyond the usual definition of an administrative building by maintaining that it should include a mixture of educational and residential spaces targeted at a whole population of the oppressed in search of their reinsertion into society. Just as his project for Trieste did not win the competition, the proposal for the University of Calabria did not make it to the second stage of the competition, leaving as its only traces three stamp-sized drawings and a short comment in Bruno Zevi's *L'architettura cronache e storia*. [68]

On 11 May 1974, Canella was allowed to enter again the university halls in Milan. Less than a month later, on 5 June, the academic board of the University of Calabria approved the results of the competition. Of course, the exploded university as imagined by Canella could not be more different to the massive physical structure that won Gregotti the first prize. Despite this, Canella remained tight-lipped on the winning design, restricting himself to criticism of academic officials and their myopic faith in a singular architectural silhouette. Twelve years after their shared experience as collaborators in Rogers's urgent wish to rethink educational institutions, Gregotti's and Canella's inquiries into the space of learning only apparently ended with opposite results. The latter's obstinacy in arguing for an activist revision of the idea of the university as a territorial and civic system remains as powerful a statement as the former's 3-kilometre bridge that eventually managed to land on the hills of Calabria.

Notes

1 The events at the Politecnico di Milano between 1963 and 1974 have been reviewed in the exhibition 'La rivoluzione culturale: La Facoltà di Architettura del Politecnico di Milano 1963–1974' curated by Fiorella Vanini and held at the Facoltà di Architettura Civile (Milan) from 23 November to 16 December 2009. See the exhibition catalogue: *La rivoluzione culturale: La Facoltà di Architettura del Politecnico di Milano 1963–1974* (Milan: Politecnico di Milano, 2009). See also Marco Biraghi, 'Università: La Facoltà di Architettura del Politecnico di Milano (1963–74)', in Marco Biraghi *et al.*, eds., *Italia 60/70: Una stagione dell'architettura* (Padua: Il poligrafo, 2010), 87–97.

2 Paolo Portoghesi, 'Perché Milano: Une saison en enfer', *Controspazio* 1 (1973): 7.

3 Quoted in *La rivoluzione culturale*, 43.

4 When Rogers took over the directorship of *Casabella* in 1953, his editorial team comprised Giancarlo De Carlo, Vittorio Gregotti and Marco Zanuso. In the late 1950s, with Gregotti promoted to editor-in-chief, Rogers set up the Centro Studi which consisted of the younger architects Aldo Rossi, Luciano Semerani, Francesco Tentori, and Silvano Tintori, to whom were later added Aurelio Cortesi and Giorgio Grassi (with Rossi and Tentori becoming editors). The Centro Studi was responsible for carrying out international case studies that constituted the backbone of the discussion on city territories and the new urban dimension on which *Casabella* focused attention in the early 1960s (see Chapter 2). Canella joined the editorial team in 1962, having already contributed with articles since 1957.

5 For a series of commentaries on Canella's work as a teacher, writer and practitioner, see Enrico Bordogna, Gentucca Canella, and Elvio Manganaro, eds., *Guido Canella, 1931–2009* (Milan: Franco Angeli, 2014).

6 See Claudio Buscaglia, ed., *Ciclo di comunicazioni sul rapporto funzioni-istituzioni: il sistema dell'istruzione* (Milan: Politecnico di Milano, 1971).

7 Portoghesi, 'Perché Milano'. 7.

8 See Claudio D'Amato Guerrieri, '*Controspazio* come "piccola rivista"', *FAmagazine* 43 (2018): 33–40. *Controspazio* originated from the student protests in Rome that reached their apex with the Battle of Valle Giulia in March 1968 (see Chapter 3). Portoghesi decided to move the magazine to Milan, where he had been a professor since 1967, after having taught Italian literature at the University of Rome. During the first two phases in the life of the magazine, between 1969 and 1972 and then between 1973 and 1976 (the latter phase following the relocation of the editorial team again to Rome), *Controspazio* played a crucial role in bringing attention to La Tendenza, the group that clustered around Aldo Rossi and found widespread recognition at the exhibition 'Architettura Razionale' at the Fifteenth Milan Triennale in 1973. See *Controspazio* 6 (1973); and Ezio Bonfanti, ed., *Architettura razionale* (Milan: Franco Angeli, 1973).

9 The letter was sent by Minister Gui on 8 July 1967. See *La rivoluzione culturale*, 27.

10 Documento dell'assemblea dei firmatari, 12 December 1967, in *Controspazio* 1 (1973): 46.

11 See Chapter 3.

12 Documento dell'assemblea dei firmatari, 47.

13 Carlo De Carli, 'La finzione, la verità', in *La rivoluzione culturale*, 32.

14 Guido Canella, 'L'epopea borghese della Scuola di Amsterdam', *Casabella* 215 (1957): 76–91.

15 From a conversation with Riccardo Canella, Milan, March 2018.

16 Paolo Portoghesi, 'L'architettura civile di Guido Canella', in *Guido Canella, 1931–2009*, 23.

17 The article on the Amsterdam School was followed in the early 1960s by other writings, including an essay on Soviet architecture, a contribution to the discussion on the planning of cities for a tertiary economy (the Italian debate on *centri direzionali*), and an issue of *Edilizia moderna* co-edited with Vittorio Gregotti on the relationship between architecture and the twentieth century: Guido Canella, 'Attesa per l'architettura sovietica', *Casabella* 262 (1962): 4–16; Guido Canella, 'Vecchie e nove ipotesi per i centri direzionali', *Casabella* 275 (1963): 42–55; *Edilizia moderna* 81(1963), 'Il Novecento e l'architettura'.

18 The other teaching assistants on the course led by Rogers in1962–63 were Piergiacomo Castiglioni, Vittorio Gregotti, Cesare Blasi, Francesco Gnecchi Ruscone, Giuliano Guiducci, Enrico Mantero, Giorgio Riva, and Ugo Rivolta (Francesco Tentori was added to the group in the academic year 1963–64). See *L'utopia della realtà: Un esperimento didattico sulla tipologia della scuola primaria* (Bari: Leonardo da Vinci Editrice, 1965).

19 Ernesto Nathan Rogers, 'Elogio dell'architettura', *Casabella* 287 (1964): 3.

20 Ernesto Nathan Rogers, 'Esperienza di un corso universitario', in *L'utopia della realtà*, 19.

21 See Ernesto Nathan Rogers, 'Continuità', *Casabella* 199 (1953): 2; and Rogers 'Continuità o crisi', *Casabella* 215 (1957): 3–4. See also Chapter 5, note 22.

22 See Guido Canella, 'Lineamenti di un programma di lavoro' (lecture, 16 December 1966), in *Alcune lezioni tenute al corso di Elementi di Composizione nell'anno accademico 1966–67* (Milan: Politecnico di Milano, 1967), 6.

23 Canella, 'Appunti per il consuntivo di un corso', in *L'utopia della realtà*, 24. Canella had first publicly commented on the course in his contribution to the special issue that *Casabella* dedicated to a discussion of the Italian architecture schools: Guido Canella, 'Due scelte per le facoltà di architettura', *Casabella* 267 (1964): 6–9.

24 Rogers had first directed attention to the problem of the school and its need for a reform in a monographic issue of *Domus* on 'Architettura educatrice' that he curated during his one-year directorship in 1947 (issue 220). Subsequently, while at *Casabella* and following the 'Piano decennale per la scuola' proposed in 1958 by the Ministry of Education, Rogers returned to the topic in 1960: see *Casabella* 245, 1960. See also Appendix 2.

25 See Guido Canella, 'Relazioni tra morfologia, tipologia dell'organismo architettonico e ambiente fisico', in *L'utopia della realtà*, 66–81.

26 See Guido Canella, 'Dal laboratorio della composizione', in *Teoria della progettazione architettonica*, ed. Antonio Locatelli (Bari: Dedalo, 1968), 83–100. The seminar included eight presentations by Guido Canella, Mario Coppa, Vittorio Gregotti, Aldo Rossi, Alberto Samonà, Gabriele Sciememi, Luciano Semerani, and Manfredo Tafuri. The book *Teoria della progettazione architettonica*, which derived from the seminar, appeared in 1968 in the 'Architettura e città' series curated by Canella for the publisher Dedalo Libri. The first volume of the series, published in 1966, had been Canella's own *Il sistema teatrale a Milano*, which stemmed from the design studios on the theatre that he delivered for two years (in parallel with Rogers) after the course on the primary school: see Guido Canella, *Il sistema teatrale a Milano* (Bari: Dedalo libri, 1966).

27 Canella, 'Dal laboratorio della progettazione', 88.

28 See ibid. and Canella, 'Vecchie e nuove ipotesi per i centri direzionali'.

29 *L'utopia della realtà*, 156.

30 See Canella, 'Attesa per l'architettura sovietica'.

31 See Guido Canella and Lucio S. D'Angiolini, eds., *Università: Ragione, contesto, tipo* (Bari: Dedalo libri, 1975), 236. The super-schools in Pittsburgh were published in *Architectural Forum* 126, no. 5 (1967).

32 An example that dates from the period of the teaching experimentation in Milan is the civic centre designed by Canella in the town of Pieve Emanuele outside Milan (1968–82).

33 *L'utopia della realtà*, 142. The book mentioned Dewey's *School and Society* (1899) among its references.

34 Ibid., 25.

35 The choice of the topic also related to Canella's personal interest in the theatre, on which he commented in the text 'L'architettura del sistema teatrale', in Carlo Quintelli, ed., *La città del teatro* (Milan: CLup, 1989), 233–249. See Gino Malacarne, 'Guido Canella e lo spazio teatrale', in *Guido Canella, 1931–2009*, 43–50.

36 See Canella, *Il sistema teatrale a Milano*.

37 Ibid., 9.

38 Ibid., 15.

39 Ibid., 165.

40 'Montaggio Didattico n.1: Architettura, città e teatro moderno' (1965–66); 'Montaggio Didattico n.2: Architettura, città e sistema penitenziario' (1966–67). See Canella, *Alcune lezioni*.

41 See Francesco Zuddas, 'The System of Learning: Guido Canella's Teaching Theatre', *Oase* 102 (2019): 52–61.

42 Canella and D'Angiolini first met in 1961 at the Lega dei Comuni Democratici di Milano, a network of municipalities in the Milanese hinterland. The two collaborated for the first time on the competition project for Turin's *centro direzionale* in 1962–63, which was followed in 1964 by the competition for the Sacca del Tronchetto in Venice. D'Angiolini served as consultant in Ernesto Nathan Rogers's course on the primary school in 1962–63 and continued collaborating with Canella during the two years of research on the theatre in 1964–66 and the subsequent two-year work on the university. See Michele Achilli, 'Il sodalizio professionale', in *Guido Canella 1931–2009*, 123–125.

43 From a conversation with Cristoforo Bono and Giorgio Fiorese, former students in the design studio on Calabria, Milan, March 2018.

44 Guido Canella, 'Alcune induzioni dal comportamento', in *Università: Ragione, contesto, tipo*, 175–182.

45 Antonio Acuto, in *Università: Ragione, contesto, tipo*, 202. See Lucio S. D'Angiolini, 'Considerazioni di macroeconomia e di macrourbanistica per un bacino industriale e un nuovo ambito metropolitano nel Mezzogiorno', in *Università: Ragione, contesto, tipo*, 123–130.

46 Antonio Locatelli *et al.*, 'Criteri generali, elementi statistici e qualitativi dell'istruzione', in *Università: Ragione, contesto, tipo*, 154.

47 Ibid., 158.

48 Ibid., 150.

49 The socio-economic context of Calabria was discussed in a session of the design course on 28 March 1969. See Claudio Buscaglia, 'Riassunzione di un'esperienza didattica sulla costruzione di un quadro macrourbanistico del Mezzogiorno', in *Università: Ragione, contesto, tipo*, 111–121.

50 Canella and D'Angiolini, *Università: Ragione, contesto, tipo*, 98.

51 Guido Canella, 'Funzione e strategia della progettazione architettonica, 1', in *Università: Ragione, contesto, tipo*, 55–56.

52 Guido Canella, 'Passato e prospettive dell'anti-città universitaria', in *Università: Ragione, contesto, tipo*, 35–50; first published as 'Passé et avenir de l'anti-ville universitaire', *L'architecture d'aujourd'hui* 137 (1968): 16–19.

53 Ibid., 38.

54 Ibid., 50.

55 Ibid.

56 Canella, 'Funzione e strategia della progettazione architettonica, 1', 55–56.

57 Guido Canella, *Un ruolo per l'architettura* (Milan: Clup, 1969), 22.

58 Law no. 442, 12 March 1968, 'Istituzione di una università statale in Calabria', *Gazzetta ufficiale della Repubblica Italiana* 103 (22 April 1968): 2514–2517.

59 See Chapter 4, Chapter 5, and Appendix 1.

60 Franco Catalano and Ermanno Rea, 'Le università del Sud: 3. Cosenza: in gara 500 architetti per la città-studi del Duemila', *Tempo* 25, no. 26 (1 July 1973), quoted in *Università: Ragione, contesto, tipo*, 12.

61 Università degli Studi di Calabria, 'Concorso internazionale per il progetto della sede dell'Università degli Studi di Calabria: Relazione illustrativa' (first competition call), 1972.

62 See *La rivoluzione culturale*.

63 Law no. 910, 11 December 1969, 'Provvedimenti urgenti per l'Università' (Legge Codignola).

64 See Guido Canella, 'Alcune induzioni dal comportamento', in *Università: Ragione, contesto, tipo*, 175–182.

65 The team comprised Guido Canella, C. Bono, A. Cristofellis, G. Di Maio, G. Fiorese, V. Parmiani, G.P. Semino, F. De Miranda, F. Gnecchi Ruscone, M. Ardita, R. Biscardini, G. Goggi, and F. Godowsky. It was assigned the competition entry number 36.

66 For the competition project for the University of Calabria by Guido Canella and collaborators, see Guido Canella *et al.*, 'Progetto per il concorso per l'Università della Calabria', in *Università: Ragione, contesto, tipo*, 423–442.

67 See Giorgio Fiorese, 'Due concorsi: Università della Calabria e Uffici Regiomali di Trieste', in *Guido Canella, 1931–2009*, 308–316. The project for Trieste, presented with the name 'Lascian gli stazzi e vanno verso il mare', was published alongside other entries in *Controspazio* 2 (1975): 41–53.

68 See Luciana de Rosa and Massimo Pica Ciamarra, 'Concorso per l'Università di Calabria: Una prima lettura dei progetti', *L'architettura cronache e storia* 20, no. 5 (1974): 318.

Epilogue II
Academic instability

In the aftermath of 1968, an intergenerational battle unfolded around the design of universities among representatives of all generations of modern Italian architects, from Giuseppe Samonà (born in 1898) to Archizoom (born between the late 1930s and early 1940s). Included between these poles that respectively represented the old power structures and their rebellious, radical sons, a middle generation tried to reflect upon itself by looking at their own images – of themselves as men and as architects – in a renewed mirror of higher education. Giancarlo De Carlo (b.1919), Vittorio Gregotti (b.1927), and Guido Canella (b.1931) oscillated between the two poles, sometimes showing clearer sympathies (as Gregotti did) for an overall maintenance of order, sometimes operating surgically on a dilution of power across a wider domain (as De Carlo did), and sometimes declaring more resolute opposition to the system (as Canella did).

In 1970–71, Vittorio Gregotti's scheme for the University of Florence suggested that a university could be concentrated in space as long as it was part of a wider territorial plan whose elements were all carefully designed. A couple of years later, faced with a slightly different brief for the University of Calabria, he ended up leaving the urbanistic plan and focusing instead on the design of the academic settlement per se. Or, more correctly, he absorbed urbanism within a massive architectural gesture. He shared this ethos with Giuseppe Samonà's project for the University of Cagliari, which took on the role of Gregotti's even more impudently gigantic precursor. Considered as a trajectory in the formulation of an idea of the university, the Florence-Cagliari-Calabria triad by Gregotti and Samonà had an inner paradox, as it ended up arguing for bottom-up appropriation of knowledge by students within the generic spaces of an academic-work-leisure park, but at the same time did not dare to desanctify the overarching principle of spatial concentration.

In a first formulation of their ideas on the nexus of architecture, city and capitalism, Archizoom entered the University of Florence competition to ridicule the academic exercises that, as students, they had been required to do on the exact same stretch of territory. Against those 'projects for roofs aimed at eatable scale models made of walnut and metal, particularly yummy and stimulating for addicted teachers',[1] the Florentine collective visualised a territory where concentration and dispersion mingled in an urbanistic dialogue that represented the capitalist combination of accumulation and continuous growth. Walking hand in hand with the deinstitutionalising theses proposed by Ivan Illich, Archizoom envisaged an exploded university, anticipating the notion of open-source information that has started materialising only in more recent times through the digital revolution, the Internet, and social media.

Whereas Archizoom's eulogy to ubiquitous knowledge depended on an over-all disbelief in the traditional conception of architecture as the figurative representation of social patterns – hence their reduction of the city to a mere juxtaposition of coexisting elements – Giancarlo De Carlo agreed about the need to dilute academic concentration. However, he did so from within a statement of trust in his own discipline. The sequence of projects he devised for universities in Urbino, Dublin, and Pavia traces a narrative about the gradual assimilation of the university as a service open to wide urban communities. His plan for the University of Pavia, in particular, demonstrates a take on academic ubiquity that is different from that of Archizoom. De Carlo's plan argued for the dilution of the traditional concentrated academic power structures through their dislocation across a vast urban territory via a mixture of repurposed buildings and new construction – and, hence, would involve some more 'projects for roofs'.

Finally, at least as far as my narrative of this story that leads to the explosion of the university is concerned, Guido Canella provides the final chapter in the form of an intricate combination of disciplinary objectives and pedagogic innovation. A disciple of Ernesto Nathan Rogers, Canella took from his master a desire to break with an understanding of education as merely concerned with professionalisation. In an anticipation of what today are called 'live-projects',[2] but moved more by intellectual anxiety than by the financial prerogatives that have often prevailed more recently, Canella's pedagogic experiments reflected the tumultuous climate of the Milanese school of architecture. For him, the university was the point of arrival in the definition of a wider system of learning that he developed institution-by-institution, proceeding through the school, the theatre, and the prison. Mirroring his activist pedagogy – in which written briefs were as long as books, confrontation was constant, and teaching took the form of a theatrical performance – Canella elaborated an idea of higher learning as constantly on the move between academic halls and advanced industries. He projected it onto the 'other' civility of the Italian south whose depression could be turned into an advantage, since it provided the ground on which a radically new system could be implemented – a system different from the one produced and constantly reproduced over a hundred years of governmental educational reforms. This was a system where the operative closure of a university was confirmed only insofar as mobility to and from an academic base-camp was guaranteed as the functioning logic of a vast territory. De Carlo's mobile poles devised as part of the project for Pavia became the overarching logic of Canella's idea of the university. It was here that the mass, technological, consumerist postwar society tried an impossible reconnection with a remote pre-modern past when the university did not enjoy the stability of life inside marvellous academic palaces but manifested itself as a network of ambulatory human beings constantly in search of some weak and temporary territorialisation.

Notes

1   Archizoom, 'Progetto di concorso per l'Università di Firenze', *Domus* 509 (1974): 11.
2   See Harriet Harriss and Lynette Widder, eds., *Architecture Live Projects: Pedagogy into Practice* (New York: Routledge, 2014).

Conclusion

Towards academic commons

Looking back at the narrative in the previous pages, a number of keywords – or, better, oppositions – emerge that bridge the two realms discussed in this book: the idea of the university, and the discourse of architecture. Professionalisation and empowerment, concentration and dilution – these are central notions around which a reform both of architecture and of higher education was attempted during the 1960s and the 1970s. It could be said that such a statement is nothing other than the confirmation that architecture partakes in the culture of its time, acting as one among many phenomena whose observation enables the decoding of a wider system of beliefs, attitudes, and objectives. But the specific story told in the preceding pages shows architecture at a moment of particular, context-specific euphoria; as such, comparisons across time are a difficult enterprise, and this includes the attempt to understand the relevance of the story to our time.

Presenting in the Introduction a disclaimer about not aiming to explicitly promote a 'learning from' approach to the topic, I have left it to the reader to decide whether and how any lesson can be gained from reassessing a historical moment that depicts a very different society from that of today. Inevitably, however, at the end of the story I feel obliged to return to the contemporary situation depicted in the introductory pages and to the question asked there: Is the university of today fundamentally different from the one our parents went to? Rather than attempting a different answer from the one I have already provided (a 'yes'), I will here reformulate the question: Is the architectural discourse on universities fundamentally different from that of fifty years ago? In this case, too, the answer should be a 'yes'. What distinguishes the two apparently identical answers, however, is that, whereas the first on the state of the university can be dissected in its positive (for example, improved mobility and personalisation of the higher learning experience) and problematic (for example, extreme corporatisation and commodification of knowledge) elements, the second on the state of architectural criticism about the university seems to be paralysed in a moment of crisis that derives from the adaptation to and semi-automatic, acritical repetition of notions derived precisely from the period discussed in this book.

Just as, today, excellence and research are labels ubiquitously and unquestioningly attached to any talk on universities, so informality and the metaphor of the building-as-city are mottos used to promote the architectural production of higher education spaces over the last two decades. The design attention has clearly shifted from the classrooms and laboratories to the creation of in-between spaces that are presented as capable of acting like real urban spaces to foster the unexpected – an element that is emphasised as being at least as important in the learning process as the traditional idea of studying books and going to lectures.[1] Yet this emphasis on in-between spaces, although usually appearing as an unquestioned truth and a constant presence in the descriptions of recent projects of higher education spaces, is hardly backed by sound pedagogical evidence.[2]

It could be counter-argued that what we are confronted with is an instance of the normal rhetoric of any project and that architectural production should be assessed on its actual results rather than on its creators' pronouncements. If we consider those results – some examples of which are provided in the Introduction to this book – we are confronted by a growing series of interiorised pseudo-urban spaces that promise endless possibilities of informal learning while almost invariably further detaching the university from its surrounding context. This context is no longer – or, at least, no longer as prevalent as it was in the 1960s and the 1970s – that of an out-of-town campus, because a changed mindset over the last few decades has 'rediscovered' the city after years of relocating its main components and institutions to the periphery. In the face of this situation, the tendency to interiorise complexity is alarming. Those projects can rightly be considered the operative arm by which late capitalism selects higher education as a favourite ground for the implementation of neoliberal logics that attach a monetary value to every sphere of human existence, in the process, promoting disparity of opportunities rather than narrowing social gaps.[3]

At the same time, recent interest in re-theorising collectiveness, and, especially, in revisiting the notion of the 'commons', as an alternative to the production of the city through the single authority of the state or the market,[4] points in a different direction, opening possibilities for reconnecting with the interrupted discourse of the 1960s and the 1970s when universities were promoted as the tools for the creation of an open democratic society. The fact that universities are 'back in town' adds further relevance to exploring this scenario today, at a time when the unstoppable forces of neoliberalism seem to shatter any possibility of real openness and democracy.

If the welfare state is no longer an option, this does not necessarily mean that its institutions also have to be left behind as either too corrupt or too starved for recovery. Reinhold Martin has tackled this question in relation to recent explorations of the commons and the concept of a hypothetical 'city as commons' beyond neoliberal capitalism.[5] Questioning what, in this hypothetical post-capitalism world, the new mediators between individuals and organised society would be, Martin argues:

public education, public health care, or public housing may indeed be vanishing into obsolescence. But these and other remnants of the socialist or reformist state remain very much part of the urban fabric and very much part of collective consciousness in many parts of the world. Emptied of their ideological force, these disused ruins also await reappropriation as instruments to redirect – to remediate, that is – the vectors of finance capital and its abstractions.[6]

The end-of-millennium words of Bill Readings, with which I opened this book, echo in the twenty-first-century statement by Martin: the university is a ruin, and, rather than dreaming of a return to the past, what we are left with is the challenge – and the drama – of learning how to dwell in its ruins.[7] Observing the university today, I am tempted to say that, even more than in 1968, a revolution shaking higher education from the ground up is happening right now, triggered by unstoppable neoliberal forces. Ironically – or, depending on perspective, tragically – the current predicament derives from a paradoxical incorporation and neutralisation of ideas (lifelong learning, mobility, self-formation, and so on) that were originally an integral part of the thinking of the 1960s and the 1970s, but which have been turned upside down to the benefit of commodifying forces that are ravishing public education all over the world.

The current Italian university[8] appears to be fortunate in not (yet) having been captured by the corporatisation, first diagnosed twenty years ago, that is a consolidated reality in other 'advanced' Western societies. While waiting for architectural thinking capable of drawing large-scale connections in a similar way to that – for all its contradictions and naivetés – accomplished half a century ago,[9] Italian universities, more broke than ever, nevertheless still survive as a public, open service. And this needs unbiased defence.

Notes

1 See Hans Ibelings, 'The Social Space of Universities', *Rassegna di architettura e urbanistica* 156 (2018): 24–31.
2 See Jos Boys, *Towards Creative Learning Spaces: Re-Thinking the Architecture of Post-Compulsory Education* (Abingdon: Routledge, 2011).
3 See Douglas Spencer, *The Architecture of Neoliberalism: How Contemporary Architecture Became an Instrument of Control and Compliance* (New York: Bloomsbury, 2016).
4 See Massimo De Angelis and Stavros Stavrides, 'On the Commons', *e-flux Journal* #17, June 2017. Available at: www.e-flux.com/journal/17/67351/on-the-commons-a-public-interview-with-massimo-de-angelis-and-stavros-stavrides/ (accessed 26 August 2019); Stavros Stavrides, *Common Space: The City as Commons* (London: Zed Books, 2016).
5 Martin refers in particular to Michael Hardt and Antonio Negri's trilogy *Empire* (2000), *Multitude* (2004), and *Commonwealth* (2009).
6 Reinhold Martin, 'Public and Common(s)', *Places Journal*, January 2013. Available at: https://doi.org/10.22269/130124 (accessed 26 August 2019).
7 Bill Readings, *The University in Ruins* (Cambridge, MA: Harvard University Press, 1996).

8 For a discussion of the contemporary Italian university and its challenges, see Juan Carlos De Martin, *Università futura: Tra democrazia e bit* (Turin: Codice Edizioni, 2017), and Sarah R. Farris, 'Cogito Ergo Insurgo! The Italian University: Laboratory of Crisis and Critique', *Site Magazine* (2012): 31–32.

9 The territorial implications of higher education in Italy have recently been discussed in two monographic issues of *Urbanistica* on university planning. See Nicola Martinelli and Michelangelo Savino, eds., 'L'università italiana tra città e territorio nel XXI secolo – Parte I', *Urbanistica*, 149 (2012): 4–67; Nicola Martinelli and Michelangelo Savino, eds., 'L'università italiana tra città e territorio nel XXI secolo – Parte II', *Urbanistica*, 150–151 (2012).

Appendix 1

Conference on university design, ISES (Istituto per lo Sviluppo dell'Edilizia Sociale), Rome, 1–2 October 1970

Thematic session: Typology and technology (*Gruppo di lavoro sulle questioni tipologiche e tecnologiche*):

Giorgio Gugliormella (coordinator), Antonio Andreuzzi, Romano Chirivi, Salvatore Dierna, Paolo Felli, Guido Ferrara, Alberto Gatti, Franco Karrer, Tomas Maldonado, Gian Mario Oliveri, Mario Preti, Ludovico Quaroni, Antonio Quistelli, Giuseppe Rebecchini, Francesca Sartogo, Piero Sartogo, Giorgio Simoncini, Luigi Spadolini, Ezio Tringali, Marco Ventura, Mario Zaffagnini, research group at Politecnico di Milano (Guido Canella, Giovanni Di Maio), research group at University of Bologna (Fernando Clemente et al.).

Thematic session: Urbanism (*Gruppo di lavoro per i problemi urbanistici*):

Corrado Beguinot, Alessando Bianchi, Umberto De Martino, Salvatore Dierna, Giuseppe Imbesi, Franco Karrer, Elio Piroddi, Sara Rossi, Renato Sorrentino, research group at Politecnico di Milano (Lucio Stellaro D'Angiolini et al.), research group at University of Rome (Paola Coppola Pignatelli et al.).

Thematic session: Quantitative issues (*Gruppo di lavoro per la determinazione del problema quantitativo*):

Albini Sacco (coordinator), Guido Cantalamessa Carboni, Emilia Cosimati, Umberto De Martino, Francesco Guidi, Giorgio Li Puma, Camillo Nucci, research group at Politecnico di Milano (Claudio Buscaglia, Marco Canesi).

Thematic session: Legislation (*Gruppo di lavoro per i problemi legislativi*):

Fabrizio Giovenale (coordinator), Michele Achilli, Franco Amorosino, Umberto De Martino, Giorgio Gugliormella, Giorgio Li Puma, Camillo Nucci, Marcello Vittorini.

Appendix 2

Designing the Italian university: Four competitions

Competition for the University of Florence

Competition call: 4 May 1970 (published as an international competition in *Gazzetta Ufficiale della Repubblica Italiana,* no.110)
  Announcement of results: 22 October 1971
  Projects received: 18 (all from Italian architects)

Jury

G. Sestini (president and rector of the University of Florence), G. Astengo, J. Barge, L. Benevolo, O. Bohigas, James Gowan, P. Carbonara, U. Cassi, V. Di Gioia, T. Maldonado, A. Mariotti, G. Michelucci, A. Montemagni, G. Morozzi, L. Piccinato, E. Salzano.

Prizes

1st prize: *Amalassunta*: Emilio Battisti, Edoardo Detti, Gian Franco Di Pietro, Giovanni Fanelli, Teresa Cobbò, Vittorio Gregotti, Raimondo Innocenti, Marco Massa, Hiromichi Matsui, Mario Mocchi, Paolo Sica, Bruno Viganò Bruno, Marica Zoppi; Collaboratori: Francesco Barbagli, Peo Calza, Gian Franco Dallerba, Franco Luis Neves, Franco Purini.

2nd prize: *Aquarius*: Pierluigi Cervellati, Italo Insolera.

3rd prize: *Sistemi Congiunti Tre*: Ludovico Quaroni, Salvatore Diema, M. Vittoria Diema, Antonio Quistelli, Francesco Karrer, Corrado Terzi, Marco Ventura, Egidio De Grossi, Pierluigi Spadolini, Mario Zaffagnini, Paolo Felli, Carlo Rocco Ferrari, Antonio Andreucci, Graziano Trippa, Carlo Guerrieri, Fernando Clemente, Leonardo Lugli, Alberto Corlaita, Luisella Gelsomino, Maurizio Mari, Carlo Monti, Giovanni Crocioni, Celestino Porrino, Piero Secondini. Consultants: Alberto Pasquinelli, Piero Barucci.

Reimbursements

Ariella: Carlo Aymonino, Giorgio Ciucci, Costantino Dardi, Vittorio De Feo, Umberto De Martino, Mario Manieri Elia, Giovanni Morabito, Francesco Pierobon.

Beltegeuse: Roberto Berardi, Fernando Faggioli, Paolo Halling, Pierluigi Marcaccini, Mauro Mugnai, Francesco Re, Salvatore Romano, Giancarlo Rossi, Resa Sadr, Wilhelm von Wolff; Consulenti: Gastone Tassinari, Domenico Sorace, Mario G. Rossi, Franco Balboni.

Continuum: Italo Gamberini, Bianca Ballestrero Paoli, Serena De Siervo Cresci, Carlo Cresti, Andrea Del Bono, Loris Macci, Piero Paoli, Rosario Vemuccio; Consulenti: Aldo Visalberghi, Tullio Seppilli.

Il rasoio di Occam: Luciana De Rosa, Massimo Pica Ciamarra, Carlo Ricci, Vittorio Biggiero, Raffaele Cozzolino, Marcello Lando; Collaboratori: Giacomo Ricci, Luciano Scotto.

Stoà: Giuseppe Rebecchini, Cesare Columba, Giangiacomo d'Ardia, Livio Quaroni: Collaboratori: Marta Calzolaretti, Andrea Vidotto.

Others

Other entries included:
I progetti si firmano: Archizoom Associati
Il Bosco: 9999
Aragosta Pellegrina (Unknown author)
Linea Verde (Unknown author)
Equipe 70 (Unknown author)
Sentieri melodiosi (Unknown author)
Unknown title: Superstudio

Competition for the University of Cagliari

Competition call: 17 July 1971 (published as a national competition in Gazzetta Ufficiale della Repubblica Italiana, no.180)
    Announcement of results: 27 July 1973
    Projects received: 17 (all from Italian architects)

Jury

Alberto Boscolo (president of the jury and rector of the university), Angelo Berio, Giuseppe Aymerich, Guido Canella, Casula, Di Gioia, Pasquale Mistretta, Giovanni Pau, Antonio Dessì, Antonio Piroddi, and others.

Prizes

1st prize: Gruppo Anversa: Luisa Anversa Ferretti (team leader), Marcello Rebecchini, Giangiacomo D'Ardia, Giuseppina Marcialis, Dario Passi, Livio Quaroni, Giuseppe Rebecchini, Pierluigi Malesani.

2nd prize: Gruppo Samonà: Giuseppe Samonà (team leader), Cesare Airoldi, Cristiana Bedoni, Mariella Di Falco, Gheta Farfaglio, Reiana Lucci, Alberto Samonà, Livia Toccafondi, Egle Tricanato, M. Alberto Chiolino, Carlo Doglio, Francesco Frattini.

3rd prize: Gruppo Aymonino: Costantino Dardi (team leader), Carlo Aymonino, Giorgio Ciucci, Bruno Conti, Vittorio De Feo, Mario Manieri Elia, Giovanni Morabito, Raffaele Panella, Maria Luisa Tugnoli.

Others

Honourable mention: Project Tharros: Uberto Siola (team leader), Carlo Alessandro Manzo, Luigi Pisciotti, Dante Rabitti.

Other entries included:

Endoxa: Giovanni Zedda

Movimento: Francesco Palpacelli

Collettivo punto zero: Carlo Di Pascasio, Alessandro Latini, Giancarlo Leoncilli;

E il Castello?: Giovanni Maria Campus, Paolo Casella; Serafino Casu, Enrico Corti, Enrico Milesi, Paolo Piga, Antonello Sanna, Gavino Dettori, Antonina Massaiu.

Competition for the University of Calabria

Competition call:

First stage, 20 July 1972 (published as an international competition in Gazzetta Ufficiale della Repubblica Italiana, no.188)

Second stage (by invitation), 20 January 1974

Announcement of results: 5 June 1974

Projects received: 67

Jury

Beniamino Andreatta (president of the jury and rector of the university), Ettore De Coro, Marcello Vittorini, Carlo Cocchia, Augusto Cavallari Murat, Aleksander Franta, George Candilis, Michael Brawne, Erdem Aksoy, J.F. Zevaco, Joseph Rykwert.

Prizes

1st prize: Vittorio Gregotti (team leader), Emilio Battisti, GM. Cassano, Hiromichi Matsui, Pierluigi Nicolin, Franco Purini, C. Rusconi Clerici, Bruno Viganò (Competition entry n.51).

2nd prize: Tarquini Martensson (team leader), M. Tarp Jensen, A. Nielsen, S. Lund, J. Engel, W. Kleemann, P. Adeler Bjarno, S. Varming, E. Hovgaard Jensen, J. Jorgensen, M. Wiingaard, D. Eliassen, F. Morelli, A. Nyvig, P. Jacobi (Competition entry n.6).

3rd prize: Jerzy Yozefowicz (team leader), E. Czyz (Competition entry n.19).

4th prize: Robert Smart (team leader), P. McGurn, R. Paoletti, A.E. Towler, F. D'Ayala Valva, I.L. Duncan, R.C. Kerr, R.J. Logan, A.A. McCrory, T.M. Murray, J.E. Pudelko, J.M. Watt (Competition entry n.46).

5th prize: Riccardo Dalisi (team leader), L. Rossi, C. Ricci, N. Polese, F. Reale (Competition entry n.13).

6th prize: Piero Sartogo (team leader), Ove Arup, S. Donato, D. Gimigliano, G. Polimeni, R. Reid, F. Sartogo, G. Gugliormella, S. Micheli, C. Hills (Competition entry n.3).

Others

Other entries included:

Costantino Dardi, Carlo Aymonino, Giorgio Ciucci, Bruno Conti, Vittorio De Feo, Mario Manieri Elia, Giovanni Morabito, Raffaele Panella, Maria Luisa Tugnoli (Competition entry n.27).

Ludovico Quaroni, S. Dierna, R.C. Ferrari, F. Karrer, P.L. Spadolini (Competition entry n.25).

Giuseppe Rebecchini, Piero Baracchi, Livio Quaroni (Competition entry n.57).

Giuseppe Samonà, Cesare Ajroldi, Cristiana Bedoni, Mariella Di Falco, Gaetana Farfaglio, Rejana Lucci, M. Salvia, M. Alberto Chiorino, Alberto Samonà, Francesco Tentori, Livia Toccafondi, G. Trincanato (Competition entry n.44).

Guido Canella, C. Bono, A. Cristofellis, G. Di Maio, G. Fiorese, V. Parmiani, G.P. Semino, F. De Miranda, F. Gnecchi Ruscone, M. Ardita, R. Biscardini, G. Goggi, F. Godowsky (Competition entry n.36).

Gianugo Polesello (competion entry number unknown).

BBPR (competion entry number unknown).

Competition for the University of Salerno

Competition call: 20 June 1973 (published as a national competition in Gazzetta Ufficiale della Repubblica Italiana, no.157)

Announcement of results: 30 June 1975

Projects received: 11 (all from Italian architects)

Jury

Nicola Cilento (president of the jury and rector of the university), Pierluigi Spadolini, Giovanni Crispo Ciccarelli, Tommaso Pelosi, Renato Sparacio, Leonardo Del Bufalo, Aniello Amendola, Ercole Gizzi, Carlo Aymonino, Lodovico Meneghetti.

Prizes

1st prize: Mario Ingrami (team leader), Giulio De Luca, Vincenzo Di Gioia, Enrico Petti, Antonietta Piemontese, Luigi Piemontese and Rolando Scarano.

2nd prize ex aequo: Massimo Pica Ciamarra (team leader), Luciana De Rosa, Renato Raguzzino, Antimo Rocereto, M. Vittoria Serpieri, Guelfo Tozzi, Elio Giangreco, Giuseppe Giordano, Nello Polese, Carlo Ricci, Francesco Reale, Carlo Viggiani and Roberto Morselli.

2nd prize ex-aequo: Uberto Siola (team leader), Giacinta Ialongo, Emilia Giaquinto, Emilio Luongo, Antonio Triglia, Rosaldo Bonicalzi, Marisa Carmini, Rejana Lucci, Carlo A. Manzo, Luigi Pisciotti, Dante Rabitti, Lidia Savares, Carlo Emanuele Callari, Renato Martellotta, Pierluigi Cattaneo, Salvatore Marano, Giancarlo Barbaro and Alfredo Plachesi.

Others

Other entries included:

Giorgio Muratore.

Carmelo Giummo.

Enrico Corti (team leader), Enrico Milesi, Paolo Piga, Serafino Casu and Antonello Sanna.

Riccardo Dalisi (team leader), Filippo Alison, Leonardo Rossi, Cesare Ulisse, Ettore Minervini and Luciano Scotto.

Virgilio Vercelloni (team leader), Demetrio Costantino, Gabriella Crivelli, Lucio Stellaro D'Angiolini, Mario Silvani, and Giancarlo Tuzzato.

Ludovico Degli Uberti (team leader), Alfonso Settimi, Sabino Staffa and Ugo Valle.

Giancarlo De Grazia.

Adalberto Dal Lago (team leader), Stefano Giannotti and Luigi Pieruzzi.

Appendix 3

Higher education: An international architectural discourse, 1960–1977

A most effective index of the extent to which higher education reform influenced the architectural discourse in the period discussed in this book is offered by the substantial number of articles and monographic issues that major international magazines devoted to the topic. Here is a synthesis of the main contributions across four countries – the UK, the US, France, and Italy – and their main architectural publications – *Architectural Design, The Architectural Review, Architectural Forum, Architectural Record, L'Architecture d'Aujourd'hui, Casabella, Controspazio, Domus,* and *Urbanistica.*

Architectural Design, UK

March 1960

Graeme Shankland, 'What Is Happening in Oxford & Cambridge? Architecture and the New University', pp. 85–93

October 1966

Cedric Price, 'Life-conditioning', p. 483
  Cedric Price, 'Potteries Thinkbelt: A Plan for an Advanced Educational Industry in North Staffordshire', pp. 484–497

December 1966

Special issue 'Living in Universities'

May 1968

Special issue 'What about Learning?' Guest edited by Cedric Price

November 1969

Sim van der Ryn, 'The University Environment', pp. 618–620

April 1972

Martin Pawley, 'Universitas', pp. 214–215
  Martin Pawley, 'The Demilitarisation of the University', pp. 216–219

November 1974

Peter Jockush, 'University Campus Design', pp. 702–717

The Architectural Review, UK

October 1957, vol. 122, no. 729

Nikolaus Pevsner, 'Universities: Yesterday', pp. 234–239
  Lionel Brett, 'Universities: Today', pp. 240–251

October 1963, vol. 134, no. 800

Special issue 'Universities'

July 1964, vol. 136, no. 809

'The University in the City', p. 9
  'Edinburgh University: A Case-study of Evolution and Planned Redevelopment' (design: Percy Johnson-Marshall)

April 1970, vol. 147, no. 878

Special issue 'The New Universities' (associate editor: Michael Brawne)

January 1974, vol. 155, no. 923

'Keep it in the city', 'University of Leeds' (design: Chamberlin, Powell & Bon), pp. 3–30

Architectural Forum, US

February 1962, vol. 116, no. 2

'Colleges: the Education Explosion', Editorial, pp. 51–73
  Warren Cox, 'The Mood of a Great Campus', pp. 74–82

March 1963, vol. 118, no. 3

David B. Carlson, 'Town and Gown', pp. 92–95
  Donald Canty, 'New Frontier of Higher Education', pp. 96–103

September 1963, vol. 119, no. 3

'N.Y.'s Big College Program Progresses', p. 11 (on the State University of New York building program)

September 1965, vol. 123, no. 2

Special issue, 'Campus City, Chicago', pp. 21–45

December 1965, vol. 123, no. 5

'Single-Building Campus', pp. 13–21

April 1966, vol. 124, no. 3

'How to Grow a Campus', pp. 57–67

May 1966, vol. 124, no. 4

'The New Campus', pp. 30–55

July–August 1967, vol. 127, no. 1

'Architecture on Campus', pp. 46–97

December 1968, vol. 129, no. 5

'Campus City Continued', pp. 29–43 (progress report on construction at Chicago Circle Campus)

April 1972, vol. 136, no. 3

Ian Brown, 'Irrelevance of University Architecture: A Forthright Discussion of Recent British Universities, with an Important Message for American Campuses', pp. 50–55

Architectural Record, US

September 1959, vol. 126, no. 3

William Wilson Wurster, 'Campus Planning', pp. 161–167

November 1960, vol. 128, no. 5

Eero Saarinen, 'Campus Planning: The Unique World of the University', pp. 123–130

February 1961, vol. 129, no. 2

'Planning the University of Baghdad', pp. 107–122 (architects: Walter Gropius and The Architects Collaborative International)

October 1961, vol. 130, no. 4

'Campus Design by Function, Not by Discipline', pp. 12–13 (on Chicago Circle Campus by SOM)

August 1963, vol. 134, no. 2

James Morrisseau, 'Some Basics of Campus Planning', pp. 125–128

May 1964, vol. 135, no. 5

'Campus Planning for the State University of New York', pp. 171–177

November 1964, vol. 136, no. 5

'California's New Campuses', pp. 175–199

July 1969, vol. 146, no. 1

'University of East Anglia', pp. 99–110

February 1970, vol. 147, no. 2

Milfred F. Schmertz, 'Designs for the Campus', pp. 101–118

L'Architecture d'Aujourd'hui, France

December 1965–January 1966, no. 123

Special issue 'Ecoles et Universités'

April–May 1968, no. 137

Special issue 'Universités'

January–February 1976, no. 183

Special issue 'Université, ville et territoire'

Casabella, Italy

August 1960, no. 242

Giulio Carlo Argan, 'La città-scuola', pp. 3–4
   'La città universitaria di Bagdad' (design: The Architects Collaborative International Limited), pp. 2–31

October 1962, no. 268

Matilde Rivolta Baffa, 'Aspetti e prospettive dei complessi universitari in Gran Bretagna', pp. 17–24

January 1968, no. 322

Carlo Pelliccia, Piero Sartogo, 'Campus design 1. Il passaggio da una struttura monofunzionale ad una struttura integrata dell'educazione', pp. 20–25. (This is the first article in a series of seven that were published in 1968 and 1969 in issues 323, 325, 326, 332, 333, and 334.)

March 1968, no. 324

Carlo Guenzi, 'Università: le assemblee propongono', pp. 58–63

June 1969, no. 337

'Mini-riforma per l'università', pp. 51–54

May 1970, no. 348

Piero Sartogo, 'Università e città: Studio sui modelli di pianificazione dell'istruzione superiore in rapporto ai modelli di pianificazione urbana', pp. 9–16

April-October 1971, no. 357

Special issue 'Studenti senza casa'

January 1972, no. 361

Issue on the University of Florence competition

March 1975, no. 399

Emilio Ambasz, 'The Univercity', pp. 8–9

March 1977, no. 423

Special issue 'Università: Progettare il mutamento'

Controspazio, Italy

January–February 1972, nos. 1–2

Issue on the University of Florence competition

September 1973, no. 3

Issue on the University of Cagliari competition

Domus, Italy

March 1960, no. 364

'L'Università di Urbino' (design: Giancarlo De Carlo), pp. 5–16

April 1963, no. 401

'Architetture universitarie in Inghilterra', pp. 2–16

April 1972, no. 509

Issue on the University of Florence competition

Urbanistica, Italy

April 1974, no. 62

Issue on the University of Florence competition

Bibliography

University, knowledge, learning and the city

Accorsi, Florence. *Universités dans la ville = Università in Città = Universities in the City*. Brussels, Paris and Milan: AAM Editions; SEMAPA; Ante Prima; SilvanaEditoriale, 2009.

Agamben, Giorgio. 'Studenti', 15 May 2017. Available at: www.quodlibet.it/giorgio-agamben-studenti (accessed 26 August 2019).

Architettura. 'La Città Universitaria di Madrid'. 10(1934): 581–596.

Architettura. 'La Città Universitaria di Roma'. 14(1935).

Bailey, Michael and Des Freedman. *The Assault on Universities: A Manifesto for Resistance*. London: Pluto Press, 2011.

Barnett, Roland. 'The Idea of the University in the Twenty-First Century: Where's the Imagination?' *Yükseköğretim Dergisi*, 1, no. 2(2011): 88–94.

Bauman, Zygmunt. 'Universities: Old, New and Different'. In *The Postmodern University? Contested Visions of Higher Education in Society*, edited by Anthony Smith and Frank Webster, 17–26. Buckingham: Society for Research into Higher Education & Open University Press, 1997.

Bender, Thomas, ed. *The University and the City: From Medieval Origins to the Present*. New York: Oxford University Press, 1988.

Bender, Thomas. 'Scholarship, Local Life, and the Necessity of Worldliness'. In *The Urban University and Its Identity*, edited by Herman van der Wusten, 17–28. Dordrecht: Springer Netherlands, 1998.

Benneworth, Paul, David Charles, and Ali Madanipour. 'Building Localized Interactions Between Universities and Cities Through University Spatial Development'. *European Planning Studies*, 18, no. 10(2010): 1611–1629.

Blanchfield, Caitlin, ed. *Columbia in Manhattanville*. New York: Columbia Books on Architecture and the City, 2016.

Bok, Derek Curtis. *Universities in the Marketplace: The Commercialization of Higher Education*. Princeton, NJ: Princeton University Press, 2003.

Boys, Jos. *Towards Creative Learning Spaces: Re-Thinking the Architecture of Post-Compulsory Education*. Abingdon: Routledge, 2011.

Brizzi, Gian Paolo, Piero Del Negro, and Andrea Romano, eds. *Storia delle università d'Italia*. 3 vols. Messina: SICANIA by GEM s.r.l., 2007.

Campos Calvo-Sotelo, Pablo. *The Journey of Utopia: The Story of the First American Style Campus in Europe*. New York: Nova Science Publishers, 2006.

Capello, Roberta, Agnieszka Olechnicka, and Grzegorz Gorzelak, eds. *Universities, Cities and Regions. Loci for Knowledge and Innovation Creation.* London: Routledge, 2013.

Carrera, Manuel, ed. *Sapienza razionalista: L'architettura degli anni '30 nella Città Universitaria.* Rome: Nuova cultura, 2013.

Casciato, Maristella. *Il campus universitario di Chieti.* Milan: Electa, 1997.

Castells, Manuel and Peter Hall. *Technopoles of the World: The Making of Twenty-First-Century Industrial Complexes.* New York: Routledge, 1994.

Chapman, M. Perry. *American Places: In Search of the Twenty-First Century Campus.* Westport, CT: Praeger Publishers, 2006.

Cole, Jonathan R. *The Great American University: Its Rise to Preeminence, Its Indispensable National Role, Why It Must be Protected.* New York: Public Affairs, 2009.

Collini, Stefan. *What Are Universities For?* London: Penguin, 2012.

De Martin, Juan Carlos. *Università futura: Tra democrazia e bit.* Turin: Codice Edizioni, 2017.

Di Pol, Redi Sante. *La scuola per tutti gli italiani: L'istruzione di base tra stato e società dal primo ottocento ad oggi.* Milan: Mondadori Università, 2016.

Eagleton, Terry. 'The Slow Death of the University'. *The Chronicle of Higher Education,* 6 April 2015.

Edu-factory. *L'università globale: Il nuovo mercato del sapere.* Rome: Manifestolibri, 2008.

Farris, Sarah R. 'Cogito Ergo Insurgo! The Italian University: Laboratory of Crisis and Critique'. *Site Magazine* (2012): 31–32.

Field, John and Mal Leicester. *Lifelong Learning: Education across the Lifespan.* London and New York: RoutledgeFalmer, 2003.

Flexner, Abraham. *The Usefulness of Useless Knowledge.* Princeton, NJ: Princeton University Press, 2017.

Gaines, Thomas A. *The Campus as a Work of Art.* New York: Praeger, 1991.

Goddard, John and Paul Vallance. *The University and the City.* New York: Routledge, 2013.

Haar, Sharon. *The City as Campus: Urbanism and Higher Education in Chicago.* Minneapolis, MN: University of Minnesota Press, 2011.

Habermas, Jürgen and John R. Blazek. 'The Idea of the University: Learning Processes'. *New German Critique,* 41(1987): 3–22.

Harriss, Harriet and Lynnette Widder, eds. *Architecture Live Projects: Pedagogy into Practice.* New York: Routledge, 2014.

Hartch, Todd. *The Prophet of Cuernavaca: Ivan Illich and the Crisis of the West.* New York: Oxford University Press, 2015.

Haskins, Charles Homer. *The Rise of Universities.* New York: H. Holt and Company, 1923.

Hoeger, Kerstin, and Kees Christiaanse, eds. *Campus and the City: Urban Design for the Knowledge Society.* Zurich: GTA Verlag, 2007.

Ibelings, Hans. 'The Social Space of Universities'. *Rassegna di architettura e urbanistica,* 156(2018): 24–31.

Illich, Ivan. *Deschooling Society.* New York: Marion Boyars, 1970.

Illich, Ivan. *After Deschooling, What?* London: Writers and Readers Publishing Cooperative, 1976.

L'architecture d'aujourd'hui, 'La Cité Universitaire de Madrid'. 6(1936): 26–33.

Madanipour, Ali. *Knowledge Economy and the City: Spaces of Knowledge.* New York: Routledge, 2011.

Martinelli, Nicola and Michelangelo Savino, eds. 'L'università italiana tra città e territorio nel XXI secolo – Parte I'. *Urbanistica*, 149(2012): 4–67.

Martinelli, Nicola and Michelangelo Savino, eds. 'L'università italiana tra città e territorio nel XXI secolo – Parte II'. *Urbanistica*, 150–151(2012): 10–43.

McNeely, Ian F. and Lisa Wolverton. *Reinventing Knowledge: From Alexandria to the Internet*. New York: W. W. Norton, 2008.

Moreno, Joaquim. *The University Is Now on Air Broadcasting Modern Architecture*. Montréal: Canadian Centre for Architecture, 2018.

Pacini, Renato. 'Cronache romane: il grandioso progetto della Città Universitaria'. *Emporium*, 459(1933): 177–182.

Pacini, Renato. 'La Città Universitaria di Roma'. *Architettura*, 8(1933).

Perry, David C. and Wim Wiewel. *The University as Urban Developer: Case Studies and Analysis*. Armonk, NY: M.E. Sharpe, 2005.

Persitz, Alexandre. 'Les Cités Universitaires'. *L'architecture d'aujourd'hui*, 6(1936): 8–11.

Pevsner, Nikolaus. 'Universities: Yesterday'. *The Architectural Review*, 122, no. 729 (1957): 234–239.

Piacentini, Marcello. 'Metodi e caratteristiche'. *Architettura*, 14(1935): 2–8.

Pisani, Mario. 'La Città Universitaria'. In *Architetture di Marcello Piacentini*, 111–118. Rome: CLEAR, 2004.

Polanyi, Michael. *Personal Knowledge: Towards a Post-Critical Philosophy*. Chicago: University of Chicago Press, 1964.

Polanyi, Michael. *The Tacit Dimension*. Garden City, NY: Doubleday, 1966.

Puddu, Sabrina. 'Campus o cittadella? Il progetto di un'eredità'. In *Territori della conoscenza: Un progetto per Cagliari e la sua università*, edited by Sabrina Puddu, Martino Tattara, and Francesco Zuddas, 134–151. Macerata: Quodlibet, 2017.

Puddu, Sabrina, and Francesco Zuddas. 'Cities and Science Parks: The Urban Experience of 22@Barcelona'. *Territorio*, 64(2013): 145–152.

Raschke, Carl A. *The Digital Revolution and the Coming of the Postmodern University*. New York: RoutledgeFalmer, 2003.

Rassegna di architettura.'La Città Universitaria di Roma'. (1936): 181–194.

Raunig, Gerald. *Factories of Knowledge: Industries of Creativity*. Los Angeles: Semiotext (e), 2013.

Readings, Bill. *The University in Ruins*. Cambridge, MA: Harvard University Press, 1996.

Spaventa, Silvio. 'L'autonomia universitaria (1884)'. In *Il resistibile declino dell'università*, edited by Gerardo Marotta and Livio Sichirollo, 123–170. Naples: Guerini e Associati, 1999.

Tiffin, John, and Lalita Rajasingham. *The Global Virtual University*. London: RoutledgeFalmer, 2003.

Turner, Paul Venable. *Campus: An American Planning Tradition*. Cambridge, MA: MIT Press, 1984.

University of California Berkeley Trustees of the Phoebe A. Hearst Architectural Plan. *The International Competition for the Phoebe A. Hearst Architectural Plan for the University of California*. San Francisco: The Trustees, 1900.

VV.AA. *1935/1985 La 'Sapienza' nella Città Universitaria: Catalogo della mostra*. Rome: Multigrafica Editrice, 1985.

Whyte, William. *Redbrick: A Social and Architectural History of Britain's Civic Universities*. Oxford: Oxford University Press, 2015.

Wilson, Richard Guy, ed. *Thomas Jefferson's Academical Village: The Creation of an Architectural Masterpiece*. Charlottesville, VA: University Press of Virginia, 1993.

Woods, Mary N. 'Thomas Jefferson and the University of Virginia: Planning the Academic Village'. *Journal of the Society of Architectural Historians*, 44, no. 3(1985): 266–283.

Higher education and university design and planning in the 1960s and 1970s

Ar-Rifai, Taleb Dia Ed-Deen. 'The New University Environment: A 20th Century Urban Ideal'. PhD thesis, University of Pennsylvania, 1983.

Aureli, Pier Vittorio. 'Labor and Architecture: Revisiting Cedric Price's Potteries Thinkbelt'. *Log*, 23(2011): 97–118.

Birks, Tony, and Michael Holford. *Building the New Universities*. Newton Abbot: David and Charles, 1972.

Brawne, Michael, ed. *University Planning and Design: A Symposium*. London: Lund Humphries for the Architectural Association, 1967.

Brett, Lionel. 'Universities: Today'. *The Architectural Review*, 122, no. 729(1957): 240–251.

Brett, Lionel. 'Site, Growth and Plan'. *The Architectural Review*, 134, no. 800(1963): 257–264.

Dober, Richard P. *Campus Planning*. New York: Reinhold, 1963.

Dormer, Peter, and Stefan Muthesius. *Concrete and Open Skies: Architecture at the University of East Anglia, 1962–2000*. London: Unicorn, 2001.

Feld, Gabriel, *et al.*, eds. *Free University, Berlin: Candilis, Josic, Woods, Schiedhelm*. London: Architectural Association, 1999.

Hardingham, Samantha, and Kester Rattenbury, eds. *Cedric Price: Potteries Thinkbelt*. Abingdon: Routledge, 2007.

Kerr, Clark. *The Uses of the University*. Cambridge, MA: Harvard University Press, 1963.

Muthesius, Stefan. *The Postwar University: Utopianist Campus and College*. New Haven, CT: Yale University Press, 2000.

Paltzonian. *Yearbook of the State of New York College of Arts and Sciences New Paltz*. New York: New Paltz, 1963.

Pawley, Martin. 'The Demilitarisation of the University'. *Architectural Design*, 4(1972): 216–219.

Price, Cedric. 'Life Conditioning'. *Architectural Design*, 5(1966a): 483.

Price, Cedric. 'PTb. Potteries Thinkbelt. A Plan for an Advanced Educational Industry in North Staffordshire'. *Architectural Design*, 5(1966b): 484–497.

Price, Cedric. 'Potteries Thinkbelt'. *New Society*, 192, no. 2(1966c): 14–17.

Rykwert, Joseph. 'Universities as Institutional Archetypes of Our Age'. *Zodiac*, 18(1968): 61–63.

Tzonis, Alexander, and Liane Lefaivre. 'Beyond Monuments, Beyond Zip-a-Tone, into Space/Time'. In *Free University Berlin: Candilis, Josic, Woods, Schiedhelm*, edited by VV.AA., 118–141. London: AA Publications, 1999.

Woods, Shadrach. *Free University Berlin*, edited by John Donat, 116–117. New York: The Viking Press, 1965.

Woods, Shadrach. 'The Education Bazaar'. *Harvard Educational Review*, 4(1969): 116–125.

Woods, Shadrach. 'Remember the Spring of the Old Days?' *Architecture Plus*, 2, no. 1 (1974): 51.

The Italian postwar architectural and urbanistic debate

Archibugi, Franco, ed. *La città regione in Italia*. Turin: Boringhieri, 1966.

Archizoom. 'No-Stop City: Residential Parkings, Climatic Universal System'. *Domus* 496 (1971): 49–54.

Archizoom Associati. 'Città, catena di montaggio del sociale: Ideologia e teoria della metropoli'. *Casabella*, 350–351(1970): 43–52.

Aureli, Pier Vittorio . *The Project of Autonomy: Politics and Architecture within and against Capitalism*. New York: Princeton Architectural Press, 2008.

Aymonino, Carlo. 'Il sistema dei centri direzionali nella capitale'. *Casabella*, 264(1962): 21–26.

Aymonino, Carlo. *Origini e sviluppo della città moderna*. Padua: Marsilio, 1965.

Aymonino, Carlo, *I centri direzionali: La teoria e la practica, gli esempi italiani e stranieri, il sistema direzionale della città di Bologna*. Bari: De Donato, 1967.

Aymonino, Carlo and Costantino Dardi. 'Roma Est: Proposta architettonica'. *Controspazio*, 12(1973): 45–49.

Aymonino, Carlo, *et al.*, eds. *La città territorio: Un esperimento didattico sul centro direzionale di Centocelle in Roma*. Bari: Leonardo da Vinci, 1964.

Bardelli, Pier Giovanni, Rinaldo Capomolla, and Rosalia Vittorini, eds. *L'architettura INA Casa (1949–1963): Aspetti e problemi di conservazione e recupero*. Rome: Gangemi, 2003.

Biraghi, Marco, *et al.*, eds. *Italia 60/70: Una stagione dell'architettura*. Padua: Il poligrafo, 2010.

Bonfanti, Ezio, ed. *Architettura razionale*. Milan: Franco Angeli, 1973.

Bordogna, Enrico, Gentucca Canella, and Elvio Manganaro, eds. *Guido Canella, 1931–2009*. Milan: Franco Angeli, 2014.

Branzi, Andrea. *Weak and Diffuse Modernity: The World of Projects at the Beginning of the 21st Century*. Milan: Skira, 2006.

Branzi, Andrea. *Una generazione esagerata: Dai radical italiani alla crisi della globalizzazione*. Milan: Baldini & Castoldi, 2014.

Bunčuga, Franco. *Conversazioni con Giancarlo De Carlo: Architettura e libertà*. Milan: Elèuthera, 2000.

Canella, Guido. 'Vecchie e nove ipotesi per i centri direzionali'. *Casabella*, 275(1963): 42–56.

Canella, Guido. 'Relazioni tra morfologia, tipologia dell'organismo architettonico e ambiente fisico'. In *L'utopia della realtà*, by Franco Basaglia, 66–81. Bari: Leonardo da Vinci Editrice, 1965.

Canella, Guido. 'Appunti per il consuntivo di un corso'. In *L'utopia della realtà* by Franco Basaglia. Bari: Leonardo da Vinci Editrice, 1965.

Canella, Guido. *Il sistema teatrale a Milano*. Bari: Dedalo, 1966.

Canella, Guido. 'Lineamenti di un programma di lavoro (lecture, 16 December 1966)'. In *Alcune lezioni tenute al corso di Elementi di Composizione nell'anno accademico 1966–67*. Milan: Politecnico di Milano, 1967.

Canella, Guido. 'Dal laboratorio della composizione'. In *Teoria della progettazione architettonica*, edited by Antonio Locatelli, 83–100. Bari: Dedalo, 1968.

Canella, Guido. *Un ruolo per l'architettura*. Milan: Clup, 1969.

Ceccarelli, Paolo. 'Urbanistica opulenta'. *Casabella*, 278(1963): 5–8.

Conforti, Claudia. *Carlo Aymonino: L'architettura non è un mito*. Rome: Officina, 1980.

Conforto, Cina, Gabriele De Giorgi, Alessandra Muntoni, and Marcello Pazzaglini. *Il dibattito architettonico in Italia, 1945–1975*. Rome: Bulzoni, 1977.

D'Amato Guerrieri, Claudio. 'Controspazio come "piccola rivista"'. *FAmagazine*, 43 (2018): 33–40.

Dardi, Costantino. *Semplice, lineare, complesso*. Rome: Magma, 1976.

De Carlo, Giancarlo. *Urbino: La storia di una città e il piano della sua evoluzione urbanistica*. Padua: Marsilio, 1966.

De Carlo, Giancarlo. 'Architecture's Public'. In *Architecture and Participation*, edited by Peter Blundell Jones, Doina Petrescu, and Jeremy Till, 3–18. London: Spon Press, 2005 (first published in Italian as 'Il pubblico dell'architettura'. *Parametro*, 5(1970): 4–12).

De Carlo, Giancarlo and Pierluigi Nicolin. 'Conversation on Urbino'. *Lotus International*, 18(1978): 6–22.

De CarloGiancarlo, *et al*. *La nuova dimensione della città: La città-regione*. Milan: ILSES, 1962.

Doglio, Carlo. *L'equivoco della città giardino*. Naples: RL, 1953.

Doglio, Carlo. *La città giardino*. Rome: Gangemi, 1985.

Ferrari, Mario. *Il progetto urbano in Italia: 1940–1990*. Florence: Alinea, 2005.

Gargiani, Roberto. *Archizoom Associati, 1966–1974: Dall'onda pop alla superficie neutra*. Milan: Electa, 2007.

Gregotti, Vittorio. *Il territorio dell'architettura*. Milan: Feltrinelli, 1966.

Gregotti, Vittorio. *New Directions in Italian Architecture*. New York: G. Braziller, 1968.

Gregotti, Vittorio. 'Territory and Architecture'. *Architectural Design Profile*, 59, nos. 5–6 (1985): 28–34.

Gregotti, Vittorio and Emilio Battisti. 'Due concorsi'. *Edilizia Moderna*, 82–83(1964): 109.

Koenig, Klaus Giovanni. 'Untitled'. *Casabella*, 370–371(1970): 43.

Malacarne, Gino. 'Guido Canella e lo spazio teatrale'. In *Guido Canella, 1931–2009*, edited by Enrico Bordogna, Gentucca Canella, and Elvio Manganaro, 43–50. Milan: Franco Angeli, 2014.

Melograni, Carlo. *Architetture nell'Italia della ricostruzione: Modernità versus modernizzazione 1945–1960*. Macerata: Quodlibet, 2015.

Ministero del Bilancio e della Programmazione Economica. *Progetto '80: Rapporto preliminare al Programma Economico Nazionale 1971–75*. Milan: Feltrinelli, 1969.

Nicolin, Paola. *Castelli di carte: La XIV Triennale di Milano*. Macerata: Quodlibet, 2011.

Pazzaglini, Marcello. 'Il dibattito sulla città e sul territorio'. In *Il dibattito architettonico in Italia, 1945–1975*, edited by Cina Conforto, Gabriele De Giorgi, Alessandra Muntoni, and Marcello Pazzaglini, 56–127. Rome: Bulzoni, 1977.

Piccinato, Luigi, Vieri Quilici, and Manfredo Tafuri. 'La città-territorio: Verso una nuova dimensione'. *Casabella*, 270(1962): 16–25.

Portoghesi, Paolo. 'Perché Milano: Une saison en enfer'. *Controspazio*, 1(1973): 6–9.

Portoghesi, Paolo. 'L'architettura civile di Guido Canella'. In *Guido Canella, 1931–2009*, edited by Enrico Bordogna, Gentucca Canella, and Elvio Manganaro, 23–32. Milan: Franco Angeli, 2014.

Renzoni, Cristina. *Il Progetto '80: Un'idea di paese nell'Italia degli anni sessanta*. Florence: Alinea, 2012.

Quaroni, Ludovico. 'Il paese dei barocchi'. *Casabella*, 215(1957a): 24–43.

Quaroni, Ludovico. 'Politica del quartiere'. *La Casa*, 4(1957b).

Quaroni, Ludovico. 'Sulla progettazione delle strutture universitarie'. In *Atti del convegno di studio sull'edilizia universitaria*. Rome: ISES (Istituto per lo Sviluppo dell'Edilizia Sociale), 1970.

Quaroni, Ludovico, Giancarlo De Carlo, Piero Moroni, and Eduardo Vittoria. 'Tavola rotonda'. *Urbanistica*, 32(1960): 6–8.

Rogers, Ernesto Nathan. 'Esperienza di un corso universitario'. In *L'utopia della realtà*, ed. Franco Basaglia. Bari: Leonardo da Vinci Editrice, 1965.

Rossi, Aldo. 'Nuovi problemi'. *Casabella*, 264(1962): 2–7.

Rossi, Aldo. *L'architettura della città*. Padua: Marsilio, 1966.

Rykwert, Joseph. 'Vittorio Gregotti e Associati: La nuova università della Calabria, il progetto vincente al concorso internazionale'. *Domus*, 540(1974): 15–16.

Rykwert, Joseph. *Gregotti Associati*. Milan: Rizzoli, 1995.

Samonà, Alberto. 'Alla ricerca di un metodo per la nuova dimensione'. *Casabella*, 277 (1963): 50–54.

Samonà, Giuseppe. *L'urbanistica e l'avvenire della città negli stati europei*. Bari: Laterza, 1959a.

Samonà, Giuseppe. 'La nuova dimensione della città'. *Urbanistica conversazioni*, May, 1959b.

Samonà, Giuseppe. 'Relazione e conclusione al seminario su città-territorio'. In *La città territorio: Un esperimento didattico sul centro direzionale di Centocelle in Roma*, edited by Carlo Aymonino et al., 90–99. Bari: Leonardo da Vinci editrice, 1964.

Samonà, Giuseppe. *L'unità architettura-urbanistica: Scritti e progetti, 1929–1973*. Milan: Franco Angeli, 1975a.

Samonà, Giuseppe. *Giuseppe Samonà: 1923–1975, Cinquant'anni di architetture*. Rome: Officina, 1975b.

Sirugo, Francesco. 'Città e regione nello sviluppo storico della città industriale'. In *La città regione in Italia*, edited by Franco Archibugi, 53–113. Turin: Boringhieri, 1966.

Tafuri, Manfredo. *Ludovico Quaroni e lo sviluppo dell'architettura moderna in Italia*. Milan: Edizioni di Comunita, 1946.

Tafuri, Manfredo. 'Studi e ipotesi di lavoro per il sistema direzionale di Roma'. *Casabella*, 264(1962): 27–35.

Tafuri, Manfredo. 'Teoria e critica nella cultura urbanistica italiana del dopoguerra'. In *La città territorio: Un esperimento didattico sul centro direzionale di Centocelle in Roma*, edited by Carlo Aymonino, 39–45. Bari: Leonardo da Vinci Editrice, 1964.

Tafuri, Manfredo. 'Per una critica dell'ideologia architettonica'. *Contropiano*, 1(1969): 31–79.

Tafuri, Manfredo. *Architecture and Utopia: Design and Capitalist Development*. Cambridge, MA: MIT Press, 1976 (first published in Italian in 1973 as *Progetto e utopia: Architettura e sviluppo capitalistico*).

Tafuri, Manfredo. 'Le avventure dell'oggetto: Architettura e progetti di Vittorio Gregotti'. In *Vittorio Gregotti: Progetti e architetture*, by Manfredo Tafuri, 7–29. Milan: Electa, 1982.

Tafuri, Manfredo. *Storia dell'architettura italiana, 1944–1985*. Turin: Einaudi, 1986.

The cultural and architectural debate on the Italian university in the 1960s–1970s

Achilli, Michele. 'Nuovi centri universitari: Rapporto sugli aspetti legislativi'. In *Atti del convegno di studio sull'edilizia universitaria*. Rome: ISES (Istituto per lo Sviluppo dell'Edilizia Sociale), 1970.

Anversa Ferretti, Luisa. *et al.* 'Concorso nazionale per il piano urbanistico di sistemazione della sede dell'Università di Cagliari: Relazione tecnica.' Rome: Studio Anversa Ferretti, 1972.

Architectural Review. 'A Florentine Fiasco'. 900(1972): 79–82.

Archizoom. 'Progetto di concorso per l'Università di Firenze'. *Domus*, 509(1974): 10–12.

Aymonino, Carlo, *et al.* 'La nuova Università di Cagliari'. *Controspazio*, 3(1973): 30–39.

Basaglia, Franco. *L'utopia della realtà: Un esperimento didattico sulla tipologia della scuola primaria.* Bari: Leonardo da Vinci Editrice, 1965.

Beguinot, Corrado. 'La rete strutturale del Mezzogiorno: Estratto dallo studio "Strutture del sapere ed edilizia universitaria in Italia"'. In *Atti del convegno di studio sull'edilizia universitaria.* Rome: ISES (Istituto per lo Sviluppo dell'Edilizia Sociale), 1970.

Beguinot, Corrado. 'Il contesto territoriale e le caratteristiche dell'area'. In *Concorso nazionale per la progettazione della nuova sede dell'Università di Salerno: Relazione tecnica allegata al bando.* Salerno, 1973 (first published in part as 'La rete strutturale del Mezzogiorno', 1970, and subsequently as 'L'università in Campania e nel Salernitano', 1971).

Biraghi, Marco. 'Università: La Facoltà di Architettura del Politecnico di Milano (1963–74)'. In *Italia 60/70: Una stagione dell'architettura*, edited by Marco Biraghi, *et al.*, 87–97. Padua: Il poligrafo, 2010.

Bohigas, Oriol. 'Considerazioni di un membro della giuria'. *Casabella*, 361(1972): 20–22, 61.

Bonani, Giampaolo. 'Fine della pianificazione universitaria'. *Parametro*, 44(1976): 4–5, 62.

Branzi, Andrea. 'The Abolition of School – Radical Note no. 4'. *Casabella*, 373 (1973): 10.

Buscaglia, Claudio, ed. *Ciclo di comunicazioni sul rapporto funzioni-istituzioni: il sistema dell'istruzione.* Milan: Politecnico di Milano, 1971.

Buzzati-Traverso, Adriano. *Un fossile denutrito: L'università italiana.* Milan: Il saggiatore, 1969.

Campus, Giovanni Maria and Paolo Casella. 'Università senza pianificazione e senza riforme'. *Casabella*, 367(1972): 3.

Canella, Guido. 'Passé et Avenir de L'anti-Ville Universitaire'. *L'architecture d'aujourd'hui*, 137(1968): 16–19 (republished in Italian as 'Passato e prospettive dell'anti-città universitaria'. In *Università. Ragione, Contesto, Tipo*, edited by Guido Canella and Lucio S. D'Angiolini, 35–50. Bari: Dedalo libri, 1975).

Canella, Guido and Lucio S. D'Angiolini, eds. *Università: Ragione, contesto, tipo.* Bari: Dedalo Libri, 1975.

Canella, Guido, *et al.* 'Progetto per il concorso per l'Università della Calabria'. In *Università: Ragione, contesto, tipo*, edited by Guido Canella and Lucio S. D'Angiolini, 423–442. Bari: Dedalo Libri, 1975.

Casabella. 'Università: Altri documenti'. 328(1968): 58–61.

Casu, Serafino, Enrico Corti, Enrico Milesi, Paolo Piga, and Antonello Sanna. 'Le strutture universitarie: Problemi di metodologia progettuale'. In *Atti della Facoltà di Ingegneria.* Cagliari: Università degli Studi di Cagliari, 1974.

Cervellati, Pier Luigi and Italo Insolera. 'Aquarius'. *Controspazio*, 1–2(1972): 14–15.

Cervellati, Pier Luigi and Italo Insolera. 'Aquarius'. *Urbanistica*, 62(1974): 56–58.

Chirivi, Romano. *Università Abruzzese, Chieti: Progetto di larga massima per la Citta Universitaria di Chieti, concorso ad inviti, anno 1966.* Venice: Istituto universitario di architettura, Istituto di urbanistica, 1967.

Chirivi, Romano, *et al.* 'Rapporto sui problemi dell'edilizia universitaria nei riguardi delle tipologie e delle tecnologie'. In *Atti del convegno di studio sull'edilizia universitaria.* Rome: ISES (Istituto per lo Sviluppo dell'Edilizia Sociale), 1970.

Clemente, Ferdinando, ed. *Università e territorio*. Bologna: S.T.E.B., 1969.

Comitato di studio dei problemi dell'università italiana. *Studi sull'università italiana*. Bologna: Società editrice Il Mulino, 1960.

Coppola Pignatelli, Paola. *L'università in espansione: orientamenti dell'edilizia universitaria*. Milan: Etas Kompass, 1969.

Coppola Pignatelli, Paola. 'Gap tra ricerca e attuazione nell'edilizia universitaria: Note su 4 concorsi'. *Parametro*, 44(1976): 13–19.

De Carlo, Giancarlo. *Proposta per una struttura universitaria*. Venice: Cluva, 1965.

De Carlo, Giancarlo. *La piramide rovesciata*. Bari: De Donato, 1968a.

De Carlo, Giancarlo, ed. *Pianificazione e disegno delle università*. Rome: Edizioni universitarie italiane, 1968b.

De Carlo, Giancarlo. 'Why/How to Build School Buildings'. *Harvard Educational Review*, 4(1969): 12–35. (Republished in Italian as 'Ordine Istituzione Educazione Disordine'. *Casabella*, 368–369 (1972): 65–71).

De Carlo, Giancarlo. 'Il territorio senza università'. *Parametro*, 21–22(1973): 38–39.

De Carlo, Giancarlo. 'Comment on the Free University'. *Architecture Plus*, 2, no. 1 (1974a): 50–51.

De Carlo, Giancarlo. 'Pavia Piano Universitario: Relazione Generale', 18 February1974b. Venice: Università IUAV, Archivio Progetti, Fondo De Carlo, pro/057.1/18/22, 040550.

De Carlo, Giancarlo. 'Un caso di studio: L'universicittà di Pavia'. *Parametro*, 44(1976): 20–22.

De Carlo, Giancarlo. 'Un ruolo diverso dell'università: Il modello multipolare per l'Università di Pavia'. In *Progettare l'università*, edited by Giuseppe Rebecchini, 144–151. Rome: Edizioni Kappa, 1981.

De Pieri, Filippo, ed. 'Il breve e il lungo '68 di Giancarlo De Carlo'. In *La piramide rovesciata: Architettura oltre il '68*, edited by Giancarlo De Carlo, 7–36. Macerata: Quodlibet, 2018.

De Rosa, Luciana, and Massimo Pica Ciamarra. 'Concorso per l'Università di Calabria: Prima lettura dei progetti'. *L'architettura cronache e storia*, 5(1974): 296–324.

Ente Studi Economici per la Calabria. *La scelta della sede dell'Università della Calabria nelle esigenze regionali e più generali*. Cosenza: Tipografia Chiappetta, 1968.

Felici, Marcello, and Giuseppe Mosciatti, eds. *Università: Le riforme promesse*. Naples: Liguori, 1978.

Fiorese, Giorgio. 'Due concorsi: Università della Calabria e Uffici Regionali di Trieste'. In *Guido Canella, 1931–2009*, edited by Enrico Bordogna, Gentucca Canella, and Elvio Manganaro, 308–316. Milan: Franco Angeli, 2014.

Frampton, Kenneth. 'City without Flags'. *Domus*, 609(1980): 18–23.

Gazzetta ufficiale della Repubblica Italiana. 'Bando di concorso internazionale per la sistemazione della Università degli Studi di Firenze'. 110(1970): 2747–2749.

Gazzetta ufficiale della Repubblica Italiana. 'Bando di concorso nazionale per il piano urbanistico di sistemazione dell'Università degli Studi di Cagliari'. 180(1971): 4453–4455.

Gazzetta ufficiale della Repubblica Italiana. 'Bando di concorso internazionale per il progetto della sede dell'Università degli Studi di Calabria'. 188(1972): 5229–5231.

Gazzetta ufficiale della Repubblica Italiana. 'Bando di concorso nazionale per la progettazione della sede dell'Università degli Studi di Salerno'. 157(1973): 4358–4360.

Gowan, James. 'Firenze università: appunti di un membro fuggiasco'. *Casabella*, 364 (1972): 10.

Gregotti, Vittorio. 'Florentine Fiasco: To the Editors'. *The Architectural Review*, 905 (1972): 63.

Gregotti, Vittorio. 'Università degli Studi della Calabria: Progetto per la costruzione del Dipartimento di Chimica. Relazione Generale'. Milan: Archivio Gregotti, 1975.

Gregotti, Vittorio, *et al.* 'Concorso internazionale per la sistemazione della Università di Firenze. Motto: Amalassunta'. Milan: Archivio Gregotti, 1970.

Guenzi, Carlo. 'Università: le assemblee propongono'. *Casabella*, 324(1968): 58–63.

Ingrami, Mario. *et al.* 'Concorso nazionale per la progettazione della sede della Università degli Studi di Salerno. Relazione'. Salerno: Università degli Studi di Salerno – Archivio di Ateneo, 1974.

ISLE (Istituto per la documentazione e gli studi legislativi). *Per il rinnovamento dell'università italiana: Atti del convegno 1–2 aprile 1965*. Rome: ISES (Istituto per lo Sviluppo dell'Edilizia Sociale), 1965.

ISES (Istituto per lo Sviluppo dell'Edilizia Sociale). *Atti del convegno di studio sull'edilizia universitaria*. Rome: ISES (Istituto per lo Sviluppo dell'Edilizia Sociale), 1970.

Koenig, Klaus Giovanni. 'La rivoluzione ad ottobre'. *Casabella*, 328(1968): 4.

Martinoli, Gino. *L'università come impresa*. Florence: La nuova Italia, 1967.

Quaroni, Ludovico. 'L'istituzione università: Che farne?' *Spazio e Società*, 4(1976): 5–32.

Quaroni, Ludovico, *et al.* 'Sistemi Congiunti 3'. *Urbanistica*, 62(1974): 58–62.

Raggi, Franco. 'Firenze università: Concorso per pochi intimi'. *Casabella*, 361(1972): 19–27.

Rebecchini, Marcello. *Progettare l'università*. Rome: Edizioni Kappa, 1981.

Richeri, Giuseppe. 'Università, territorio e televisione'. *Casabella*, 423(1977): 26–27.

Romano, Andrea. 'A trent'anni dal '68: "Questione Universitaria" e "Riforma Universitaria"'. *Annali di storia delle università italiane*, 2(1998). Available at: www.cisui. unibo.it/annali/02/testi/01Romano_frameset.htm (accessed 26 August 2019).

Rota, Italo, ed. *Il progetto per l'Universita delle Calabrie e altre architetture di Vittorio Gregotti/The Project for Calabria University and Other Architectural Works by Vittorio Gregotti*. Milan: Electa International, 1979.

Russo, Giovanni. *Università anno zero*. Rome: Armando Editore, 1966.

Samonà, Giuseppe, *et al.* 'Concorso nazionale per il piano urbanistico di sistemazione della sede dell'Università di Cagliari: Relazione illustrativa dei concetti informatori della proposta, con le fasi e i metodi di realizzazione e il piano finanziario di massima'. Samonà 1.pro/1/069, Venice: Università IUAV – Archivio Progetti, Fondo Giuseppe e Alberto Samonà, 1972.

Sartogo, Piero. 'Campus Design 6: Modelli di sviluppo territoriale urbanistico ed architettonico della istruzione superiore in Italia'. *Casabella*, 333(1969a): 16–21.

Sartogo, Piero. 'Campus Design 7: Concorso per la Libera Università abruzzese "Gabriele D'Annunzio" a Chieti'. *Casabella*, 334(1969b): 20–25.

Sartogo, Piero and Carlo Pelliccia. 'Campus Design 1: Il passaggio da una struttura monofunzionale ad una struttura integrata dell'educazione'. *Casabella*, 322(1968): 20–25.

Sartogo, Piero and Carlo Pelliccia. 'Campus Design 2: Analisi ed ipotesi di sviluppo dell'istruzione superiore negli USA'. *Casabella*, 323(1968a): 10–19.

Sartogo, Piero and Carlo Pelliccia. 'Campus Design 3: Finalità e componenti specifiche dell'istruzione superiore negli USA'. *Casabella*, 325 (1968b): 32–37.

Scolari, Massimo. 'Progetti per due città'. *Controspazio*, 1–2(1972): 2–4.

Sicignano, Enrico. *I campus di Fisciano e Lancusi*. Rome: Gangemi, 2011.

Siola, Uberto, *et al.* 'Università di Salerno: Concorso nazionale per la progettazione della nuova sede. Relazione illustrativa'. Salerno: Università degli Studi di Salerno – Archivio di Ateneo, 1973.

Spadolini, Pierluigi. 'Metodologia della industrializzazione dell'edilizia universitaria'. In *Atti del convegno di studio sull'edilizia universitaria*. Rome: ISES (Istituto per lo Sviluppo dell'Edilizia Sociale), 1970.

Università degli Studi di Cagliari. 'Consiglio di amministrazione integrato del 2 Maggio 1968, relazione sulla scelta delle aree per l'Università di Cagliari del gruppo di studio incaricato del piano edilizio universitario (22/4/1968)'. Cagliari: Università degli Studi di Cagliari, 22 April1968.

Università degli Studi della Calabria. 'Concorso internazionale per il progetto della sede dell'Università degli Studi di Calabria. Relazione Illustrativa'. Calabria: Università degli Studi di Calabria, 1972.

Università degli Studi della Calabria. 'Jury Report on the International Competition for the Design of the Seat of the University of Calabria'. Calabria: Università degli Studi di Calabria, December1973.

Università degli Studi di Salerno. 'Consiglio di amministrazione, riunione del 31.10.1972'. Salerno: Università degli Studi di Salerno, 31 October1972.

Università degli Studi di Salerno. 'Concorso Nazionale per la progettazione della sede dell'Università degli Studi di Salerno: Relazione tecnica allegata al bando'. Salerno: Università degli Studi di Salerno, 1973.

Viale, Guido. *Il sessantotto: Tra rivoluzione e restaurazione*. Milan: Gabriele Mazzotta Editore, 1978.

VV.AA. *Università: L'ipotesi rivoluzionaria. Documenti delle lotte studentesche. Trento, Torino, Napoli, Pisa, Milano, Roma*. Padua: Marsilio, 1968.

VV.AA. *Contro l'università: I principali documenti della critica radicale alle istituzioni accademiche del sessantotto*. Milan: Mimesis, 2008.

VV.AA. *La rivoluzione culturale: La Facoltà di Architettura del Politecnico di Milano 1963–1974*. Milan: Politecnico di Milano, 2009.

Zuddas, Francesco. 'Pretentious Equivalence: De Carlo, Woods and Mat-Building'. *FA Magazine*, 34(2015): 45–65.

Zuddas, Francesco. 'The Idea of the Università'. *AA Files*, 75(2017): 119–131.

Zuddas, Francesco. 'The System of Learning: Guido Canella's Teaching Theatre'. *Oase*, 102(2019): 52–61.

General

Avermaete, Tom. *Another Modern: The Post-War Architecture and Urbanism of Candilis-Josic-Woods*. Rotterdam: NAi, 2005.

Banham, Reyner. *Megastructure: Urban Futures of the Recent Past*. London: Thames and Hudson, 1976.

Bell, Daniel. 'Notes on the Post-Industrial Society'. *The Public Interest*, 6(1967): 24–35.

Cacciari, Massimo. *La Città*. N.P.: Pazzini, 2004.

De Angelis, Massimo and Stavros Stavrides. 'On the Commons'. *eFlux Journal*, 17, June 2017. Available at: www.e-flux.com/journal/17/67351/on-the-commons-a-public-interview-with -massimo-de-angelis-and-stavros-stavrides/ (accessed 26 August 2019).

Ferguson, Francis. *Architecture, Cities and the Systems Approach*. New York: G. Braziller, 1975.

Forty, Adrian. *Words and Buildings: A Vocabulary of Modern Architecture*. New York: Thames & Hudson, 2000.

Ginsborg, Paul. *Storia d'Italia dal dopoguerra a oggi*. Turin: Einaudi, 1989.

Gottmann, Jean. *Megalopolis: The Urbanized Northeastern Seaboard of the United States*. New York: Twentieth Century Fund, 1961.

Habermas, Jürgen. *The Structural Transformation of the Public Sphere: An Inquiry into a Category of Bourgeois Society*. Cambridge: Polity, 1992.

Lefebvre, Henri. 'The Right to the City'. In *Writings on Cities*, 61–181. Oxford: Blackwell, 1996 (originally published in French as *Le droit à la ville*, 1968).

Lefebvre, Henri. *The Urban Revolution*. Minneapolis, MN: University of Minnesota Press, 2003 (originally published in French as *La révolution urbaine*, 1970).

Lorey, Isabell. 'Becoming Common: Precarization as Political Constituting'. *eFlux Journal*, 17(2010). Available at: www.e-flux.com/journal/17/67385/becoming-common-precarization-as-political-constituting/ (accessed 26 August 2019).

Lyotard, Jean-François. *The Postmodern Condition: A Report on Knowledge*. Minneapolis, MN: University of Minnesota Press, 1979.

Marcuse, Herbert. *One-Dimensional Man: Studies in the Ideology of Advanced Industrial Society*. Boston: Beacon Press, 1966 [1964].

Martin, Leslie. 'The Grid as Generator'. In *Urban Space and Structures*, edited by Leslie Martin and Lionel March, 6–27. London: Cambridge University Press, 1972.

Martin, Reinhold. *The Organizational Complex: Architecture, Media, and Corporate Space*. Cambridge, MA: MIT Press, 2003.

Martin, Reinhold. 'Public and Common(s)'. *Places Journal*, January 2013. doi:10.22269/130124.

Mumford, Lewis. 'A New Regional Plan to Arrest Megalopolis'. *Architectural Record*, 137, no. 3(1965): 147–152.

Mumford, Lewis. *The Culture of Cities*. New York: Harcourt, Brace & World, 1966 [1938].

Ockman, Joan. 'Slashed'. *eFlux Journal*, 27 October 2017. Available at: www.e-flux.com/architecture/history-theory/159236/slashed/ (accessed 26 August 2019).

Rowe, Colin, and Fred Koetter. *Collage City*. Cambridge, MA: MIT Press, 1978.

Rykwert, Joseph. *On Adam's House in Paradise: The Idea of the Primitive Hut in Architectural History*. New York: Museum of Modern Art, 1972.

Sarkis, Hashim, ed. *Le Corbusier's Venice Hospital and the Mat Building Revival*. Munich: Prestel Verlag, 2001.

Smithson, Alison. 'How to Recognise and Read Mat Building'. *Architectural Design*, 9 (1974): 573–590.

Smithson, Alison. *The Charged Void: Architecture*. New York: Monacelli Press, 2000.

Smithson, Alison. *The Charged Void: Urbanism*. New York: Monacelli Press, 2005.

Spencer, Douglas. *The Architecture of Neoliberalism: How Contemporary Architecture Became an Instrument of Control and Compliance*. New York: Bloomsbury, 2016.

Standing, Guy. *The Precariat: The New Dangerous Class*. London: Bloomsbury Academic, 2011.

Stavrides, Stavros. *Common Space: The City as Commons*. London: Zed Books, 2016.

Swenarton, Mark, Tom Avermaete, Dirk van den Heuvel, and Eve Blau, eds. *Architecture and the Welfare State*. New York: Routledge, 2015.

Vidler, Anthony, Léon Krier, and Massimo Scolari. *Rational Architecture: The Reconstruction of the European City/Architecture rationnelle: La reconstruction de la ville européenne*. Brussels: Éditions des Archives d'architecture moderne, 1985.

Woods, Shadrach. *The Man in the Street: A Polemic on Urbanism*. Baltimore, MD: Penguin Books, 1975.

Index

Page numbers in italics indicate figures

Agamben, G. 3
Amalassunta (project by Gregotti and Detti) 77–8 129–35, *130*, *132*, *133*, *134*, 147, 149
ambiente totale 120–2, 128
anthropogeographical project 120–2
anti-city 183, 196–7; *see also* Canella, G.
Anversa Ferretti, L. 84–6, *85*, *87*, 99, 108
Aquarius (project by Cervellati ad Insolera) 80, *81*
archetype 4, 31, 100, 114
Archiginnasio 17
Archigram 50, 69, 93, 149
archipelago (as an urbanistic principle) 80, 82, 84, 86, 191
Architectural Design 34, 69
architecture as ordering 43, 46, 50, 86, 90, 99, 116, 119
architecture/city nexus 145, 149
Archizoom, 8–9, 70, 82, 84, 86, 115, 129, 141–56, 160–1, 177, 205–6; *see also* I progetti *si firmano*
ARUP 86, 90, 96, 128, 168
asse attrezzato 49, *130*
AUA (Architetti e Urbanisti Associati) 47
authority 7, 21, 23, 34, 42, 52, 56, 60, 76, 115, 137, 174, 187, 209
autonomy: of the university (academic) 17, 28, 29, 56–9, 174; of architecture (formal) 4, 94, 100, 109
Autunno caldo 146
Aymonino, C. 8–9, 44, 47, *48*, 49, 50, 52, 66, 75–6, 80, 90, *91*, 92–3, 100, 108, 120, 129

baby boomer generation 18, 190
Banham, R. 50, 69, 93, 96, 128
Barbiana 61; *see also* Milani, L.
bas-relief 86, 92, 116, 137, 147
Basaglia, F. 60–1, 200
base-camp 195, 206; *see also* Canella, G.
Battle of Valle Giulia *see* Valle Giulia
Bauman, Z. 1, 2; *see also* Postmodern: university
Beguinot, C. 95
Berlin Free University 67, 86, 96, 155, 162, 165, 168–70
Bo, C. 162
Bohigas, O. 78
Bologna Process 2, 109
Branzi, A. 147–8, 151, 153, 155–6
Brawne, M. 90
British New Universities 27–31, 89, 131, 163; *also* plateglass
building system 96–7, 99
Buzzati-Traverso, A. 58–9, 70

Calvino, I. 40
Candilis, Josic & Woods 67, 86, 96, 155, 162, 165, 175
Canella, G. 8–9, 47, 6–8, 75, 92, 115, 183–201, 205–6; taught studios and pedagogical approach 185, 187–97; competition project for the University of Calabria *93*, 200 ; competition project for the regional offices in Trieste 200
Casabella 43, 44, 46, 48, 50, *51*, 52, 62, 69, 78, 109, 119, 121–3, 145, 149, 151, 184, 188
Ceccarelli, P. 48–9, 121

centro direzionale 40, 47, 49, 52–3, 68, 76–7, 87, 119–20, 122, 131, 189; of Turin 47–9, *48*; *sistema dei centri direzionali* 49
Centro di Studi e Piani Economici *see* Centro Piani
Centro Piani 46, 68
centro universitario 40, 53, 170;
Cervellati, P.L. 80, *81*, 82, 129
Christian Democratic Party 59
CIAM 50, 161
CIDOC (Centro Cultural de Documentación) 152
città regione 40, 45–7, 67, 119, 147, 160, 163, 166, 170, 176; book by Centro Piani 46
città territorio 40, 45, 47–50, 52, 53, 87, 90, 92, 119, 147; article by Piccinato, Quilici and Tafuri 50, *51*; book by Carlo Aymonino 49
Città Universitaria in Rome 64–6, *65*
city of parts 121
city-factory 82, 86
city-territorialists 68, 75, 93, 113
city-territory 20, 47, 49, 50, *51*, 52, 77, 82, 92; *see also città territorio*
Ciudad Universitaria in Madrid 64
Clemente, F. 67
Collegio del Colle (project by De Carlo) 163, *164*
commodification 21, 32, 152, 208
commons 208–9
competition: controversy of competitions 75–7; for the University of Bochum 67; for the University of Cagliari 84–7; for the University of Calabria 87–94; for the University of Florence 77–84; for the University of Salerno 94–102; for Turin's *Centro Direzionale* 47–9, *48*; for University College Dublin 165–70
Comunità 45
Continuum (project by Gamberini) 82
Contropiano 146
Controspazio 78, 82, 185
Copcutt, G. 189–90
Coppola Pignatelli, P. 67, 107
Cravino (University of Pavia) 170, 172
Cuernavaca 151–2

Dalisi, R. 90
D'Angiolini, L.S. 68, 194–5, *196*
Dardi, C. 9, 75–6, 80, 90, *91*, 129
DC *see* Christian Democratic Party

De Carli, C. 183, 185, 187
De Carlo, G. 8–9, 41, 46, 53, 62, 67, 75, 86, 96, 109, 115, 134–5, 160–77, 205, 206; competition project for University College Dublin 165–70, *167*; plan for the University of Pavia 170–4, *173*; project for Collegio del Colle (Urbino) 162–5, *164*
De Sica, V. 40, 42
decentralisation 21, 45, 109
decongesting 131
de-institutionalisation 141, 162
deschooling 151–5
deterritorialisation 21
Detti, E. 77–8, 107, 129, 131, 134, 166
Diller & Scofidio + Renfro 7
disegno 86
disorder 47, 168, 177
Dober, R. 26–7, *28*, 69, 98
Doglio, C. 44–5, 135, 137, 162

economic miracle 39, 194
Edilizia moderna 47, 120–1, 123
education as a method of distorting mental and behavioural life span 34; *see also* deschooling
Eliot, T.S. 123
esamificio 60
excellence 3, 209; *see also* Readings, B.

Fanon, F. 197
fascist 8, 40, 57, 64, 66, 115, 116, 174
Ferguson, F. 94–5, 108, 128
figurative role of architecture 99, 109, 122, 127, 131, 148–9, 166, 169, 206
Fisciano (University of Salerno) 95
Florentine fiasco 78, *79*, 129
Florentine radical movement 69, 145
forced socialisation 33, 165
Frampton, K. 92, 99, 127–8
Freire, P. 61

Garden City 44–5, 119, 131, 135, 149
generic: as a general category 136; intellectual capabilities 87; skills 87, 144; spaces 90, 122, 205
Gentile, G. *see* Gentile Reform of Education
Gentile Reform of Education 57
German idealism 1; German university reform 18, 113–14; *see also* Von Humboldt, W.
Global Tools 151
Gottman, J. 41

Gowan, J. 78, 80, 129
Grafton Architects 7
Greco, S. 49, 52, 120
Gregotti, V. 8, 10, 44, 47, 75–7, 84, 88, 92,
    99, 107, 108, 115–38, 144, 147–9, 161,
    166, 187, 197, 200, 205; project for the
    University of Calabria *117*, 124–8, *125*,
    126; project for the University of
    Florence 77–8 129–35, *130*, *132*, *133*,
    134, 147, 149
grid as a design principle 69, 86,
    96, 99, 124, 127, 141, 166,
    168, 177
Gui, G. 59, 186

Habermas, J. 56, 113
habitat 21–2
Haskins, C.H. 56
Howard, E. 44–6, 119, 131, 135

I progetti si firmano (Archizoom project)
    141, 149, 151, 153
Illich, I. 61, 151–6, 162, 176, 206
INA Casa 42
Ingrami, M. 96, 97, *98*, 99, 108
Insolera, I. 80, *81*, 82, 129
instability 42, 172, 205
institution: convivial 153; interrupted 176;
    manipulative 153; public 57
International Competition for the Phoebe
    A. Hearst Architectural Plan for the
    University of California 114
INU Congress in Lecce 41, 67
ISES (Istituto per lo Sviluppo dell'Edilizia
    Sociale) 67, 82, 96
Italian Constitution 57
IUAV (Institute of Architecture in Venice)
    44, 116, 135,
ivory tower 17, 168

Japanese Metabolists 50
Jefferson, T. 23–7, *25*
Johns Hopkins University 114
Josefowicz, J. 90

Kahn, L. 50, 77, 122, 131
Kerr, C. 26, 33, 58, 69
knowledge: Aristotelian structure of 113;
    cluster 17; democratic access to 109;
    district 17, 20; economy 4–5; factories
    of 6; hub 6, 17; marketisation of 59;
    mercantilization of 148; park 17;
    tacit 152
know-how 143

Koenig, G.K. 145–6
Koolhaas, R. 7, 121

L'architecture d'aujourd'hui 64, 196
La Tendenza 100
Lasdun, D. 29, *30*, 163
Laurea 60, 183
Le Corbusier 44, 46, 123, 149
learning webs 155–6; *see also* Illich, I.
Lefebvre, H. 21–2, 34, 36
Levi, C. 88
Libera, A. 43
lifelong learning 33, 210
live-projects 206
Lotta continua 146
Loughborough Technical University 86,
    97, 128, 168
Lynch, K. 122
Lyotard, J.F. 1, 143–5

Mao Tse-tung 60
Marcuse, H. 60–1
Martensson, T. 90
mass: departments 197–8; university 61,
    135, 165, 185
mat-building 86, 155, 168, 170
Meda, L. 47, *48*
megastructure 20, 47, 50, 93, 119, 122, 127
Mendini, A. 145, 185
metaprogetto 82
Middle Ages 17, 56
Milan Triennale 91, 131, 175
Milani, L. 60–1
MIT (Massachusetts Institute of
    Technology) 88, 122, 194
mobility 2, 206, 208, 210
Montaggi didattici 191, *192*, *193*; *see also*
    Canella, G.
MOOCS (Massive Open Online
    Courses) 114
Moro, A. 59
morphology 93, 100, 185
Morphosis 7
Movimento Studentesco 60–2, 146, 185–7
multi-scalar 41, 95, 121, 124
multiversity 26, 29, 33, 58
Mumford, L. 44–5
Mussolini, B. 57, 64
Muthesius, S. 27–8

National Economic Plan 46, 68
Neo-Rationalist 42, 121, 128
neutralisation 7, 23, 57, 82, 189, 210
New Paltz 18

new towns 22–3, 45, 131
new urban dimension 40, 41–6, 49, 50, 52, 66, 68, 77, 80, 116, 119, 160, 163; see also *nuova dimensione urbana*
Nikolskij, A. 86
No-Stop City (project by Archizoom) 143, 149, 155
nuova dimensione urbana 40, 50, 147; article by Alberto Samonà 52

Olivetti, A. 45
OMA 7
Open University 109
Operaist movement 82, 145–6, 148, 151, 155, 161
origin of architecture 126
Oxbridge 27, 29, 89, 163, 196

paradigm 4, 10, 31, 40, 99, 119, 128, 152, 160, 175
Parametro 108
participatory planning 171
Pasolini, P.P. 39–40, 42, 61–2
Philipps Universität in Marburg 95, 97
Piacentini, M. 64, 65, 66
Plan for the Center of Philadelphia (project by Kahn) 50, 77, 131
Polanyi, M. 152
Polesello, G. 47, *48*
Politecnico di Milano 50, 60, 62, 68, 92, 120, 183, *184*, *192*, 193–4, *196*, 198, *199*; teaching experimentation 185–7
politica del quartiere 42; *also* politics of the neighbourhood
Portoghesi, P. 183, *184*, 185, 187–8, 198
Postmodern: condition 1, 143–4, 148; university 1, 3
Potteries Thinkbelt 32–6, *33*, 67, 162; *see also* Price, C.
Price, C. 31–6, *33*, 61, 67, 69, 162, 172
principle of concentration 113–15
professionalism 87
Progetto '80 68, 69–70, 90
Proposta architettonica per Roma Est (project by Aymonino and Dardi) 91

Quaroni, L. 8–9, 41–2, *43*, 44, 47, *48*, 50, 75, 82, *83*, 96, 108, 109, 116, 120, 129, 149
quartiere 22, 40, 42–3, 89, 92, 108; Barene di San Giuliano 41–2, *43*, 50, 82; Tiburtino 42; Tuscolano 43; also *quartieri*

Radical Notes (articles by Branzi) 151
rationalising will 84, 95
Readings, B. 1, 3–4, 8, 210
Red Vienna 66
Rebecchini, G. 129
reterritorialisation 34
Robbins Report on Higher Education 27–8, 32–3, 59
Rogers, E.N. 69, 116, 119, 120–3, 128, 145, 184–5, 187–2, 200, 206
Rosi, F. 40
Rossi, A. 46–7, *48*, 49, 50, 120–1, 183–4, 188
Rykwert, J. 4, 31, 90, 124, 126, 128, 160

Samonà, A. 49, 52–3, 68, 84, 87, 92, 116, 122
Samonà, G. 8–10, 41, 44–7, *48*, 49, 52, 75, 84, 86, 92, 108, 115–16, *118*, 119, 135, *136*, 137–8, 144, 147, 148, 161, 169, 205; project for the University of Cagliari 116, 135–138, *118*, *136*
Sartogo, P. 68
Scolari, M. 76, 78, 82
self-contained 19, 22–4, 32–3, 35, 42, 69, 88, 90, 131, 135
self-formation 115, 137, 175
Sesto Fiorentino (University of Florence) 129, *130*
settlement principle 10–11
signification 121–2, 124, 149
Siola, U. 100, *101*, 108
Smart, R. 90
Smithsons (Alison and Peter) 165
Snow, C.P. 170
social condenser 64, 129, 169
SOM 7, 67, 133
Spadolini, P. 96–7
spatial units 97, 128
staircase principle *30*, 163
Stanton Williams 7
State University of New York 18
Stresa 160, 163
student protest 35, 62, 108, 115, 137, 151, *161*, 174–6
SUNY see State University of New York
super-schools in Pittsburgh 190
systems approach 94

Tafuri, M. 42, 44, 47, 49, 50, 51, 52, 99, 147–9, 151
Tange, K. 50, 122
Team X 96, 161–2, 165, 168, 175
technopoles 5
territory of architecture 123
tertiary: activities 52, 77, 131, 147; armature 84; economy 136; education 27, 194; functions 52; offices 87; services 119, 134; society 22, 48, 121; workers 50, 52
The Architectural Review 78, 79, 129, 131
Tokyo Bay Plan (project by Tange) 50
total experience of learning 176
town-and-gown 17, 196
Trojan horse 149
Tronti, M. 146, 155
Tschumi, B. 7
Turner, J. 162
Turner, P.V. 23
two cultures 170; *see also* Snow, C.P.
typology 67, 82, 96, 100, 128, 137, 172, 185, 189, 191, 195; university typology 68–9; *also* building type

Universicittà 160, 162
university: as a special place or experience 33, 136; as a working environment 33, 86; corporate 2; disarticulated 170–1; entrepreneurial 2; global 2; Harvard 6, 23, 114; idea of 24, 32–4, 64, 80, 86–7, 90, 100, 107–9, 115, 119, 137, 162, 165, 169, 172, 197, 201, 206, 208; in ruins 1, 6, 210; militarised 174; multi-polar 171–2, 224; nomadic 113–14, 172, 183, 195, 200; of Berlin 1, 18; of Bologna 68, 135; of Cagliari 8, 19, 70, 75, 76, 84–7, 107, 116, 118, 135, 136, 147, 205; of Calabria 8, 10, 19, 70, 75, 87–94, 95, 117, 124, 125, 126, 128, 194, 196, 205; of California 26, 114; of East Anglia 28–9, 30, 163; of Essex 28–9, 30, 86, 166; of Florence 8, 19, 68, 70, 75–84, 96, 107, 116, 129, 130, 132, 133, 134, 141, 142, 145, 149, 150, 151, 152, 160, 166, 205; of Illinois at Chicago Circle 67, 133; of Kent 28; of Lancaster 28–9, 30, 166; of Naples 58, 95; of Pavia 58, 75, 161, 173, 206; of Salerno 8, 10, 70, 75, 94–102, 128; of Sheffield 165; of Sussex 28; of Trento 60; of Urbino 75; of Virginia 23–5, 27, 69; plateglass 9, 28–9, 33, 127, 137; Princeton 23, 114; redbrick 27, 29; transational 1–2; of Warwick 28; Yale 23, 114; of York 28
University College Dublin 96, 161, 165, 167
urban revolution 19; *see also* Lefebvre, H.
utopia 7, 22, 31, 46, 49, 88, 100, 109, 146–8

Valle Giulia 61–2, 63
Villaggio Matteotti (project by De Carlo) 171
Ville radieuse (project by Le Corbusier) 149
Von Erlach, F. 123, 126
Von Humboldt, W. 1, 3, 113–14, 143–4, 175

Ward, C. 162
weak urbanisation 148
Woods, S. 86, 165, 168–70